D1060264

IBSEN

IBSEN

The Intellectual Background

BY

BRIAN W. DOWNS, M.A.

*Fellow and Tutor of Christ's College,
Sometime Director of Scandinavian Studies
in the
University of Cambridge*

15

CAMBRIDGE
AT THE UNIVERSITY PRESS
1946

Printed in Great Britain at the University Press, Cambridge
(Brooke Crutchley, University Printer)
and published by the Cambridge University Press
Cambridge, and Bentley House, London
Agents for U.S.A., Canada, and India: Macmillan

To

MY MOTHER
ETHEL ESTER DOWNS

CONTENTS

PREFACE

The present study does not aim at supplying a biography of Henrik Ibsen or a criticism of his writings. My purpose in writing it has been to give an account, where it seemed relevant, of the background of ideas, artistic conventions and historical events before which he moved. The attempt, at least, stands in no need of an apology. Ibsen is a very great author, one of the supreme dramatists of all time. His development is multifarious, interesting and well-attested, but it is not fully comprehensible without reference to the intellectual and moral life of his time. For, contrary to what is often believed outside Scandinavia, he was not a sudden, causeless phenomenon, born in a hyperborean desert with no traceable ancestry, but stood well in the stream of the ethical, religious, political and sociological thought of his time and, besides making notable contributions to it, took a lively interest in many of its aspects. I wish, however, to make it plain that I am not presenting him as the mere product of such-and-such clearly distinguishable 'influences', nor has it been my design to track down all the 'sources' of his plays and poems.

I have to acknowledge the courtesy of Messrs William Heinemann and of the American Scandinavian Foundation for allowing me to quote freely from *The Collected Works of Henrik Ibsen* and *Early Plays by Henrik Ibsen* respectively and of Messrs J. M. Dent & Sons for leave to reproduce one of the translations from *Lyrics and Poems from Ibsen*.

I am deeply in debt for advice and encouragement during the writing of my study to my friends Joan and Stanley Bennett and to my Mother. And to my Mother, who was an Ibsenite at a time when it was a much more unconventional and hazardous thing to be than it is now for her son, I take leave to dedicate the book.

B. W. D.

Goathland
September 1944

NOTE

Except where otherwise stated, Ibsen's writings are quoted, by volume and page only, from the Standardutgave of his *Samlede Digter Verker* (7 volumes, Christiania, 1918) and, prefaced by the word 'Archer', from the English *Collected Works of Henrik Ibsen* (edited by William Archer, 12 volumes, London, 1910–12). Other works quoted in an abbreviated form are the three volumes of Ibsen's *Efterladte Skrifter* (Copenhagen, 1909) and the two volumes of his letters, *Breve* (Copenhagen, 1904).

The two chief biographies of Ibsen, Gran, G., *Henrik Ibsen* (Christiania, 1918) and Koht, H., *Henrik Ibsen* (Oslo, 1928), are cited merely by author's surname, with volume and page numbers.

CHRONOLOGICAL LIST OF IBSEN'S WRITINGS

CHAPTER ONE

THE REVOLUTION OF 1848

Catiline (1850)

OF all the great revolutions that have disturbed the civic peace
of nations those of the year 1848 arouse to-day as languid an
interest as any. Revolutions they were, however, in the plural,
creating a prodigious and very far-reaching commotion. Dr
Gooch's *Annals of Politics and Culture* devotes more space to the
year 1848 than to any other. Not only did the trembling citizen
behold marchings, barricades, the dismissal of all-powerful
ministers, executions, novel constitutions, sociological experiments, the flight of old princes and the convocation of new
parliaments, but those active in creating this millennium were,
as a rule, animated by a quite exceptional zeal. The congenital
revolutionary felt that all was at stake, that his ideals and
activities now had the completest scope with a more fervid conviction than his predecessor had done in 1688, in 1830 and even
in 1789. The economic and political issues were more obviously
combined. The disappearance of a regimen that had promulgated 'enrichissez-vous' as a watchword made it clear that at
any rate in Paris (where the mischief started) the lists were
definitely fixed for trial by combat between those who possessed
and those who craved to possess. 1848 was the year of Marx
and Engels's Communist Manifesto.

By the time that they reached Norway the repercussions of
the big events in Paris, Vienna, Budapest and Berlin had lost
almost all their force. As far in Thule as Stockholm there had
been riots; even the King of Denmark had been forced to grant
his excited subjects a constitution. Norway stood in no need
of this soothing specific, having indeed since 1814 enjoyed what
in many respects was the most enlightened constitution in
Europe. No barricades were thrown up in Christiania, there
was no resident monarch to drive away or summon to the
balcony of his palace.

Nevertheless, the liberal daily of the Norwegian capital,
Morgenbladet, so enthusiastically hailed the news of the Paris

revolution that its editor, Adolf Bredo Stabell, suffered a 'demonstration' beneath his windows sufficient for military intervention.[1] This Stabell, with four other members of Parliament, gave notice of a motion of no-confidence in the government, an 'address'; but after it had been remitted to a special committee it was shelved, and Norwegians of a political idiosyncrasy concentrated their attention on one of the remoter after-effects of the flight of Louis-Philippe, the first war over the duchies of Slesvig and Holstein.

On Ibsen, however, the news of the revolution and manifestos, as he vividly remembered twenty-seven years later,[2] left so deep and lasting a mark that they who see in him first and foremost the apologist of revolt might attribute the most vital part of his genius to the germ which was then implanted. One of his close friends at this time, Due, reports[3] that before some select spirits he launched a diatribe *in tyrannos*,[4] upholding the republican form of government as the 'only possible' one, and their elders really thought him a dangerous firebrand. Though it cannot be maintained that the pen was actually forced into his hand by the contemplation of these events (since he had certainly begun to indulge in poetry before), they did give the impulse to his playwriting. For, in addition to what he calls 'ringing poems', encouraging the Magyars (who in 1848 seemed in the van of progress), and a series of hortatory sonnets addressed to King Oscar of Sweden and Norway, his excitement urged him to compose the three-act verse-tragedy of *Catiline* (*Catilina*, his earliest work to appear in book-form, 1850).[5] It remained the only echo of that year of revolution which Norwegian *belles-lettres* returned.[6]

[1] Mørch, E., *Da Kristiania var Smaaby* (1901), p. 161.

[2] When he wrote the Introduction to the second, revised, edition of *Catilina* (1875).

[3] Due, C., *Erindringer fra Henrik Ibsens Ungdomsaar* (1909), p. 42.

[4] Though it is not, as German authors think, self-evident that Ibsen knew *The Robbers* by Schiller (who calls his hero a Catiline), it is by no means improbable; he seems to have known Schiller's *William Tell* before this time (cf. F. Bull's note in Berggrav, E., *Ibsens Sjelelige Krise*, 1937, p. 54).

[5] It was published pseudonymously, as the work of Brynjolf Bjarme. This seems to have been in accordance with Northern conventions; Strindberg remarks in *Röda Rummet* (1879) on an author's immodesty in publishing his first work under his own name.

[6] Gran, I, p. 21, who adds that of the two leading authors of the times Welhaven was just peevish at the threat to his tranquillity, while Andreas Munch rubbed his hands with satisfaction that such things could not happen in respectable Norway.

THE REVOLUTION OF 1848

The author of *Catiline*, then completing his twentieth year, was living in Grimstad as assistant to the pharmacist of that small seaport. He had recently renounced his intention of entering the doctor's surgery through the chemist's shop (as was still just possible at that date)[1] and, with the aid of a tutor, he was preparing himself for the matriculation examination (*examen artium*) of the university of Christiania. Latin was a compulsory subject; and Ibsen, having digested Caesar's *Gallic War* (from which he derived a couple of names for *Catiline*), now proceeded to grapple with Sallust and Cicero. The historian as well as the orator informed him of the formation and detection of the memorable conspiracy against the state and senate of republican Rome, the times caused his imagination to kindle at this subject, and the early sportings of that spirit which made his last recorded speech "On the contrary" (*tvert-imot*)[2] determined his attitude towards it. What helped him to his form and manner we shall consider in a later chapter.

Catiline, however, raises two questions of immediate interest. How and why did the circumstances of the time move the young dramatist to celebrate such a hero? and what reasons had he for shaping that hero's doom in the way he did?

The name of Catiline hung in the air at that time like a portent; and it is no coincidence that the Cosmopolitan Night-Watchman, as Franz Dingelstedt called himself, should run together a *scenario* around him or that so astute a caterer to the public taste as Alexandre Dumas the elder, immediately after theatre-going in Paris became safe again, should offer his public a new melodrama commemorating the man of whom the historian of Rome[3] declares that his knavish tricks are proper to the Newgate Calendar rather than the style of Clio. "Villain, bawdy, bawdy, kindless villain" Catiline had proverbially become in the mouths of the literate of all countries. His duplicate they thought to discern behind every barricade and on the rostrum of every public assembly. He was nevertheless a villain from whom some portion of the community could not withhold a certain sympathy. The story goes[4] that just about the time when *Catiline* was published, though knowing as little of Ibsen's

[1] Koht, I, p. 40.　　　　[2] Koht, II, p. 384.
[3] Mommsen, T., *Römische Geschichte*, III (7th edition, 1882), p. 175.
[4] Skard, E., in *Edda*, XXI (1924), p. 82, quoting Nielsen, Y., *En Christianiensers Erindringer*, p. 103.

play as Ibsen did of Dumas's (which was nothing),[1] the pupils
of the venerable Cathedral School could be heard glorifying its
central character in the tranquil streets of Christiania.

The reason for such indulgence is not far to seek. Ibsen sup-
plies it himself[2] when he calls Catiline's adversary "the majority's
indefatigable attorney Cicero"—Cicero doubly hateful to stu-
dious youth as the successful repressor of enterprise in the past
and as the occasion for much tedious construing in the present,
offensive to a liberal taste through the unction of his self-
congratulations. Ibsen, moreover, was urged by a more personal
motive than these to celebrate a character to which in fact he
attached much the same value as Cicero and Sallust—debauched,
violent, restless, appetitive of troubled waters. With whatever
degree of detachment, Catiline fought in the ranks of the dis-
possessed and despised, among whom the Grimstad chemist's
boy (*apotekerdreng*) reckoned himself in the indigence which
often deprived him of stockings and underwear and excluded
him from the society of that "aristocratic sea-port".[3] He could
not but remember that he had been born into the aristocracy
of a considerably larger community, that of Skien, and he had
been old enough when his father became bankrupt[4] to feel
acutely the contrast between his family's former varied, care-
free life and the cramped, isolated, shabby-genteel existence
of the *déclassés*.

For the historical outlines of that long-protracted crisis in
Roman history which terminated in 62 B.C. Ibsen did not
widely depart from his school-books, though he took a subtle
revenge on his bugbear Cicero in excluding him and his
loquacity entirely from the dialogue. He exhibited the un-
deserving and the deserving malcontents, with nothing to lose
and everything to gain by the overthrow of the aristocratic
oligarchy that ruled through the Senate, their determination to
stick at nothing, not even at an alliance with the external enemies
of the republic, the Gauls. He indicated the betrayal of the

---

[1] Ibsen was almost certainly unfamiliar with the innumerable dramatisations
of Catiline's story; though he had read some of Voltaire's writings at this time,
that *Rome Sauvée* was one of them is most unlikely.

[2] Introduction to 2nd edition of *Catiline*; VII, p. 115.

[3] "Aristokratiske sjøfartsby" (Eitrem, H., in *Edda*, III, 1915, p. 69). For all
its smallness, Grimstad could boast several 'ruling dynasties'; on this and the
like cf. Bergwitz, J. K., *Grimstad 1800–1850 som Type paa Norsk Smaaby* (1916).

[4] Knud Ibsen finally broke in 1836, when Henrik was eight years old; but he
had been in difficulties for about two years.

4

conspiracy by those in its counsels, the necessity of removing its operations from the confines of Rome and its final overthrow by force of arms in the battle of Pistoria; and, as has been said, he kept to the traditional view of Catiline's character.

Yet in arranging for his hero's death, at least in the major features, Ibsen departed from his historical sources. In accordance with fact, he represents Catiline as married to Aurelia, whom he makes a devoted and respectable female, not at all the sort in whom, as Sallust says, men find nothing to praise but their figures; for this Aurelia Catiline has a quite sincere affection, but at the same time he is presented as passionately enamoured of the Vestal Virgin Furia. The infatuation brings him to grief, not as a bigamist, but because this fictitious Furia uses it to hound him through the authentic conspiracy to his ruin, in revenge for the seduction and abandonment, years ago, of her dead sister. When his companions have been defeated and slain, Furia comes to him on the battlefield and, after an ineffectual attempt to drive him to self-slaughter, stabs him dead herself.

Catiline presents, essentially, the belated, catastrophic effect of a misdeed committed long ago, the kind of situation underlying almost without exception all the author's later tragedies. It equally shows a man erotically linked to two women, as are also Alfred Allmers, with Rita and Asta (*Little Eyolf*), Johannes Rosmer, with Rebecca West and Beata, Arnold Rubek with Irene and Maja. A close parallel to the dual situation occurs in *Peer Gynt* when The Green-Clad One appears with her and Peer's misbegotten brat just as he is about to set up house with Solvejg and so drives him to a lifetime of wandering and futility. At the time that he was composing *Catiline* Ibsen had ever present in his mind an experience of which the parish-register of Vestre Moland recorded the outcome among the christenings: "Hans Jacob, born October 9, 1846, of the unmarried chemist's assistant of Skien, Henrik Johan Ibsen, and the unmarried servant-girl Else Sofie Jensdatter Borkedalen."[1]

[1] Ibsen had to pay for the maintenance of the bastard during fourteen financially difficult years and may well have thought from time to time that his future was hopelessly compromised. Else Sofie was ten years the senior of her partner in sin, so that if there was any seduction in the case it is unlikely that he behaved as Catiline did to Furia's sister. The record is reproduced by Bishop Berggrav in *Ibsens Sjelelige Krise* (1937), p. 11.

Furia's purely private vengeance for a purely private wrong is of a piece with the rest of the play. Catiline does not come forward as the advocate of any social programme,[1] nor even of his fellow-malcontents, whom he knows to be as contemptible as their adversaries. He is prepared to gain personal, even regal, power by bribery. He stands as a self-conscious individual not against the senatorial majority and their attorney alone, but against the opponents of these also, wresting the leadership from them after he has bearded them by himself and all but suffered death at their daggers. The conflict in which his hero is represented by Ibsen is one of personalities at the lowest political level:

> Now in the senate has my adversary,
> The crafty Cicero, trampled me to earth.
> His speech was a portrayal of my life
> So glaring that I, even I, must gasp.[2]

The term 'freedom' that spurs Catiline to his fatal efforts has himself for its sole true object.

The interpretation which he gave to the events of 63 and 62 B.C. shows the constant bias of Ibsen's mind. In so far as radicalism and the cry for political liberty meant anything to him personally, they always implied the emancipation of the individual from the restraint of magistrates and majorities. That could not be better illustrated than by what is reckoned the most 'social' of his plays, *An Enemy of the People*, at the end of which the ratepayers of the little spa, the visitors' hygiene and the morality of communal advertisement suffer complete eclipse behind Thomas Stockmann's single-handed defiance of the 'compact majority' and their indefatigable attorney, his brother. In the revolution of 1848, as in Catiline's conspiracy, Ibsen saw primarily not the cause, but the revolutionary, and the things which permanently interested him were not the aims of a Lamartine, a Kossuth, a Daniele Manin or a Stabell. The men, their spirit, the possibility of their success, however, electrified him, and without their example he himself would, very likely, never have become the great questioner and iconoclast, in short

---

[1] Unless loot could be counted such. Sokolowsky, R., 'Henrik Ibsens Römerdramen' in *Euphorion*, IX (1902) seems to me quite astray when he names (p. 601) "Bürgerfreiheit, Recht und allgemeines Staatswohl" as Ibsen's leading ideals in this play.

[2] VII, p. 38. *Early Plays*, p. 26.

6

THE REVOLUTION OF 1848

the great revolutionary, overjoyed, as he declared, to torpedo
the Ark itself.[1]

*   *   *   *

Looking back twenty-five years afterwards[2] upon his 'prentice
work Ibsen could discern in it other germs which later developments were to bring to maturity—the contrast between desire
and performance, and the coexistence in the individual as well
as in humanity of tragic and comic, for instance. Full of
significance, too, are the lines uttered by Catiline towards his end:

> And is not life an everlasting fight
> Between the hostile forces in the soul?—
> And this fight is the soul's own life.[3]

To these themes, little as they have to do with the February
Revolution, we shall return at a more fitting opportunity.

[1] "Jeg lægger med lyst torpedo under arken" (vi, p. 372, 'Til min ven Revolutions-taleren').
[2] In the Introduction to the 2nd edition, 1875 (vii, pp. 114 ff.).
[3] vii, p. 109. These lines have no equivalent in the revised version and therefore
are not translated in the *Early Plays*: the translation is my own.

CHAPTER TWO

EARLY IMPRESSIONS OF PUBLIC LIFE

Andhrimner (1851) and *Norma* (1851)

SINCE he took small interest in them as such, it would prove an unnecessary task to review at any length the constitution of Norway and the system by which that country was governed in Ibsen's early manhood. A few factors in them, however, may summarily be mentioned, since they have a bearing on the formation of his ideas.

A new regimen had come into existence in 1814, when Norway ceased to be a dependency of Denmark and its crown was united with that of Sweden, both countries otherwise maintaining (except in foreign affairs) an absolute independence. The constitution which the fathers of the country promulgated at Eidsvold iron-works on 17 May 1814[1] rigorously separated the supreme executive, legislative and judiciary powers after the manner which Montesquieu had advocated and Benjamin Franklin had elaborated. It ensured almost as perfect an example of bureaucracy as may be imagined. The executive had no place in parliament (the *Storthing*), to which it was not responsible; it consisted of the permanent heads (*statsraader*) of the different government departments, who had their offices in Christiania; they received their appointments from the crown, and the foremost among them, the *statsminster*, as their joint representative, was personally attendant on the king and for that reason usually resided in Stockholm. Schooled administrators, not politicians, the *statsraader* had usually advanced through the civil service and, when they reached the summit of their ambition, had as little contact with the people as with parliament. Representative local government scarcely existed, and at every stage the administration lay in the hands of civil servants appointed and controlled in Christiania. Peter Stockmann in *An Enemy of the People* often goes by the name of 'mayor' in English commentaries; but his functions would be to

---

[1] This day has ever since been celebrated with much solemnity and speechmaking; *The League of Youth* begins at such a celebration.

implement the decrees of the central government, to command the police of the town and to act as criminal magistrate in the first instance; he is a servant of the Home Office.[1] Farthermore, since the crown enjoyed the sole patronage of the national Lutheran church, the ecclesiastical department (*kirkedeparte-ment*) formed a government office like any other.

Though the appointment and control of the ministry were quite out of its hands, the legislature[2] proved effective both in theory and in practice. It was no mere piece of democratic trimming, and its members held an honoured position in the land. Besides requiring (on the advice of the *statsraader*) royal sanction, all laws and fiscal measures had first to pass parliament, which actually had the power to enact them without sanction if they had been voted in the identical form by three successive assemblies. These however were, during the first fifty-five years of the new dispensation, only convoked in every third year, and the franchise, though liberal according to the standards of the time, was far from universal. It was withheld from the rural labourer and the artisan of the town. Election was 'indirect', those entitled to the franchise voting for members of an electoral college, in whom was vested the final choice of the member of parliament. (In Ibsen's *League of Youth* the matter at issue is not the ordinary voters' but the electoral college's election of Stensgaard to the *Storthing*.)

Not until the eighth decade of the nineteenth century did the Norwegian parliament know anything like a developed party-system. There were no 'whips', no location of benches in the house according to principles, no programmes, no central offices for the dissemination of parliamentary candidates. Members appear to have been elected primarily for their personalities, secondarily for a somewhat indeterminate political 'colouring'. For, even in the earliest days of the *Storthing*, the germs from which the later parties grew appear to have been present. Though their official chiefs might not sit in parliament, minor civil servants and clergy were frequently elected and naturally gravitated to the government's programme.[3] The

---

[1] The same is true of Fogden in *Brand*, who is likewise called 'The Mayor' in English translations.

[2] Though divided for certain purposes, the *Storthing* was in effect unicameral.

[3] Not all did so; and it is greatly to the credit of Norwegian public life that they were not only dispensed from their administrative duties during the parliamentary session, but were not penalised either for voting against ministerial proposals.

other members were at first usually peasants and farmers, as the rural constituencies greatly preponderated. They tended to form the opposition. But, as always seems to happen when a legislature is divorced from the executive, that was the tendency of the *Storthing* as a whole. The political structure made the lieges' habitual attitude to politics a purely critical one and weak not only in constructive notions (since the opposition as such could never be called on to form a government), but even in tenacious co-operation to negative ends. Though the constitution enabled parliament ultimately to have its way, the processes were tedious and cumbrous, and only on the rarest occasion did it summon the necessary resolution to brave royal disapprobation by passing vetoed bills three times running or to impeach ministers before the supreme court (*riksret*).

The illuminations and conflagrations of 1848 had shone into little Grimstad by a double reflection, through newspaper reports of events that were foreign and remote. When in April 1850 Ibsen removed to Christiania[1] with the intention of studying at its university, though a small town it was a capital to which he came, the seat of government offices and parliament, the place where the policies affecting his own country were actually framed, debated and enacted; he could himself establish contact of a sort with those responsible for them. It was an opportunity he did not miss; his failure to pass the matriculation examination[2] and consequent resolve to renounce a learned profession in favour of literature gave him the leisure he wanted to continue the political education begun under the auspices of Cicero and Sallust.

He found quite an amount of fire still burning. It had, in Norway, been farther fanned by Marcus Møller Thrane, at that time occupied in combining in an active alliance the work-

---

[1] For descriptions of Christiania at this time, cf. the first volume of Lorentz Dietrichson's *Svundne Tider* (1896) and Mørch, E., *Da Kristiania var Smaaby* (1901).

[2] Ibsen's academic position was a trifle anomalous, at least in English eyes, and may call for a moment's elucidation. In August 1850 he passed in all except two of the subjects of the matriculation examination and obtained the general character of *non contemnendus* (i.e. a 'third class'); but he would have had successfully to offer Greek and Arithmetic again (and these two subjects alone) in order to qualify for the status of matriculated student. I fancy, however, that even before this he would have been entitled to attend university lectures, and he certainly became a member of the university club (*Studenter-foreningen*). He counted as an undergraduate, a university man, "Student Ibsen", and that is important. In later life, after the university of Upsala had honoured him, he had himself invariably addressed as "Hr. Doktor".

men's clubs which he had begun to found in the year of revolution. When the franchise was later extended, the members of
the workmen's clubs stood in the same relation to the Socialist
party as the *statsraader*'s friends to the Conservative and the
peasants to the Liberal. Thrane had acquired considerable
influence, and it was anticipated that the 1851 session of
parliament—the next after that which had shelved Stabell's
'address'—would be all the stormier as a general conference of
the workmen's clubs had been convoked to Christiania, to sit
contemporaneously for the purpose of negotiating with it. But
Norway, it quickly appeared, afforded no exception to the
universal ebb of revolutionary fortunes. The new parliament
showed itself the mildest ever summoned, and the members
who, like Stabell, had been sent to it with mandates more or
less radical tumbled over one another in the scramble to drop
them in the vestibule.

In proportion as the legislature cringed, the government,
having nothing to fear, began to show its teeth. Seeking whom
it might devour, it lighted on a single individual, who had the
advantage of being a foreigner, and deported this fairly in-
nocuous Danish subject[1] on the grounds that he was incubating
Catilinarian projects; in his support Student Henrik Ibsen
signed a petition and took part in the only political meeting
he is known ever to have attended.[2] Flushed with their easy
triumph the authorities then directed their severity upon the
labour conference itself and, after due and protracted process of
law, had above one hundred members of it sentenced to varying,
but relatively harsh, sentences of imprisonment.[3] Among them
was Thrane himself, also his lieutenant Abildgaard.[4] With the
latter Ibsen had shared lodgings and for his paper, *Arbeider-
Foreningernes Blad*,[5] written some articles, and, indeed, only a
cunning press-overseer's presence of mind prevented some of

[1] Harro Harring, who came from the duchy of Slesvig.
[2] Jæger, H., *Life of Henrik Ibsen* (English translation, 1890), pp. 54 f. Perhaps,
then, it is partly ignorance on the author's part which makes the proceedings at
the public meeting in Act IV of *An Enemy of the People* so peculiarly disgusting.
[3] With *excès de zèle* the secretary of the conference had noted in the minutes
the words 'revolution' and 'revolutionary' every time they occurred in its transactions; that it was a revolutionary assembly formed the gravamen of the charge
against Thrane, who had convened it, but taken no part in its debates, and who
was sent to gaol for four years.
[4] After having been remanded in custody for four years, Abildgaard was sentenced to four years' hard labour.
[5] I.e. *The Labour Clubs' Sheet*.

them from falling into the hands of the police and exposing the author to the risk of prosecution and conviction.

On Ibsen's writings the patent effect of these interesting events was small. Socialistic programmes—especially when, like Thrane's, they could hardly be distinguished from liberal[1]— and the welfare of the working man never made a great appeal to him. He worked such subjects into the fabric of no play or poem. The rascally carpenter Engstrand of *Ghosts*, who aspires to rise to *bourgeois* wealth and dignity through keeping a brothel, is the only developed lower-class character which he presented in them. None of the multifarious questions which they disengage are of the order of those argued by his successors Hauptmann and Galsworthy, in *The Weavers* and in *Strife*.

They likewise bear small resemblance to that at issue in his contemporary Bjørnson's *Paul Lange and Tora Parsberg* or in Sir Harley Granville-Barker's *Waste*. Ibsen draws no portrait of a *statsraad* in his public or private capacity, and of politicians only two: pastor Straamand of *Love's Comedy* (1862) and lawyer[2] Stensgaard of *The League of Youth* (1869). The former, a member of parliament for a rural constituency, avails himself of the comparative leisure of the session (and a member's monetary allowance) for taking his wife and their unconscionably vast progeny of girls to the capital for a holiday; the audience do not learn that he has a policy or even a mandate, but, as in him has been discerned[3] the priestly ideal of Bishop Riddervold, at that time minister for ecclesiastical affairs, it may be presumed that he supports the government. Stensgaard is the typical 'carpet-bagger', glib and unprincipled, the obscure politician intent only to gain the emoluments of his profession at the cheapest and most speedy rate, in whose character Ibsen could distinguish no redeeming trait.—We shall have to consider other aspects of Stensgaard on examining Ibsen's connection with Bjørnson and other factors in the political life of Norway when this study proceeds to *An Enemy of the People* and *Rosmersholm*.[4]

[1] This is the complaint of Koht, H., *Henrik Ibsen*, 1 (1928), p. 74.

[2] That Stensgaard should follow this calling is probably not chance; attorneys became prominent in the Norwegian parliament in the 1860's; the future prime minister, Johan Sverdrup, was one.

[3] Ording, F., *Henrik Ibsen's "Kærlighedens Komedie"* (1914), p. 33. Riddersvold was supposed to have been inimical to Ibsen and so contributed perhaps to his anticlerical bias.

[4] See pp. 170 f. and 175 f., below.

In a more insidious fashion, however, the experiences which Ibsen underwent in 1851 affected him strongly. They encouraged and fixed the spirit of rebellion against constituted authority which is the common prerogative of spirited and ambitious youth and to which *Catiline* had borne no abstruse testimony. For this the soulless, crushing state-machinery was responsible, while simultaneously the vapourings and gesticulations of the popular representatives destroyed any hopes he may have felt of resistance to those brute forces where opposition most naturally might have been looked for. The defiant rebel, he saw, had neither friends nor expectation of justice—a point which he made with too improbable an insistence when he sketched the fortunes of Dr Stockmann in *An Enemy of the People*. Conversely, the realisation was forced upon him how readily the ordinary man will abandon an isolated position and with what impudence he will go back on old convictions and pro-mises, protesting that nothing is changed. In Stabell and his friends he saw at close quarters the phenomenon of apostasy; what he hated in them was not the opinions they expressed at one time or another, but the fact that, right or wrong, they did not stick to their guns.

On his personality, farthermore, the eighteen months from April 1850 to October 1851 which Ibsen spent in Christiania had an effect which was equally far-reaching. At Grimstad he had been, it seems, a bold, a lively, sometimes even a sportive, lad, ready to publish lampoons and frighten good folk with proclaiming heterodox opinions; a few years later, at Bergen, he was universally known for aloof, old-maidish and personally timid. He had seen the most squalid side of Nor-wegian life, in cheap undergraduate's lodgings,[1] he had cadged and starved. But, worst of all, some inadvised words had brought the whiff of gaol to his very nostrils. He had had a horrible fright.

We will leave it to moralists to determine how much the character is strengthened and ennobled by such a trial. But to the world of aesthetics it brought a gain. The timidity which hereafter Ibsen could only on the rarest occasions shake off[2]

[1] It seems that the poorer members of the university of Christiania often lodged in the quarters otherwise given up to prostitution.

[2] There were one or two isolated periods of Ibsen's late life worthy the physio-logists' attention, e.g. 1864–6 and 1885, when he exhibited a quite unusual loquacity and personal combativeness.

led him to disguise the convictions which burnt with un-
diminished fire in his breast. He contented himself with putting
them forward through the mouth and actions of invented personages. In brief, his fears nurtured the dramatist within him.

*   *   *   *

The contempt for politicians and politics conceived in that year
of petty degradation was the fruit of fairly close observation in
the strangers' gallery of the *Storthing* and colloquies between
Abildgaard and his associates. Ibsen was by no means ignorant
of what he learned to scorn, and for a time he was put in charge
of the political side of the little weekly periodical which his
friend Botten Hansen set up at New Year, 1851. *Andhrimner*—
or *Manden*,[1] as it was generally called—was a satirical miscellany
inspired by *The Corsair (Korsaren)*, the Danish periodical (1846)
of Meir Aron Goldschmidt, a fervent admirer of Heine. Its
general tone has an interesting bearing on undergraduate
opinion at the time and also on the development of its most
celebrated contributor. In politics it was entirely critical,
unfettered by allegiance to any party or faction or leader; any
programme of its own which it may have had was only in-
sinuated obliquely, and its main shafts were directed against
the majority in parliament, the opposition, that is to say—not
because it *was* the opposition or the majority, but because the
liberalism which it presumed itself to possess by virtue of forming
the opposition was so dilute as to be imperceptible and because
through cowardice it failed to exercise that pressure on the
government which its numbers would have warranted; in short,
Andhrimner cavilled at the opposition because it did not oppose
stoutly *enough*.

No glory or success helped *Andhrimner* on its way; it never
sold more than a hundred copies.[2] Journalism of the kind in
which Ibsen involved himself was an affair of trivial con-
fabulations and jobbing printers' back-premises; but so, with
the fewest exceptions, was journalism in the whole of the North
not only in the 1850's, but for several decades still to come, and
in a great many countries besides the Scandinavian.

[1] *Manden* (= The Man) was a nickname suggested by the woodcut (reproduced
in Lothar, R., *Henrik Ibsen*, 2nd edition, 1902, p. 25) of a quizzical observer on the
title-page. Andhrimner was the cook who served messes to the heroes of Valhalla.
[2] Koht, H., 'Henrik Ibsen i "Manden"', being No. 1 of *Avhandlinger utgitt av
Det Norske Videnskaps-Akademi* (1928), *ii, historisk-filosofiske Klasse* (Oslo, 1929), p. 3.

The journalists and master-printers, who are their con-
federates when they are not their employers, leave an impression in Ibsen's pages as disgusting and sordid as do the
politicians. Open and acid contempt of the press runs like a
recurrent theme through modern Norwegian literature, though
Norwegian journalism does not seem any more undesirable
than that of other countries: Bjørnson exhibits it in *The Editor*
(*Redaktøren*), Kielland in *The Feast of St John* (*Sanct Hans Festen*),
Knut Hamsun in *Editor Lynge* (*Redaktør Lynge*). Indefatigable
reader of newspapers as he was, Ibsen shared it to the full.
Of all the vile toadies and turncoats, Billing, the 'Folkebudet'[1]
reporter in *An Enemy of the People* is the worst, and his principal,
the editor Hovstad, scarcely improves upon him. We are
allowed to conceive little good of Hammer in *Pillars of Society*.
No one could call Mortensgaard, the radical publicist of
Rosmersholm, a man of honour or integrity, but Ibsen here goes
out of his way to explain his degradation, through sordid
persecution; and in *The League of Youth* the obvious conclusion
is advanced through the premisses that "the great public" is
"the bad public" and that the bad public wants bad newspapers. This is the argument of Aslaksen, the printer of such
a sheet, who figures again as the capitalist behind *The People's
Messenger* in *An Enemy of the People*, alike contemptible in the
older play as a starveling and, in the later, as a man with a
stake in the country.

✻   ✻   ✻   ✻

The assertion that Ibsen's early commerce with practical politics
produced small patent effect on his imaginative writing would
have been more unreservedly made had it not been for a trifle—
the only purely comic piece he ever wrote—which has never
been translated and is not widely known in the original either.[2]
It is a squib called *Norma* after Bellini's opera,[3] whose *scenario*
it follows fairly closely, though in parody, as the following notes
to the *dramatis personae* show: the hero Severus, to be played
by a Liberal "or, in default of one, by Hr. Stabell", after having
had two consumptive children ("the Addresses of 1848 and
1851") by Norma ("the Opposition"), begins to carry on with

---

[1] I.e. *The People's Messenger*.

[2] It was first published in *Manden* for 1 and 8 June 1851 and not again, after
that, before volume 1 of *Efterladte Skrifter* (1909).

[3] Which was played at Christiania in May 1851.

Norma's good friend Adalgisa (the government party); the Chorus of Druids ("sensible men of the opposition, together with Skjerkholdt")[1] vow condign vengeance, and nothing preserves Severus's life but the happy intervention of his second mistress in the form of an angel, who "turns him into a demi-god or, as we should express ourselves today, a cabinet-minister"— that expectation being the motive which popular scurrility assigned to Stabell's tergiversation.[2]

[1] Halvor Skjerkholdt was M.P. for Nedenes from 1851 to 1873.
[2] Norma's father was supposed to be played by the peasant-politician Ueland, who will come into consideration again in connection with *Peer Gynt* and *The League of Youth* (see pp. 111 and 132 n., and below).

CHAPTER THREE

IBSEN'S LITERARY EDUCATION:

(i) THE DANISH DRAMATISTS

The Warrior's Barrow (1850) and *St John's Eve* (1853)

THE time has now come, after considering some specific stimuli
to which young Ibsen was exposed at the outset of his literary
career and which proved of ephemeral importance in the
shaping of his sympathies, his judgement and his personality,
to take a somewhat more general view of the formative influences operative upon any Norwegian of Ibsen's age and
station in life—in other words, to gain some notion of the
civilisation and culture in which he grew up.

All discussion of Norwegian civilisation involves the relations
between Denmark and Norway. The questions which they raise
are sometimes ticklish and impose caution especially on the
foreigner; in attempting to answer them he will certainly give
offence, however candid his intention. The risks that he incurs
closely resemble those with which, in a study of the civilisation
of Eire, an analysis of Anglo-Irish relations is fraught, and in
what follows an English reader will perceive numerous parallels
between the history of Norway and that of Ireland.

In Norway as elsewhere the feuds of the latter middle ages
had left the royal power supreme and its enemies, the feudal
lords, weak in power and in numbers. Norway now boasts
itself a country without a nobility, and the process by which
in 1824[1] it finally ensured that it should become so had been
going on for a long while. When the Norwegian crown passed
to the royal dynasty of Denmark in 1387 and, *a fortiori*, when,
pursuant to the despotic ideals then prevalent, that dynasty one
hundred and fifty years later organised a centralised, autocratic
rule, it had virtually no opposition to meet in a poor, thinly popu-
lated, inordinately scattered country of farmers and peasants.
No burgess class existed in the towns to resist its encroachments

---

[1] In that year the *Storthing*, recognising two living counts, six living barons and
a few others of hereditary rank, forbade the descent of their dignities.

D I   17   2

either; for the Norwegians had at that epoch lost the maritime power which they were to regain only in the nineteenth century, and what trade touched their shores had for generations been in the hands of foreign merchants, chiefly the Hanseatic community at Bergen.

The Danish kings exercised their rule in Norway through a viceroy at Akershus (the castle of Christiania), a department for Norwegian affairs in Copenhagen and a civil and military service, the members of which were all responsible to the crown and to the crown alone. The ecclesiastical organisation ran closely parallel to the political; for the Lutheran reformers, in abolishing papal jurisdiction throughout Norway, had also destroyed the virtual independence of ecclesiastical bodies which it had often ensured thereby giving the crown an almost absolute sway over the church too. The principal offices in the hierarchies of state and church—and many of the lesser positions too—were held by Danes or by the Low Germans whom the royal house's connections with Holstein and Oldenburg constantly attracted northwards. This course was not dictated by jealous statecraft alone, but also by practical necessity. Even if there had been the wish to govern Norway through Norwegians, there was not a sufficiency of Norwegians competent to receive the necessary training. Farthermore, such Norwegians as there might be, capable and wishful of preparing themselves for responsible office in the church, the army, the navy, the civil service or the teaching profession, were obliged to attend for long years in the royal court or the university of Copenhagen. Some of the ablest of such men—Holberg, for instance, the Molière of the North, a native of Bergen, who rose to high academic office—never returned; and those who did return were Danicised.

This state of affairs continued for centuries, up to the time of the separation of Norway from Denmark by the peace of Kiel in 1814, the Danish monarchy then still remaining an autocracy. Only one year before had a university been established at Christiania, which in the course of time might, irrespective of other considerations, have effected some of the changes about to be described.

In consequence of the conditions so summarily indicated, the educated stratum of Norwegian society, when it was not actually made up of immigrant Danes, was formed and constantly replenished from 'dynasties' of public servants long settled in

Norway or from Norwegians whose manners, ideas and tastes a Dane could scarcely distinguish from his own; in this category are comprised the sheriffs and sheriffs-substitute, judges, military and naval commanders, bishops, masters of grammar-schools, physicians, as well as their families and those taking their tone from intercourse with them, like the inferior clergy, ushers and those members of the rising merchant class who had received their education at the grammar-schools or from university-bred tutors. This would apparently represent a formidable aggregate of individuals, but even on a relative estimate the educated stratum of a community which, in 1814, counted not much above a million souls was a thin one. The middle class of brokers, agents, dealers, professional men humble of extraction as well as of powers, industrialists on a similar small scale, chief clerks and *rentiers*, which laid claim to some culture and had assumed considerable proportions by the end of the nineteenth century, developing an *ethos* distinct from and often antagonistic to their social superiors and inferiors, had virtually not come into existence at the epoch now under consideration. At the time of Ibsen's birth (1828) and just before and after, we must imagine on the one hand the mass of the people and, on the other, what by no great licence of expression was denominated an aristocracy and what it would be tempting to call a patriciate if that term were not commonly associated with rigid caste and an economic foundation upon urban ground-rents.

Preponderantly urban, none the less, was the aspect which this Dano-Norwegian aristocracy wore, and in the towns it reigned supreme. The contrast with the countryside was absolute. We see in the newly found state of Norway not a rural civilisation opposed to an urban civilisation, but (to all intents and purposes) a situation of no civilisation *versus* Danish civilisation.

The first events of importance to Norway that ensued upon the battles of Leipzig and Waterloo and the lifting of the British blockade[1] have been specified: the substitution of a union of the Norwegian and Swedish crowns for Danish abso-lute rule, the enactment of the Eidsvold constitution and the stablishment of the university of Christiania. But their effect on Norwegian civilisation could not but be tardy. True, the strong rural representation in the *Storthing*, by devolving

---

[1] How effective it could be and how devastating in its results may be inferred from Ibsen's ballad of 'Terje Vigen' (vi, p. 340).

responsibility and parliamentary power on to the farmers, at once set up a potential equipoise to the Danicised towns. But to breed an aboriginal official class in the lecture-rooms of Christiania would of necessity prove the labour of accumulated years; and, if in the meanwhile the country was to be governed at all, the administration must still lie in the hands of those who had exercised it as agents of Denmark or (it is almost literally true) in the hands of their sons; as a matter of course, it was from the families of officials, clerics and their social compeers that the first undergraduates went up to Christiania. Outside these only an occasional farmer in the east could command the resources for maintaining a son at the university, and even he would then have first to put him through one of the old-established grammar-schools or employ a graduate of Copenhagen to coach him for the matriculation examination at home. The Dano-Norwegian aristocracy, accordingly, were not expelled from their hegemony by the signatories of Kiel and the constitution-makers at Eidsvold iron-works; the working of the constitution, with its genuine bureaucracy, confirmed them for some decades in it and gave them an enhanced political consciousness. For many years still, in order to be a civilisation at all, the civilisation of Norway had to be Danish civilisation.

A grandfather of Ibsen's mother had been a clergyman, but there were no lawyers, doctors, mayors or civil servants in his ancestry; as far, however, as we can trace it[1] (upwards of a century and a half before his birth) that ancestry is, on the whole, urban and well-to-do; its small merchants and sea-captains are extremely typical[2] of the social strata in southern Norwegian coast-towns which by upward permeation often supplied their aristocracy. Ibsen's father's father had allied himself by marriage to one of the ruling 'dynasties'[3] of Skien, and, until the son was involved in bankruptcy, he could be properly reckoned among that aristocracy[4] and consequently as a participant in Dano-Norwegian culture.

Such too is substantially the situation of the personages whom Ibsen was to present in his 'modern'[5] dramas. They belong

[1] Bergwitz, J. K., *Henrik Ibsen i sin Avstamning* (1916).
[2] This is the view of Koht, 1 (1928), p. 13.
[3] The Paus family.
[4] Jæger, H., *Life of Henrik Ibsen* (English translation, 1890), p. 14.
[5] I exclude from present consideration (as practically 'timeless') *Brand* and *Peer Gynt*.

to this urban, Danicised Norwegian society, even when like
Fru Alving or Rosmer they have their homes in the country.
In these plays, which do not leave the confines of Norway,
Ibsen never deals, even by allusion, with farmers and peasants—
unless it be in *The League of Youth*, where, however, Lundestad
and some others of his kidney are seen only in their purely
political capacity. Norway, at no time a rich country, exhibits
few uncomfortable contrasts between the very opulent and the
completely destitute. Nevertheless, the theatrical managers of
wealthier lands commit an error when (as they often do) they
represent the persons whom Ibsen puts upon the stage as
shabbily-genteel or as unpretending members of the lower
middle class throughout. They may not be cabinet ministers,
sheriffs (*amtmænd*) or bishops, but short of these dignitaries they
represent the cream of the land. In default of baronesses and
belted earls, factually extinct, Chamberlain (*Kammerherre*)[1]
Bratsberg and Hedda Gabler's late father, the general, gained
the highest temporal honours to which a Norwegian might
aspire, the dinner-party which Herr Werle senior gave in honour
of his son represented hundreds of thousands of pounds of
capital, Borkman's cell was a great ball-room of the rococo
period, the Alvings and Allmers' lived in a large way. Too
frequently we have seen in English theatres Hedda Gabler—
whose admirer is 'Mr Justice' Brack—provided with a sitting-
room suitable to lodgings in a side street, whereas an illustration
of the first production shows it to be adorned with palms and
rich hangings; and we cannot understand Head Master Kroll's
consternation at his friend's apostasy until it becomes clear to
us that Johannes Rosmer's English counterpart would be styled
'the Reverend and Honourable'.[2]

*   *   *   *

The poverty and humiliation involved by his father's bankruptcy
and the endeavours of the family to keep up appearances might

---

[1] A personal distinction implying periodical attendance at court.

[2] I do not wish it to be inferred that Ibsen was a snob even in the sense in which
one might (mistakenly) label Pinero or Henry James a snob, or that, for instance,
Hjalmar Ekdal's establishment should be staged as Christiania's equivalent to the
studio of Messrs Elliott & Fry. In *The Wild Duck* the *petit-bourgeois milieu* is of course
obvious and deliberate; Dr Thomas Stockmann is too charitable on a small income
to live luxuriously; and Nora Helmer (who clearly likes everything about her
pretty and who has been to Italy) is emerging after a hard struggle to make ends
meet into the comparative affluence of a provincial bank-manager's wife.

well have left deep traces on Ibsen's sentiments. But, if anything in this order of speculation, he must be regarded not as an upstart or as someone genuinely submerged, but as a temporary *déclassé*, clinging after the loss of worldly goods all the more tenaciously to that cultural heritage, which was among the best that could be offered him in the part of the world where he was born.

By the beginning of the nineteenth century, whatever may be true about an earlier era, Denmark was sharing fully in the general culture of Europe. On the Danish civilisation which Ibsen inherited therefore only two points need be made now. The first is that, centred in a capital city always extremely populous in relation to the country as a whole,[1] it was eminently urban and for that reason propitious to the theatre. In the second place, it has at all times shown itself highly susceptible to foreign influences and, situated as it is at the junction of important lines of communication, in the direction both of south to north and east to west, Denmark has assumed something of the character of an *entrepôt* also in moral wares. Not least through its well-developed book-market, Copenhagen has acted very efficiently as the distributing centre throughout the north for ideas and more specifically literary products.

If the term 'Norwegian literature' be interpreted liberally, it would be unjust to deny its existence during the interval between the remote ballad age and the separation from Denmark in 1814. In that space falls the career of one great author of Norwegian provenance, Holberg (1684–1754); there were also, a little after Holberg, respectable writers of lesser note, like Wessel and Nordahl Brun, and these actually founded a Norwegian literary society (Det Norske Selskab, 1772); but they spent most of their lives in Denmark, they wrote a language indistinguishable from that employed by the Danes, the meetings of the Norske Selskab took place in Copenhagen. In the literary world around 1800, Norway could not front Denmark with so much as the shadow of a counterpart to Edinburgh Castle rearing its head over against the Tower of London.

Naturally, then, a young Norwegian of literary tastes and ambitions, growing up in a society that generally derived its preceptors and its books from Copenhagen, would assume the

---

[1] At present the capital contains about 800,000 of a total population of 3½ millions, a higher proportion than in over-centralised England or France.

same literary heritage as his counterpart in Odense or Aarhus, though he might take a peculiar pride in Holberg, just as a young Caledonian of the time, deep in Wordsworth and Jane Austen and Byron, could yet feel more strongly drawn to Sir Walter Scott—even if Holberg made no appeal, as Scott persistently did, by virtue of 'local colour'. The virtual identity of Norwegian and Danish literature would, in changed political conditions, doubtless have come to an end sooner or later—the more readily as the artistic ideals of the age were so deeply tinctured by the same spirit of nationalism that had animated the constitution-makers of Eidsvold; but the establishment of a flourishing Norwegian literature proved a slower process than that of the Norwegian state. Meanwhile, for the school-boy at Skien and the pharmacist's assistant at Grimstad in the 1830's and 1840's, the literature which he would rightfully look upon as 'his' literature was Danish literature. The great names in its annals, besides those mentioned, were Ewald, Baggesen, Œhlenschläger, Johan Ludvig Heiberg, Hertz and Frederik Paludan-Müller.[1]

Newspapers apart, Ibsen was no great reader in his maturity[2] and always gave way to a notable irritability when any suggestion of literary indebtedness on his part came to his notice. Partly, no doubt, that was an aspect of the sensitiveness which his timidity and proud poverty had bred, but in part it could plead a better excuse. Ibsen's was not at all the kind of mind that reflects from its surface whatever has just been cast upon it from the outer world; everything that passed out of him was the effect of a greatly protracted rumination and thorough assimilation into his moral being; what he wrote, he said, had not been experienced, but *lived*.[3] Nevertheless with him, as everywhere else, exports represent imports, and the finished product was sometimes conditioned by the raw materials to a degree which flat denials cannot diminish.[4] His critics must therefore, without unduly pressing any charge of mendacity,

[1] For Ibsen's relations with Paludan-Müller see pp. 56 f., below.
[2] "Books", he is reported to have said (Koht, II, p. 198), "I leave them to my wife and Sigurd [his son] to read." As a matter of fact, I think that Ibsen's abstention from book-reading has been exaggerated; his correspondence bears witness to quite a number of exceptions.
[3] *Breve*, I, p. 207; cf. also ibid. p. 205.
[4] Ibsen read, it seems, everything in the newspapers from the first words to the last; and even from them it is possible to learn something of what is occurring in the realms of the mind.

hold themselves free, on occasions, to disregard such disclaimers of indebtedness.

*   *   *   *

At the time that he composed *Catiline* Ibsen, according to his own admission,[1] was acquainted with at least two Danish classics, Holberg and Œhlenschläger. He cherished all his life[2] a predilection for the comedies of the former and for his satire *Peder Paars.* But the distinctive and all-pervading element in Holberg's works of imagination, his classical humour, was incompatible with the tragic and individualistic strain proper to Ibsen, and it would prove a profitless undertaking to argue a formative ascendancy of the older over the younger man. Still, Ibsen can scarcely have helped admiring Holberg's economy, his power of rigidly subordinating means to the twofold end of theatrical entertainment and social criticism; and his own tendency in that direction may well have been promoted thereby.

Œhlenschläger stood nearer to him in every sense. As a boy at Skien he enjoyed opportunities of seeing plays of his acted by theatrical strollers.[3] In his country's temple of fame Adam Gottlob Œhlenschläger (1779–1850) occupies a position analogous to that claimed elsewhere for Victor Hugo, Pushkin and (shall we say?) Walter Scott, though his genius, for all its fecundity in drama, lyric and narrative verse, may not quite attain to the sublimity of theirs. He is the great romantic poet of Denmark and conspicuous in his generation for one thing— the celebration of the legendary and romantic historical past of the Scandinavian peoples.[4] For that reason too he commended himself very strongly to the Norwegians who, in rivalry with the Swedes and the Danes, have always claimed to be *par excellence* the heirs to Valhalla and the Vikings.

Œhlenschläger's example had plainly stood before the author of *Catiline.* Though fortified by the fictitious scenes concerned with Furia, the appeal of that tragedy resembles one of Œhlen-

[1] Cf. Koht, I, p. 54.
[2] Paulsen, J., *Samliv med Ibsen,* II (1913), p. 21.
[3] Mosfjeld, O., 'Ibsen og Skien' in *Edda,* XXX (1930), p. 63, where it is stated that other authors so presented were Scribe, Kotzebue and Heiberg.
[4] In his own country he had been anticipated by Ewald; Britons will remember Gray.

24

(i) THE DANISH DRAMATISTS

schläger's in being declamatory rather than dramatic, and his prosody is reproduced, both in the flaccid, rather monotonous, blank verse and in the infrequent relief therefrom. To the same source of inspiration Ibsen subsequently resorted for subject-matter. His next dramatic project, a lost play on the Norwegian king Olaf Trygveson, it is plausibly conjectured, was to form a pendant to Œhlenschläger's best drama on a Norse subject, *Earl Hakon (Hakon Jarl)*. *Olaf Trygveson* was never completed; but in the dramatic experiment with which its author followed it up, *The Warrior's Barrow (Kjæmpehøjen,* 1850), he selected a theme perfectly consonant with Œhlenschläger's prepossessions.

A Romantic poet as believing with Mme de Staël[1] that Romantic poetry was Christian poetry, Œhlenschläger endeavoured to reconcile that principle with historical matter of such peculiar appeal to himself by repeated dwelling on the phase in early Scandinavian history in which the devotees of Odin and Thor were becoming converted to Christianity. He felt it incumbent upon him to represent this as a development, not as a clean break with the past, and to show by how easy a transition the virtues of the Viking could pass into those of the Christian. Under his pencil, the bloody butchers too well known to their neighbours' chronicles readily took on the lineaments of their congeners in *Idylls of the King*.

The Warrior's Barrow, then, once more mainly couched in blank verse, takes up an Œhlenschlägeresque subject and treats it in the manner of the master. In its single act Gandalf, a 'sea-king from Norway', lands on Pantelleria or some other island near Sicily in order to exact vengeance for the fate suffered by his father some time before. He mistakes for his quarry an old man living there with his foster-daughter, but the veteran's self-sacrificing magnanimity—an effect of his conversion to Christianity—so strongly impresses Gandalf that he abandons his fell design and, a convert himself,[2] sails off again. He takes with him the old man's daughter Blanka, who speaks these last lines, closely parallel to those spoken by Maria at the

---

[1] At one time Ibsen appears to have accepted Mme de Staël's equation: romantic=modern=Christian (see his lecture 'On the Heroic Ballad and its Significance for Artificial Poetry', 1857, first reprinted in *Samlede Værker*, x, 1902, pp. 350 ff.).

[2] Not to Christianity, but to the cult of Balder, which in complete accordance with Œhlenschläger's ideas is conceived as a half-way house.

25

end of Œhlenschläger's *Varangians in Miklagard* (*Væringerne i Miklagard*):

> Soon is the viking life a memory bleak!
> Already sits the hero on his mound;
> The time is past when he could sail around
> With sword and battle cry from strand to strand.
> Thor's hammer will no longer rule the land,
> The North will be itself a giant grave.
> But bear in mind the pledge All-Fader [*sic*] gave:
> When moss and flowers shall the barrow hide,
> To Idavold the hero's ghost shall ride,—
> Then Norway too shall from the grave be brought
> To chastened deeds within the realm of thought![1]

Henrik Jæger too is doubtless right in observing[2] that Œhlenschläger furnished the models for a not very valuable cycle of poems on the Old Norse legend of Helge Hundingsbane which Ibsen contributed to *Manden* (in 1851) and never had reprinted during his lifetime.[3]

Gandalf's renunciation of vengeance finds a parallel in Ibsen's later play, *The Vikings in Helgeland*, where Sigurd's refusal to obey the ferocious, self-seeking code of the battle-axe and the spread-eagle is explained by his secret acceptance of the cross. But Œhlenschläger's influence on Ibsen waned rapidly. A sign of it is the abandonment of blank verse; acute ears have even made out[4] that the echoes of Œhlenschläger's music have already become fainter in the second of the two surviving versions of *The Warrior's Barrow*. Many more persistent impressions left their mark on *Peer Gynt*, but there are good grounds for thinking that certain scenes in it constitute a parody and criticism of the good-for-nothing of genius whom Œhlenschläger glorified in *Aladdin*, Danish romanticism's *Hernani*.[5]

*　　　*　　　*　　　*

[1] *Early Plays*, pp. 125 f.
[2] *Life of Henrik Ibsen* (English translation, 1890), p. 64.
[3] It can be found in *Efterladte Skrifter*, 1, p. 91.
[4] Incompetence makes me, as a rule, unwilling to judge Ibsen's style or to base any arguments of my own on it. Paasche, F., 'Ibsen og Nationalromantiken' in *Samtiden*, x (Bergen, 1909), observes (p. 649) that the style of *Kjæmpehøjen*, particularly in the earlier version, is Œhlenschläger's, but that the accents of Welhaven and J. L. Heiberg have penetrated into the second.
[5] With his accustomed skill Georg Brandes elaborates (*Henrik Ibsen*, 1898, p. 22) a parallel of the antithesis which Œhlenschläger set up between Aladdin and Noureddin with the antithesis Haakon-Skule in Ibsen's *Pretenders*. The actual impulse to which *The Pretenders* was due was another (see pp. 67 f., below), but Brandes scores a good point (p. 105) when he likens Skule's appropriation of Haakon's 'royal thought' to Noureddin's theft of the magical lamp.

Several pieces by Œhlenschläger have been translated into
foreign languages, and Holberg enjoys an even greater international repute. But, apart from theirs, Danish plays have
remained almost unknown outside their own country. That
does not imply, however, that they are negligible. The lively interest taken in the theatre by the Danes has indeed ensured a
somewhat remarkable dramatic activity of an intensity and at
a level to which probably none of the smaller countries of
Europe can afford a parallel in modern times.[1] After the first
great Romantic outburst in the first years of the nineteenth
century, the chief names in the dramatic field were Johan
Ludvig Heiberg and Henrik Hertz, and with both of them
Ibsen was brought into contact.

Heiberg (1797–1861) occupies an odd, amphibious position.
He was both the accredited representative of the Hegelian
philosophy in Denmark and the perfecter of a form of art by
no means commonly associated with philosophy, the so-called
vaudeville, by which term, in Danish parlance, is meant a kind
of ballad-opera kin in many essentials to *The Beggar's Opera*,
though more fanciful. Heiberg not only composed some most
excellent specimens of this sort, but likewise defended it theo-
retically at considerable length. For he was also a literary
critic; and to his diverse occupations he added that of manager
of the Royal Theatre in Copenhagen which experts[2] have
held up as the model playhouse.[3]

To Heiberg Ibsen had an introduction when he first visited
Copenhagen, and the great man received his humble colleague
with his accustomed courtesy, even though he confined his conversation to gastronomic topics.[4] It is highly probable that
Ibsen's determination to force himself a path to public eminence
and to power in the realm of thought through the theatre was

---

[1] During the six weeks which Ibsen spent in Copenhagen in 1852 he could
have seen (and pretty certainly did see) the following Danish plays at the Royal
Theatre: Beyer's *Flugt og Fare*, Buntzen's *For Ti Aar Siden*, Hartnack's *Bevægede Tid*,
Heiberg's *Recensenten og Dyret* and *Nej*, Fru Heiberg's *Søndag paa Amager* and
Abekatten, Hertz's *Stifbørnene*, *Scheik Hassan* and *Kong René's Datter*, Holberg's
Pernilles korte Frøkenstand, *Barselstuen*, *Henrik og Pernille* and *Vægelsindede*, Hostrup's
Soldaterløjer, Nielsen's *Slægtningene* and Œhlenschläger's *Hakon Jarl*.
[2] Archer, W. and Granville-Barker, H., *A National Theatre* (1909).
[3] His equally distinguished wife, Johanne Louise Heiberg, was the leading
actress and towards the end of her career sometimes acted as 'producer' there.
Ibsen wrote one of his rhymed epistles to her (VI, p. 389).
[4] Paulsen, J., *Samliv med Ibsen*, I (1906), p. 44.

given supreme encouragement by Heiberg's brilliant figure and condescension.[1] But more specific effects followed also.

Ibsen began the play that was to succeed *The Warrior's Barrow* at Copenhagen during the visit just alluded to. This *St John's Eve* (*Sancthansnatten*, 1853), a comedy in three acts, for which the scene is laid in the Norwegian countryside and the time of action is the present, owes several features to the so-called *Huldreromantik* (i.e. fairy-romanticism) and cognate Norwegian phenomena shortly to be reviewed, but the nature of the whole was plainly suggested by Heiberg's example, and it may justly be considered from the title downward as a pendant to his *Seven Sleepers' Day* (*Syvsoverdag*),[2] even in the circumstances that both draw in substantial measure on Shakespeare's *Midsummer Night's Dream*:[3] *St John's Eve* and *Seven Sleepers' Day* each exhibit a blend of the lyric with the dramatic, of the fantastical and the respectably *bourgeois*;[4] mortals have dealings with beings from another world at a time traditionally appropriated to the latter, and (in consequence of this commerce) undergo swift changes of affection and parental approbation, to the end that, in the teeth of great odds, the worthiest young man becomes affianced to the worthiest young woman at the same time as another betrothal takes place.

It is not the present purpose to particularise the reminiscences from Heiberg's plays which have plausibly been traced elsewhere in the works of Ibsen, but a few words may be here devoted to the effect exerted on him by Heiberg's aesthetic essay 'On the Vaudeville',[5] which he certainly knew.[6] Ibsen was clearly impressed at once by the cardinal theory which that 'dramaturgical investigation' advances, viz. that drama repre-

[1] On Heiberg's death Ibsen wrote a not very felicitous poem, which he excluded from his collection of *Digte*; it is to be found in the *Efterladte Skrifter*, I, p. 180.

[2] Heiberg's most celebrated play, *The Elfin Mound* (*Elverhøj*), also has many of these features.

[3] Shakespeare's comedy had received special commendation from Hermann Hettner, whom Ibsen met in Dresden a few weeks after the meeting with Heiberg (cf. also pp. 49 f. below).

[4] But by no means rudely mechanical. This double blend was effected also by Heiberg's junior, Hostrup, in his *Master and Apprentice* (*Mester og Lærling*) which was being performed at the Casino precisely during the weeks that Ibsen was in Copenhagen and incubating *St John's Eve*.

[5] 'Om Vaudevillen' (1826), in his *Prosaiske Skrifter*, VI (1861), pp. 1 ff.

[6] Koht, I, pp. 87 f., insists that during his time at Christiania in 1850 and 1851 Ibsen was steeped in Heibergian aesthetics, which had received a great impetus just then by the appointment of M. J. Monrad to the professorship of philosophy.

sents[1] a synthesis of the lyrical (or narrowly poetic and self-revelatory) and the epic (or narrative and objective) elements of literature; for in his paper on the Heroic Ballads, which was read in 1856,[2] he accepts it virtually as an axiom, and, beginning with *St John's Eve*, all his dramas for the next fifteen years exhibit an unmistakable determination to comprise both these sets of elements—until, after the completion of *Peer Gynt*, other considerations of the relations between the subjective and the objective were brought to his notice by Georg Brandes (another Dane!).

'Om Vaudevillen' contained other passages on which Ibsen no doubt meditated—Heiberg's gibe at poetic justice, for instance, which demanded before the final curtain fell a manifest reward of virtue and punishment of vice, the accompanying complaint that the North[3] understood not satire and the doctrine for which the illustrious support of Holberg was claimed:– "Comedy[4] should be a portrayal of the manners of the age, that is to say should be local and, by attaching itself to the manners of the nation and the age, gain historical validity and, with it, true poetic objectivity." Nevertheless, though in these respects too *St John's Eve* had some interesting premonitions, it was some time before Ibsen's own practice showed him to have rejected the conventions against which Heiberg's pleas were urged.[5]

Henrik Hertz (1805–71), the junior contemporary of Heiberg and great admirer of his wife, came upon the scene rather later than he, and Ibsen quite probably knew little about him till after the first Christiania days. His is a less interesting figure

[1] Ibsen's own phrase is "Notoriously...a higher combination of lyric and epic" ("som bekendt...en højere forbindelse af lyrik og epos", *Samlede Værker*, x, 1902, p. 356).

[2] To the 'Foreningen af 22 December' in Bergen (first printed in his *Samlede Værker*, x, 1902, p. 350); a companion paper on Shakespeare has unfortunately been lost.

[3] Heiberg, *op. cit.* p. 95, actually says "Denmark"; but I have no doubt that Ibsen took Norway to be homogeneous with Denmark in this respect.

[4] The word should probably be taken as the equivalent of the French *comédie*; for *comedy*, as commonly understood in English, Heiberg's term would be *lystspil*. The passage runs in the original: "Comedien skulde være en Skildring af Tidsalderens Sæder, det er at sige, at den skulde være local, og ved at slutte sig til Nationens og Tidsalderens Sæder, faae historisk Gyldighed, og derved den sande poetiske Objectivitet" (*op. cit.* vi, p. 81).

[5] The conclusions which Heiberg reached commend themselves more strongly than his cumbrous, doctrinaire method. It is perhaps a sly dig at his interpreter when Ibsen makes the pedantic bore of *St John's Eve*, Paulsen, discourse the language of Hegel.

than Heiberg's, and even on the purely dramatic side he does not rise to the same heights. But, by aping the manner of Baggesen,[1] he led a conscious reaction against Œhlenschläger's full-blooded Romanticism, which could not fail to evoke sympathy from a younger generation, and he scored at least two outstanding stage successes with *The House of Svend Dyring* (*Svend Dyrings Hus*) and *King René's Daughter* (*Kong René's Datter*)—the latter of which enjoyed an international vogue.[2] The debt of Ibsen's *Feast at Solhaug* (*Gildet paa Solhaug*, 1856) to the former has formed a subject for acute, even acrimonious, debate from the start, and Danish partisans are almost certainly in the right against their opponents in advertising its existence, even if some may over-estimate its magnitude and significance. In *The House of Svend Dyring* (1837) Hertz presented no ballad-opera after the style of Gay or Heiberg, but converted to dramatic uses some of the much less sophisticated conventions of the old ballad-ages, the casting of magical (and efficacious) spells, the returning of ghosts from the dead to watch over those dear to them and so forth. Ibsen's *Olaf Liljekrans* (1857) and, more particularly, *The Feast at Solhaug*, rationalise such supernatural elements, but they lay their scene in the remote society which accepted them together with homicide and outlawry, and their style and language too are a far-going adaptation of the heroic ballad manner. When writing his two pieces Ibsen could not be unaware of a similar experiment made with such resounding success twenty years earlier.[3]

*   *   *   *

There is no point in insisting farther[4] on the readiness with which Ibsen and his collaborators in *Manden* adopted the purely critical viewpoint of Goldschmidt; and Ibsen's very important relations with Kierkegaard and Georg Brandes, as touching a much more advanced stage in his career, must be relegated to a subsequent chapter. Enough, however, has been said to demonstrate how firmly Ibsen, as an author, was rooted in the

---

[1] Who is supposed to be the Noureddin, the villain, of Œhlenschläger's *Aladdin*.
[2] There were, for instance, several English translations.
[3] Arguments have been based on the plea that both *The Feast at Solhaug* and *The House of Svend Dyring* derive from Kleist's *Katie of Heilbronn* (*Das Käthchen von Heilbronn*) and that *The House of Svend Dyring* was presented at the Bergen Theatre just after *The Feast at Solhaug*, also on Ibsen's vastly superior style; but, whatever their force, they scarcely, in my opinion, invalidate the main contention.
[4] Cf. p. 14, above.

Danish civilisation to which the Norway of his youth was still tributary. His sentiments towards Denmark were liable to fluctuations in later life, but his greatest and most enduring political passion, his 'Scandinavianism',[1] ensured their general friendliness. As an old man, when he was making his last journey to Copenhagen, he remarked[2] to his companion that to come from Norway to the shores of the Sound was like emerging from a tunnel into the sunlit day, and we may be sure that the observation had metaphorical overtones. Yet, however deep the roots may have gone by which he was attached to the civilisation of Denmark, to look upon him as entirely alien from his native land, unconcerned with the specifically Norwegian developments that during his lifetime were going forward in the moral domain, as elsewhere, would be a gross error. To these developments we must now direct our attention.

[1] On this see chapter VIII, below.
[2] Vogt, N., 'Paa Reise med Henrik Ibsen' in *Samtiden*, XVII (Christiania, 1906), p. 331.

CHAPTER FOUR

IBSEN'S LITERARY EDUCATION:

(ii) THE NORWEGIANS

St John's Eve (1853), *The Feast at Solhaug* (1856),
Olaf Liljekrans (1857)

IN the autumn of 1851, while *Manden* (or *Andhrimner*) was still in being, the University Club at Christiania held a *conversazione* for the purpose of contributing funds to a new theatrical enterprise that had come into being at Bergen.[1] The famous violinist Ole Bull, then actively concerned in its management, came over from Bergen to play at the *conversazione*, and young Henrik Ibsen contributed a 'Prologue'.[2] The two men were introduced to one another, with the result that the junior was at once given a post at the Bergen theatre. By this means Ibsen was brought directly into contact with the latest and, in some ways, the most vigorous manifestation of the new Norwegian nationalist spirit in the arts. That spirit was in a measure engendered by a revulsion against the whole Danish tradition in which, as has been indicated, Ibsen had been bred,[3] and his new experiences could not but give a sharp jolt to many of his prepossessions. Before proceeding to a discussion of its consequences, as far as they affect Ibsen, we must give some idea of this nationalist spirit in its origins and aims.

Like so many a secession state a hundred years later, the Norwegian began its existence in 1814 under the least favourable auspices—impoverished, its old life-lines cut, founded on a constitution which was pure 'bed-work and mappery', implicated

---

[1] Shortly before this, parliament had rejected a petition for a grant in aid of this; *Andhrimner* commented on the rejection in its usual satirical style, but I do not think that it has been ascertained whether Ibsen wrote the comment.

[2] The Prologue (in *Efterladte Skrifter*, i, p. 116) was recited by the actress Laura Svendsen who, under her married name of Gundersen, was later to become one of the most distinguished interpreters of Ibsen's female *rôles*.

[3] He was not unaware of what was going on. The commotion occasioned by the appointment in 1851 of the Dane, Carl Borgaard, to the direction of the theatre at Christiania proved to him the strength of the nationalist movement in the domain he was to make his own; but at that time he had merely sneered at it. (Review of *Haarpidsk og Kaarde* reprinted from *Manden* in *Samlede Værker*, x (1902), pp. 319 ff.)

in a new order of which the determining conditions remained
obscure, prone to identify tradition in public affairs with lack
of patriotism if not with treason, knowing no international
relations that were not based on hatred and suspicion. A thou-
sand and one small things which seem almost automatic had
to be devised and laboriously set going. Progress nevertheless
was made also in greater matters; the constitution was found
to be workable and was worked, a not unsatisfactory *modus
vivendi* established with the new king and with his other people,
the Swedes; trade was put on its legs again, the budget balanced,
the currency stabilised. No spectacular triumphs attended these
early advances, no calamitous setbacks; after a quarter of a
century in which nothing much seemed to have happened, the
engine's parts had been in effect assembled and tested, a head
of steam raised, the regulator slowly opened and all made ready
for a run which, allowing for some occasional decelerations,
even a minor stoppage or two, continued satisfactorily until 1940.

An ideal of the Eidsvold assembly had been the yeoman of
Norway, the *odelsbonde*, seen in the double radiance of the
historical reverie which circled about the old medieval kingdoms and of the Rousseauistic enthusiasm for the primitive and
natural. He had been given considerable political responsibility
and, though he could not always avoid detraction on grounds
more or less colourable, he showed himself worthy of his trust.
The latter is one of the dominant facts in the history of Norway
during the two generations after 1814 and was bound up by
reciprocal cause and effect with both the cultural and the
economic progress of the countryside.

Nevertheless, for long enough, the advance in the moral
realm that had been so confidently expected to accompany
national independence proceeded even more sluggishly than the
advance elsewhere. An impartial modern observer has described
it [1] not as advance at all, but mere stagnation; in view, however,
of the scantiness of the available forces and the necessity of their
being primarily employed to construct the new machinery of
society, he rightly forbears surprise that in the fifteen or
twenty years after the Eidsvold assembly no one of eminence
was found to concoct a specifically Norwegian philosophy, to
compose the new Norwegian music, to paint the new Norwegian
pictures, even to build the public buildings, deliver university

[1] Boer, R. C., *Norwegens Letterkunde* (1922), p. 7.

lectures or reinvigorate the national church. Something of
course was done in all these departments of the national life,
but the will was often, with a great deal of fervour, taken for
the deed, and the deed was of poor quality, speedily forgotten.[1]
In this general stagnation literature also partook.

* * * *

From 1829 onwards, however, a critic is justified in speaking
of Norwegian literature, without reservations or euphemism.
Its originators are generally held to be Welhaven and Wergeland, two respectable, but minor writers, whose distinctive
contributions a foreigner does not always find it too easy to
discern, more especially since, in later life, Welhaven modified
his outlook and, in certain essential respects, drew nearer to his
traditional opponent than he had been in their youth. For
opponents they were, when they were both alive, in a sense
decidedly more actual than the oppugnancy that is vulgarly
assumed between a Dickens and a Thackeray (their contemporaries) or a Goethe and a Schiller.

Johan Sebastian Cammermeyer Welhaven (1807–73), who
eventually graced a professorial chair at the university of
Christiania and indeed signed that certificate which half rejected Ibsen in his matriculation examination, represented,
with the modifications which a short lapse of time brought with
it, the Dano-Norwegian tradition that had prevailed down to
1814.[2] In his youth, he was looked upon as a spokesman
of those young and generally practical university men who were
to take the lead in their country's administration when the
generation of Eidsvold had passed away.[3] With the general
public Welhaven made a name by means of a slim volume of
carefully turned sonnets which bore the ominous title *The Half-
Light of Norway* (*Norges Dæmring*, 1834),[4] wherein, amid a good
deal of fine natural appreciation for which he always preserved
a *penchant*, he coldly and severely surveyed the moral realm

[1] A reservation of importance must be made for the great mathematician Abel,
who died, aged only 27, in 1829.
[2] His mother was a first cousin of Johan Ludvig Heiberg.
[3] Their leader in many other respects was Schweigaard, polymath and later
statsraad, to whom Ibsen addressed the poem 'Til Professor Schweigaard' (vi,
p. 323), in which he hailed him as a pioneer.
[4] 'Dæmring' is usually rendered 'Twilight'; but Welhaven is referring to the
half-light before the (doubtful) dawn. Welhaven had previously published *Poetics
and Polemics* (*Digtekunst og Polemik*, 1832).

about him and pronounced it a desert. *The Half-Light of Norway* was directed mainly against the strident self-gratulations of his contemporaries and especially against those of them who circled round Henrik Arnold Wergeland (1808–44). Welhaven saw mere barbarism and lack of principle in the debaucheries of Wergeland and his friends and in the corresponding extravagance of their expressions, which culminated in Wergeland's hastily penned, scarcely revised *Creation, Man and Messiah* (*Skabelsen, Mennesket og Messias,* 1829), a poem as vast almost in its length as in its subject; and the justice of his strictures was borne out by an all but murderous ambush which these patriotic rowdies then proceeded to lay; luckily for the sonneteer, they cudgelled the wrong man.

With these two so dissimilar works the new Norwegian literature was safely launched, albeit launched on to ruffled waters (for the hostilities between Welhaven and Wergeland were by no means confined to this single occasion nor, as we have seen, to their two persons); but the hurly-burly had the advantage in the eyes of all the participants in it of attaching attention to moral and intellectual questions even if placidity should be rudely broken.

In this place it is unnecessary to follow farther the careers of Welhaven and Wergeland. But the nature of their opposition should be noted since it has been held symptomatic of an antinomy in that nebulous entity, the national character. On the one hand, there is Wergeland's sanguine spirit (apt to degenerate into boastful self-satisfaction), nourished by the real, but remote feats of the Viking ancestors and by the contemplated virtues of honest industry, steadiness and piety in the contemporary populace, particularly that of the countryside— virtues disdained by other observers either as illusory or nowise special to the country. Against it is ranged Welhaven's spirit of criticism, which certainly has the merit of trying the critic's own heart and reins as well as others', but whose severity induces pessimism and is, to some tastes, tainted with sheer nihilism. The former attitude of mind readily accepts formal carelessness as a token of sincerity, if not of genius, the latter joins pregnancy of expression to strictness of judgement. The discrepancy just indicated found many years later its completest expression in the rivalry, both real and imagined, between Bjørnson, the warm admirer of Wergeland, and Ibsen, heir to

35   3-2

much that was best in Welhaven, whose style he very carefully studied.[1]

Among the progenitors of the new Norway's literature, rather earlier in the field than Wergeland and Welhaven, we should rank the minor novelist Mauritz Christopher Hansen, who skilfully utilised the device of a sinister, gradually disclosed secret, which may have impressed the imagination of Ibsen when he was young and helped to determine a very noteworthy feature in the plots of his plays.[2]

After Wergeland and Welhaven come another couple of great stimulatory effect and celebrated, not for their collisions and incompatibility, but for the success of their co-operation. They are the later Bishop Jørgen Moe (1813–82) and his jovial, sometimes Rabelaisian friend, Peter Christen Asbjørnsen (1812–85). Preceded by the reverend Andreas Faye, who published *Norwegian Tales* (*Norske Sagn*) in 1833,[3] Asbjørnsen and Moe gave to the world in 1841 the first of their *Norwegian Popular Fairy Tales*[4] (*Norske Folkeeventyr*). In this series of volumes they assembled the current, traditional stories, which they had had narrated to them on extensive excursions through the Norwegian countryside. The tales which they cast into an enduring form enjoyed a vast vogue and possessed for some doctrinaire minds the additional merit of affording vital links between the historical past and that repository of modern Norwegian virtue, the peasant. The efforts of Asbjørnsen and Moe were seconded by other collections of Folk-Songs and Ballads, first that of Landstad, then that of the learned Bugge.[5]

*   *   *   *

The antiquaries' labours, whether in prose or in verse, raised

[1] Bull, F., in Berggrav, E., *Ibsens Sjelelige Krise* (1937), p. 49.

[2] The case for this has been ably argued by Collin, C., 'Henrik Ibsens Dramatiske Bygningstil' in *Tilskueren* (1906), p. 610.

[3] From the second edition (1844) of this, Ibsen took the theme of his unfinished play, *The Grouse in Justedal* (*Rypen i Justedal*), which he modified and worked into *Olaf Liljekrans*.

[4] The sobriety of the English people has included no word in their vocabulary exactly corresponding to the Norwegian and Danish *Eventyr* (etymologically connected with the French *aventure*) and to the German *Märchen*. We are obliged to use the terms 'fairy-tale' or 'fairy-story' for a class of prose narratives in which there need be neither fairies nor indeed supernatural agents and occurrences, provided only they be phantastical enough. I take this opportunity to apologise likewise for the hideous, but unavoidable, neologisms of 'Folk-Tale' and 'Folk-Song'.

[5] *Norske Folkeviser* (1853) and *Gamle Norske Folkeviser* (1858) respectively.

in peremptory form a question of language. As long as Norwegian literature formed a branch of the Danish civilisation, no such question had obtruded, and writers like Welhaven, Wergeland and their coevals were content with the language of Œhlenschläger, Heiberg, even of Hans Andersen. However, where a Galt or a Moir employs the word 'bonny' in place of 'pretty', a Norwegian author, even when praising the works of the Holy Spirit,[1] might say 'vakker' rather than 'smuk', and such trifling deviations became more numerous as time went on, especially when the necessity arose of reporting local speech. For even among town-dwellers, besides marked differences in pronunciation, discrepancies in vocabulary and idiom occurred more frequently in proportion as, in one sense or another, the old Danish metropolis seemed to recede into the distance.[2] When now authors like Asbjørnsen and Moe felt the necessity of reproducing *in extenso* narratives and poems that hitherto had subsisted entirely in the mouths of the uneducated and rustic, a linguistic difficulty of quite a novel order confronted them. To attempt a paraphrase into the accepted literary language meant sacrificing the raciness of the original and even accuracy; if, on the other hand, stories and verses were set down as nearly as possible in the form in which they had been communicated, they often would remain intelligible only in the district in which they had survived, and the intention of forming, for the benefit of a reading public, a truly national store-house of traditional literature would be defeated. The idea naturally presented itself then of fashioning a new literary language which, it might be said, should represent the highest common factor of the principal spoken dialects and at the same time not prove of insuperable difficulty to readers of the old Danish literary language.

This new *landsmaal* was adumbrated by J. A. Hielm in *Almindelig Norsk Maanedsskrift* (1831), advocated (as it is natural to expect) by Wergeland, encouraged by the collections of Asbjørnsen and Moe and, by the end of the nineteenth century, generally admitted to all the uses of a literary language. There

[1] See on this point an amusing passage of arms between Georg Brandes and the theologians when he first visited Christiania (Brandes, *Levned*, ii, 1907, pp. 207 ff.).
[2] Koht, however, makes the interesting observation (ii, p. 147) that after 1830 what he calls the "book-language" (i.e. Dano-Norwegian) advanced so far that members of the official and urban class naturally spoke it, while the preceding generation had adhered to *patois*.

is no need to enter into details of this new development, which became for the first time a matter of widespread interest in the 1850's, beyond remarking for the satisfaction of the reader that Ibsen always wrote in the old established Dano-Norwegian *riksmaal*[1] (as did Bjørnson, Lie, Kielland, Knut Hamsun, Sigrid Undset), while the *landsmaal* won notable triumphs through the genius of Vinje and Arne Garborg. Of the two standard biographies of Ibsen, Gran's is couched in *riksmaal*, Professor Koht's in *landsmaal*.

*   *   *   *

Since it was the spoken word that had brought this literary question to a head, it inevitably and speedily obtruded itself on to the stage. The Norwegian theatre of the early nineteenth century, in so far as it existed at all, was a dependency of the Danish theatre, by reason both of the eminence to which the latter had attained and of the general cultural situation. That this relationship should continue indefinitely seemed probable; for it was the urban populace which supported the stage and delighted to hear the professional recitation of the language which formed its own ideal, naturally preferring Danish-born actors, who could best subserve their requirements, and the Danish repertory[2] which the players had no choice but to present. In his biography of Ibsen Gerhard Gran observes that "as late as 1850 our theatre was to all intents and purposes wholly and completely Danish: Danish pieces, Danish translations, Danish actors, Danish direction".[3] A Danish manager guided the fortunes of the Christiania Theatre until the end of 1862.[4]

[1] For that reason his plays could always be presented in the author's own words on the premier stage of the North, the Royal Theatre (Kongelig Theater) of Copenhagen. Round about 1860 Ibsen's work shows the greatest absorption of purely Norwegian words, it seems. The acute ear of Karl Larsen, a Dane and a philologist, could only detect two slight 'Norwegianisms' in the first version of *Catiline*. Brandes (*Henrik Ibsen*, 1898, p. 129) calls all Ibsen's *juvenilia* "pure Danish" and notes that in *Olaf Liljekrans* there were scarcely a dozen 'Norwegian' words nor a single un-Danish expression. For familiar intercourse Ibsen used "modern riksmaal" (according to Løken, H., *Ibsen og Kjærligheten*, 1923, p. 77).

[2] The translations from the French, German, etc. were those originally prepared for a Copenhagen public.

[3] "...endnu i 1850 [var] vort teater saagodtsom helt og holdent dansk; danske stykker, danske oversættelser, danske skuespillere, dansk scene-ledelse" (Gran, I., p. 132).

[4] According to at any rate one trustworthy historian (Mørch, E., *Da Kristiania var Smaaby*, 1901, p. 128) the period just before the end of the Danish hegemony in the Christiania Theatre was its most lustrous.

The weakest link at which to break this chain of cause and effect (if it was thought proper to do so) was that represented by the players. As long as they were Danes, capable only of speaking Danish with the sounds and intonations of their countrymen, the formation of a Norwegian repertory of Norwegian plays as distinct from a Danish repertory could only be effected at the expense of making it a travesty. We need only imagine how impossible it would be (in the event of a desire to do any such thing) to set up a Scottish national theatre in Edinburgh, presenting a Scottish national drama, before there was a sufficiency of authentic Scottish players to fill all the parts. Certain patriotic enthusiasts in Christiania were accordingly well advised to commence the operations that eventually secured complete success, when they first founded a national school of acting there, which, through the public rehearsals of its pupils, by degrees grew into a regular theatre. This school dates from 1852.[1]

Two years previously an enterprise directed to the same end, but more ambitious in its scope, had been inaugurated[2] in the most advanced city of Norway, Bergen. The historian of the Norwegian stage thinks the place peculiarly apt, partly because of the high standard reached there by the acting of *amateurs*, partly because of the denizens' "natural wit and suppleness, their innate humour and geniality, the softness and pliability of their speech".[3]

For all the ambitions that promoted, and the devotion that sustained, the Norske Theater at Bergen, it must be owned, proved a primitive and rather disappointing affair. Not only were nearly all those employed in it completely inexperienced, but they soon discovered alarming difficulties in the way of

---

[1] The first public performance of 'Den Norske Dramatiske Skoles Theater (i Huset Nr. 1 i Möllergaden)' took place on 11 October 1852, Bjerregaard's *Krydsbetjenten* being presented.

[2] The private inauguration took place on 21 November 1849, the public ceremony on 2 January 1850.

[3] Blanc, T., *Norges Første Nationale Scene* (1884), p. 7. Henrik Jæger says in his biography of Ibsen: "The theatre in Bergen was an outcome of the National feeling, which in the forties and fifties had risen to enthusiasm. The treasures of popular poetry brought to light by Asbjørnsen and Moe had fired the people with a transport of Nationalism, and Northern art and Northern romance were the result. Painters were to depict Northern nature, musicians were to play or harmonise Northern melodies, poets were to show us the people of the North—of the present or the past. The *Volkslied* [i.e. folk-song] style was the style of the day, and the Scandinavian peasant its literary ideal" (English translation, 1890, p. 70).

carrying out their intended programme. The meagre repertory of genuinely national pieces at their disposal when they began[1] did not very notably increase during the period of their activity, at almost every performance a Danish pronunciation still conveyed a Danish text,[2] and the presentation was often as rough as the culture of the players. In his delightful recollections,[3] Lorentz Dietrichson gives several amusing illustrations of the last-named defect—for instance the scene in which an actor, about to disclose his exalted identity by flinging back the cloak that concealed the insignia of majesty, found himself baffled by its buttons and attempted to pull it over his head like a shirt, from whose folds a muffled voice exclaimed: "Know ye not the Holy Roman Emperor?"[4] Nevertheless it redounds greatly to the credit of a community comprising no more than 25,000 souls that (even if on two or three evenings a week and during the darker months only) it could keep solvent for fourteen years an institution[5] which was essentially an idealistic experiment.[6]

The Norske Theater at Bergen is often identified with one of the most famous sons of that community, Ole Bull. But the great genius of the violin can, it seems, most fitly be described as a mascot or advertisement of the enterprise, for all the interest which, by fits and starts, he certainly took in it. The idea of launching it was by no means exclusively his; he was either travelling abroad or excluded from the management of the theatre during most of its history; the financial support which it derived from him never amounted to all that he and his admirers would have liked it to be believed. He cannot, nevertheless, be robbed of the distinction of having personally recruited Ibsen to its banner.

*   *   *   *

[1] Koht estimates (I, p. 63) that when *Catiline* was published there were in existence only about a dozen truly Norwegian plays of any magnitude; of these there figured in the repertory at Bergen: Wergeland's *Fjeldstuen*, C. P. Riis's *Til Sæters* and *Julegjæsten*, Jensen's *Huldrens Hjem* and A. Munch's *Aften paa Giske*.

[2] Koht, I, p. 108.

[3] *Svundne Tider* (3 vols., Christiania, 1896–1901).

[4] Dietrichson says (I, p. 149) that the play was a translation of Deinhardstein's *Hans Sachs*.

[5] It was the only regular theatre in the city.

[6] Bjørnson was appointed producer of the theatre after Ibsen's departure and remained in that position till the autumn of 1859; even his galvanic spirit failed to impart lasting health to that institution. The full history is given in commendable detail by Blanc (*op. cit.*). The documents relative to Ibsen's appointment are reproduced *in extenso* by Wiesener, A. M., 'Henrik Ibsen og Det Norske Theater i Bergen' in Transactions of *Bergens Historiske Forening*, XXXIV (1928), pp. 5 ff.

(ii) THE NORWEGIANS

To Bergen then Ibsen travelled in November 1851, "to assist the theatre as dramatic author".[1] Brought up hitherto (as we have seen) entirely in the 'Danish' tradition, with as little knowledge of the Norwegian 'artistic revival' as sympathy for it, he found himself engaged to farther its dramatic aspirations in their only existing focus.

The first play which Ibsen wrote for production at the Norske Theater was *St John's Eve* (*Sancthansnatten*, 1853). In it he turned to theatrical account the *Huldreromantik*, the fairy-romanticism, of recently popularised Norwegian folk-lore—the continued lighting of bale-fires at midsummer (St John's Eve), once a pagan rite, and the belief not only in magic potions, but also in domestic goblins and sylvan elves, which have the power to show themselves to mortals and even to affect their destiny. The balladry which Landstad was collecting and the stories which Asbjørnsen and Moe had begun to publish abounded in such creatures and their antics. Some songs introduced in the course of the play reproduce the style of the old popular poetry. In assembling all these elements Ibsen had to some extent been forestalled by two earlier experiments in drama-tising *Huldreromantik*, P. A. Jensen's *The Fairy's Home* (*Huldrens Hjem*) and his friend Botten Hansen's *The Fairy Wedding* (*Huldre-brylluppet*).[2]

Ibsen laboured to bring in the features that might be expected as sedulously as Nicholas Nickleby did to fulfil the demands of Mr Crummles, and in the performance they loomed larger than, for instance, a few lines of stage-direction like the following do in the printed text:

Soft music is heard from the background; the mountain opens, and in its interior a great, brilliantly illumined hall is seen; the mountain-king is seated on a throne at the back; elves and goblins (*hougfolk*) dance around him.[3]

[1] "til at assistere Theatret som dramatisk Forfatter" (Blytt, P., *Minder fra den første Norske Scene*, 2nd ed. 1907, p. 5, quoting from the minute-book of the managing committee). The post was a new one, and its duties consisted in preparing a new play for the theatre's official 'birthday' every second of January and writing special prologues whenever they should be needed (some of the latter are to be found in *Efterladte Skrifter*, 1, pp. 117 ff.). Ibsen soon took on also the office of assistant stage-manager and helped in coaching the players; he superintended and sometimes designed the scenery and costumes. He was never either manager or producer at this house.
[2] The former had been performed at Christiania while he was there (and he had not liked it), the latter first appeared in *Manden*.
[3] *Efterladte Skrifter*, 1 (1909), p. 407.

41

But such attractions remained adventitious; they had small dramatic effect beyond revealing the characters of the flesh-and-blood actors who witnessed them. Ibsen certainly toiled dutifully at the 'national' task which his contract and the programme of his theatre enjoined upon him. The main interest, nevertheless, which *St John's Eve* has for the historian lies less in the nationalistic ingredients than in the implied criticism of these which transpired and in the elements that came into it from other quarters. In the previous chapter it was demonstrated how deeply *St John's Eve* stood in the debt of Heiberg, Hertz and Shakespeare; and, similarly, the very ballads on which Ibsen drew mostly came from Denmark and Sweden, only one, apparently, being of genuinely Norwegian provenance.[1] Finally, in the discomfited and hypocritical Julian Paulsen, a quite unlovely personage in the play, Ibsen held up to ridicule certain peculiarities which were nothing else than the manifestations of his local patriotism. Paulsen is firmly identified with it as the founder of a Society for the Restoration of the Norse Tongue[2] and is "particularly strong in the National";[3] he calls himself "a Man of the People" and establishes that proud title by going about with a clasp-knife on his hip and refusing to spell nouns with capital letters;[4] he confesses moreover that his motive for such eccentricities is just to make himself "damned interesting" ("forbandet interessant") and that he takes care to draw sharp distinction between his theory and his practice;[5] with him, in other words, who talks most about it 'the National' is a mere caprice.

When, three years later, Ibsen brought out *The Feast at Solhaug* (*Gildet paa Solhaug*, 1856) as his second experiment[6] in adapting elements from Norwegian traditions to the uses of the stage, he showed himself more thorough and whole-hearted. The national story of Audun of Hegrenaes is used in the fable,

[1] In the Introduction to the play in vol. II of the Centenary Edition, F. Bull declares (p. 16) that the "folk-song-like" (*folkeviseaktige*) stanzas sung by Anne and Birk seem Danish, those about Erik and Svanhvide Swedish, while the ballad about "Liten Karin" is the Norwegian 'Liti Kjersti'.

[2] Selskabet til Norronatungens Restitution (*ed. cit.* p. 380).

[3] "især stærk i det Nationale" (*ed. cit.* p. 381).

[4] It was (and is) the *Danish* practice to use capital initials for all nouns.

[5] There may be a sly thrust implied in Juliane's artless remark (*ed. cit.* p. 374) that the scene which is meant to be so unexceptionably Norwegian, reminds her of a *Swedish* novel.

[6] For 2 January 1854 a revised version of *The Warrior's Barrow* had to do service, for 2 January 1855 *Lady Inger* (on which see pp. 47 f, below).

and the ballads drawn on are no longer of miscellaneous Scandi-navian origin, but all autochthonous, found in Landstad's *Norwegian Folk-Songs* of 1853.[1] More important are features already mentioned in connection with *The House of Svend Dyring*, but for all that not specifically Danish: the removal of the time of action from the nineteenth century to the ballad-age itself, the use of a plot quite consonant with the spirit of that age and the extensive employment (side by side with prose) of a verse form definitely modelled on that of traditional popular poetry, so that the whole leaves the impression of an expanded ballad.[2] Nothing either in the text itself or in what Ibsen himself remarked on it in any way suggests the satirical criticism so insistent in *St John's Eve*.[3]

That after some years in the service of the Norske Theater the playwright's hand had (after a manner of speaking) become subdued to what it worked in is shown also by Ibsen's *Olaf Liljekrans* (1857), the fable of which results from the combin-ation of one of Landstad's ballads, 'Olaf Liljukrans',[4] with a story narrated by Faye in *Norwegian Folk-Tales*, style and time of action remaining much the same as in *The Feast at Solhaug*.

St John's Eve, *The Feast at Solhaug* and *Olaf Liljekrans* hang together by virtue of their common 'Huldreromantik' or at least through presenting the sort of environment associated with it. In the fourth play of the Bergen series—actually the second in chronological order—in *Lady Inger of Østraat* (*Fru Inger til Østerraad*,[5] 1855), a patriotic ideal is again pursued, but with the choice of subject Ibsen ventured on to a different terrain.

---

[1] F. Bull, Introduction in Centenary Edition, III, p. 13, instances those of Margit Hjuxe, Gudmund and Signelita, Little Kersti, King Endel, Sir Peer and Proud Margaret, Hendrik and Aarolilja.

[2] This was the view which Bjørnson most enthusiastically, if rather one-sidedly, put forward in his eloquent defence of the play against the Christiania critics, particularly in his notice in *Morgenbladet* reprinted in his *Artikler og Taler*, I (1912), p. 108.

[3] Certain Danish elements in *The Feast at Solhaug* were discussed in the preceding chapter, and a connection with Scribe will shortly be mentioned. It is observable that, apart from these, F. Bull's exhaustive discussion of the sources of this piece (*ed. cit.* vol. III, p. 15) names works all associated in one way or another with Norway: Hauch's *Sisters of Kinnekullen*, Jørgen Moe's *Fanitullen*, Welhaven's verse-romances and A. Munch's *Donna Clara*.

[4] For 'Olaf Liljukrans' the English reader may consult Jæger, H., *Life of Henrik Ibsen* (English translation, 1890, p. 93). It is a ballad turning on the supernatural, but in his handling Ibsen rationalises the supernatural, as he had not done in *St John's Eve*.

[5] Ibsen adopted the form Østråt for the second edition; the place is variously spelled.

The action is not placed either in the present or in an indeterminate period of the Middle Ages, but at a definite point in the national history of Norway, the time of the last determined opposition to Danish rule round about the year 1525,[1] and in fashioning his fable, which he couched in prose throughout, the author was not guided by the collections of ballads and old wives' tales, but by the historians.[2] Though these, as it happened, were Danes again,[3] Ibsen neglected on this occasion the devices and conventions employed by Œhlenschläger,[4] Johan Ludvig Heiberg and Hertz. In their place he adopted certain features of the technique of Scribe—a debt which calls for some special attention.

       ＊   ＊   ＊   ＊

Before, however, we pass on to consider to what influences, besides those of Norwegian nationalism, Ibsen was exposed during his five and a half years' sojourn at Bergen, it will be convenient briefly to formulate some general observations on the quartette of plays first presented there and to indicate the degree to which in his later career the ideas persisted which he absorbed at the time of their composition.

St John's Eve, Lady Inger of Østraat, The Feast at Solhaug, Olaf Liljekrans represent a genuine effort to fulfil the prime purpose for which Ibsen had been summoned to Bergen, the provision of drama satisfactory to Norwegian nationalistic aspirations. The progressive diminution of elements in them either critical of these aspirations or foreign to them suggests in Ibsen a growing conviction of their tenability. Yet they do not mark a corresponding advance in theatrical or literary value: the last of them, *Olaf Liljekrans*, is perhaps the weakest, certainly the

---

[1] In 1873 Ibsen submitted *Lady Inger* to his old friend, the historian Ludvig Daae, for his expert opinion on the matter. Daae then investigated the sources (cf. his paper 'Fru Inger Ottesdatter og hendes Døtre' in *Historisk Tidsskrift* for 1874), and pronounced Ibsen's version of them to be erroneous and mischievous. For his second edition (1874) Ibsen toned down the anti-Danish sentiments.

[2] The fable of *The Warrior's Barrow*, such as it is, is freely invented.

[3] G. F. Lundh (*Samlinger til det Norske Folks Sprog og Historie*, 1833–9) and C. P. Paludan-Müller (*Grevens Feide*, part II, 1854).

[4] In his admirable 'Studiar over Fru Inger til Østerrad', Dalgard, O., in *Edda*, XXX (1930), pp. 1 ff., insists on the following points of resemblance between Ibsen's play and Œhlenschläger's *Queen Margaret* (*Dronning Margareta*): (i) the Norwegians' doomed resistance to the Danish monarchy; (ii) the resolute highborn lady's endeavour to win the crown for her son; (iii) the outwardly indistinguishable half-brothers; (iv) the horrible secret of the vault; but, striking as they are, they seem to me to lie on the surface only. Dalgard likewise adduces (p. 21) some ballad-reminiscences in *Lady Inger*.

least interesting, and most promise was shown by the second of the series, *Lady Inger*, which stands aside from the direct line of development. The conclusion is irresistible that Norwegian National Romanticism and the specific 'Norse-Norse', as it was called (*norsk-norsk*, to distinguish it from the *dansk-norsk* prevalent before), had led Ibsen's art into a blind alley. It came perhaps as a relief to him when the dramatic aspect of the movement was laughed into limbo by a parody of one of his own productions, by Olaf Skavlan's *Gildet paa Mærrahaug*,[1] which the students of Christiania presented in 1857.[2]

Any seeming depreciation of this nationalistic phase in Ibsen's career must, however, be balanced by some important considerations. The history of Norway, to which *Lady Inger* owed its origin, furnished also, after nine years, the subject of his *Pretenders*. His preoccupation with ballads as literary material, on which, he told his friend Botten Hansen, he could compose a dissertation, roused in him an interest sufficiently strong to drive him to a tour for collecting folk-lore in the summer of 1862—and traces of those investigations are abundantly clear in *Peer Gynt*.[3] Lastly, the study of his country's older literature had brought him into contact with the sagas, which he was not merely to turn to immediate account in *The Vikings in Helgeland* (*Hærmændene paa Helgeland*, 1858), but which were also to sharpen, it would seem, the insight into the dramatic potentialities of human character informing all his own major works. Interestingly enough, however, even the sagas came to him in Danish guise. What he knew in that field were N. M. Petersen's paraphrases, Œhlenschläger's *Kjartan and Gudrun*, Hauch's *Saga of Thorvald Vidføre* and the same author's essay on the family-sagas.

If we endeavour to bring Ibsen's development at this stage into relation with the incipient neo-Norwegian literature which we touched upon earlier in the present chapter, we can say that *grosso modo* it represents a forced attempt to follow up the indications given by Wergeland. That it was unsuccessful is implied in the disparity of the two authors' temperaments. Ibsen, none the less, held Wergeland, for all his distasteful

---

[1] The title might fairly be translated as *The Feast in the Mare's Nest*.

[2] That Ibsen bore the author no grudge is attested by the fact that in later life he was one of the very few persons with whom he stood on the familiar footing of *Du* (thou, in place of *De*, you).

[3] Both in the personality of the hero and in certain of the episodes, like the Hall of the Mountain King, the encounter with the Bøjg, cf. p. 107.

extravagances, in high esteem as a public figure, and the only known dinner party at which he acted as host was given in Rome, on 17 May 1881, to celebrate the unveiling of Wergeland's statue in Christiania—when Ibsen's speech was not wanting in ironic salt.[1] For by nature he was of the tribe of meticulous Welhaven, whom he quoted in so late a piece as *Little Eyolf*,[2] whose Wild Duck[3] lives again in the play of that name and whose handsome appearance and distinguished address he would gratefully call to mind, as he lectured before the university of Christiania during the session 1850–1—on Danish literature.[4]

*   *   *   *

One manifestation of the revived national life has so far received no attention in this chapter and can only receive the briefest notice at the end of it. That is the very strong pietistic revival in the religious sphere, at first associated with the missionary efforts of the great lay-preacher Hans Nilsen Hauge[5] (1771–1824) and then branching out in a number of not very dissimilar connexions. One of these stood under the aegis of the reverend Gustav Adolf Lammers (1802–78), at first a priest of the official church, who inaugurated the more active phase of his ministry in 1849, precisely in Ibsen's native town of Skien. Ibsen could not be unaware of a movement which developed into a great power in the land, stimulating especially those who took the political lead among the peasantry and which assumed a puritanically hostile attitude towards culture and the arts,[6] towards the theatre in especial: his own family were numbered among Lammers's devoted adherents and counted their Henrik as one of the damned. The time for a literary handling of religious revivalism had not yet come, but the self-questionings and private unhappiness which it provoked in Ibsen's breast were to find their metamorphosed outcome in *Brand*.

[1] Paulsen, J., *Mine Erindringer* (1900), p. 191.
[2] vi, p. 110; Archer, xi, p. 52.
[3] "En Vildand Svømmer Stille" ('Søfuglen' in Welhaven's *Samlede Digterverker*, ii (1921), p. 35.
[4] Paulsen, J., *Samliv med Ibsen*, ii (1913), p. 211.
[5] The reader of *belles-lettres* will find a sympathetic account of the Haugians, at the time of their genuine spiritual and social significance, in Kielland's fine novel *Skipper Worse* (1882); the dreadful side of this 'Hell-fire Christianity' is studied in the fiction of Arne Garborg and Amalie Skram (after 1887).
[6] The later leader of the peasants, Ueland, consistently voted against all public grants to the arts and their practitioners.

CHAPTER FIVE

IBSEN'S LITERARY EDUCATION:

(iii) OTHERS

Lady Inger (1855)

IBSEN's literary education, so far as preceding chapters have endeavoured to define it, lay in the hands of his sparse Norwegian precursors and of the Danish playwrights approximately contemporaneous with himself. There were also other preceptors, models and idols, and these it will be natural to consider now.

What went to the stylistic formation of *Catiline* and *The Warrior's Barrow*, those firstlings in which the mere determination to write a play was the predominant impulse, has received a consideration which may seem excessive. Even so, however, the tale is not complete. Shakespeare[1] had treated in dramatic form a Roman conspiracy yet more memorable than that of Catiline, and the nocturnal setting of Ibsen's play,[2] the devoted anxiety of the conspirator's wife, the spirit come from beyond the grave to warn him suggest no accidental resemblance to *Julius Caesar*.[3] Similarly, the situation at the outset of *The Warrior's Barrow*, of the old man and the young girl on their remote southern island to which violent men and a wooer are about to resort, calls to mind the second scene of *The Tempest*. Gosse felt[4] the atmosphere of Østraat to be that of Dunsinane, and the originally noble and then insanely deteriorating character of Skule (in *The Pretenders*), his rivalry and contrast with the calm legitimacy of Haakon, the ghost-rid hallucination towards his end corroborate a guess that *Macbeth* deeply

---

[1] It may be observed that Œhlenschläger had made translations of *A Midsummer Night's Dream* (and of substantial portions of *Venus and Adonis*).

[2] He himself attributed (VII, p. 116) that peculiarity to the hours he had stolen from sleep to compose his tragedy.

[3] There is even the verbal parallelism between Manlius's adjuration of his junior Statillius: "Nei sov Du kuns! den Unge trænger til en kvægsom Søvn" (VII, p. 80: i.e. "Nay, sleep on; the young need reviving sleep"), and Brutus's remark to his page: "I know young bloods look for a time of rest."

[4] *Ibsen* (1907), p. 61, but declares the resemblance to be unconscious.

47

interested Ibsen, though he certainly became at no time of his life an obsequious student of the English master.[1]

Schiller's dramaturgy may similarly have found a way into his imagination less indirectly than by way of Œhlenschläger. The rebellion against law and order which Ibsen was so often to personify, beginning with his Catiline, is to be found not only in *The Robbers*, with its band of tippling desperadoes, but also in the 'modern' *Love and Intrigue* (*Kabale und Liebe*), in *Fiesco*, *Don Carlos* and in *William Tell*, of which we know[2] that, as a youth, he possessed a copy and to whose celebrated storm, defied by the hero, he furnishes a striking counterpart in Act II of *Brand*. In talk Ibsen felt himself on safe enough ground to contrast[3] (in the spirit of Brandes) the heroes of Schiller, who act as their creator's mouthpieces, with the objectively presented personages of Goethe. Heinrich von Kleist, whose *Kathie of Heilbronn* he prayed in aid[4] against Hertz, also served him, by virtue of his early suicide, to clinch the argument that Prussia could foster no poet,[5] and John Paulsen could vividly call to mind,[6] twenty years afterwards, the enthusiasm with which Ibsen expatiated on Otto Ludwig's *Hereditary Forester* (*Erbförster*, 1850) and Hebbel's *Mary Magdalene* (1844), two interesting German experiments in 'modern', everyday tragedy, very destitute of theatrical tricks; his son once told an interviewer[7] that his father never would acknowledge himself indebted for technical proficiency to anyone except Hebbel, but to Ibsen's particular technique it does not, in effect, seem that Hebbel had much to contribute; it is unlikely that he owed much more to these two German dramatists than the encouragement of their example.[8]

Towards Goethe—so radically different from himself in temperament,[9] education, experience and aim—Ibsen's attitude

[1] His wife's step-mother, in whose drawing-room at Bergen he was not infrequently seen, keenly admired Shakespeare, of whom Ibsen may have learned something from a Jomfru Crawfurd, resident in Grimstad, who lent him books by Kierkegaard. When he was in Copenhagen in 1852 he had opportunities for seeing *Hamlet*, *King Lear*, *Romeo and Juliet* and *As You Like It* and probably saw them.
[2] Cf. Berggrav, E., *Ibsens Sjelelige Krise* (1937), p. 45.
[3] Cf. Janson, K., *Hvad Jeg Har Oplevet* (1913), p. 80.
[4] VII, p. 123. Cf. also p. 30 n., above.
[5] Paulsen, J., *Mine Erindringer* (1900), p. 162.
[6] *Mine Erindringer* (1900), p. 162.
[7] Henderson, A., *The Changing Drama* (1914), p. 74.
[8] But cf. Paulsen, J., *Mine Erindringer* (1900), p. 162.
[9] To Ibsen, the man Goethe was simply "a goat" (Paulsen, J., *Samliv med Ibsen*, I, 1906, p. 73).

was ambiguous. He praised him, as has just been remarked, at the expense of Schiller. In *Love's Comedy* Goethe is referred to as the Right Honourable Herr Goethe[1]—scarcely the address of a true devotee; and *Peer Gynt* contains a sly, not to say malicious, misquotation from *Faust*, which William Archer, not over-endowed with a sense of humour, corrected.[2] (Faust makes the notorious observation "Das Ewig-Weibliche zieht uns hinan" which English paraphrase usually has to render in some such terms as 'The Eternal-Feminine draws us upwards and onwards'; the fornicating rogue Peer, posing as a prophet and philosopher, pontificates, in German: "Das Ewig Weibliche zieht uns an!"[3] i.e. 'The eternally feminine attracts us'.) The same play bears, however, the imprint of a deeper acquaintance with *Faust*, one perhaps not altogether to its advantage. For, like the completed drama of the Weimar sage, *Peer Gynt* grew into the amorphous study of an enterprising man's course from early manhood to senescence, at the point of death brought once more into contact with the woman whom long ago he loved and abandoned—Solvejg in the one case, Gretchen in the other; both women have retained their faith in and devotion to their lover, and the suggestion cannot be shirked that, like Faust, Peer is 'redeemed' by this love; and such a 'redemption' would go far to stultify[4] whatever argument can be construed from the rest of the play, where in Goethe's it merely adds a sentimental sugaring.[5]

After the belletrists there is a critic from the land of Goethe to be taken into account in the formation of Ibsen's mind. Herman Hettner, one of the most respectable of the German aestheticians, had published in 1851 his pithy dissertation on the modern drama, *Das Moderne Drama*.[6] It fell into Ibsen's hands already while he was visiting Copenhagen in the spring

[1] "geheimeråd Goethe" (I, p. 345); Archer, I, p. 428.
[2] He later withdrew, and apologised for, the correction (Archer, IV, p. 156).
[3] II, p. 358; Goethe is here "en agtet forfatter", "a much esteemed author".
[4] This moral weakness is faithfully dealt with by Gilliland, M. S., *Ibsen's Women* (1894), p. 25.
[5] Ibsen, with his skill for putting the full onus of interpretation on the reader, has probably, while assuming no responsibility for it, deliberately 'led' him to this parallel. According to Paulsen (*Samliv med Ibsen*, I, 1906, p. 79, and II, 1913, p. 171), Ibsen would have preferred the obliteration of Germany to that of *Faust* and had, in his youth, "studied Goethe more closely than anybody knows".
[6] I have used the edition of Merbach, P. A., No. 151 of *Deutsche Literaturdenkmale des 18. und 19. Jahrhunderts* (n.d.).

of 1852,[1] not with immediate effect, but (we may reasonably conclude) for subjection to his characteristic, slow, but thorough mode of assimilation.

Hettner had no pedantic or solemn mind. But he was convinced of the serious mission of drama and turned resolutely against the anecdotic in every shape or form, whether it was that of pure comedy of intrigue or of historical chronicle or of 'fate-tragedy'; the lighter plays of Scribe,[2] Tieck's pageants and Ludwig's *Hereditary Forester* stood equally condemned in his sight. If a new drama is possible, Hettner contended that it must be "historical or social", and, as he proceeded to demonstrate that there is no true *genre* of historical drama, but that, to be of value, it must be a variant of tragedy, the inference to be drawn is that it must be tragical or critical. He did not rule out comedy, where he even put in a good word for the Aristophanic type, which could be as gay and fanciful as might be, but never forget that it "should deal with a substantial theme"[3]—suggestions not without effect upon the verve and the social criticism of *Love's Comedy*.

In tragedy, similarly, Hettner reserved his highest admiration for the 'tragedy of ideas', in which "the antitheses forming the tragic conflict...are implicit in the innermost nature of mankind and the laws of its development"[4] and as examples of which he adduces Goethe's *Faust*, Sophocles's *Electra* and, in spite of its many faults, Hebbel's *Mary Magdalene*. In connection with the last named he insists that the tragedy of everyday life (*bürgerliche Tragödie*) needs not, as hitherto it usually has done, deal with sentimental trumpery like gambling-debts and falsely suspected innocence, but can pierce to the profoundest depths of human nature, provided that it do so with a poet's eye; Shakespeare's *Romeo and Juliet*, *Timon of Athens*, *Othello*, even *Lear* are domestic tragedies in his definition. Of the licence herewith (so to speak) granted the dramatic author to forsake the realms of conventional sublimity, without forfeiting the title of tragic poet, the great series of plays bears witness which Ibsen inaugurated with *The Pillars of Society* and *A Doll's House*.

---

[1] Neiiendam, R., in *Politiken* for 29 December 1928, *cit.* Dalgard, O., in *Edda*, xxx (1930), p. 30 n.

[2] He bestowed cordial, though discriminating, praise on Scribe's more substantial plays, like *A Glass of Water* (p. 162).

[3] "dass das Lustspiel einen bedeutenden Stoff habe" (p. 168).

[4] *Op. cit.* p. 100.

These two do not end in death; and another, too often neglected, point made by Hettner was the reminder[1] that, as the authors of the *Oresteia*, *Philoctetes* and *Tasso* had shown, the conclusion of a tragedy need not be a suicide or an execution. Again, Hettner's doctrine that "the great poets never employ any motives that are not simple and clear", so that "the spectators have a clear view of all the personages and situations",[2] Ibsen found enforced on a lower plane by the practice of Scribe; but it took him a little time to absorb it.[3]

*   *   *   *

Candour must allow that any impress which Ibsen's thought or imagination received from the belletristic sources hitherto considered in the present chapter was superficial. The same is true also of the Swedish literature of the early nineteenth century, on which (in connection with Ibsen) Hr. Svensson has written[4] learnedly, without, however, carrying conviction. But two other streams of influence to which he was exposed in the early part of his life left a considerably deeper mark, that, on the one hand, emanating from the French dramatist Scribe[5] and, on the other, that originating in certain non-dramatic Danish authors.

Neither Ejder nor Kattegat had halted the triumphal progress of Scribe's plays. Peter Blytt, director of the Bergen Theatre, was not alone among Northerners in confessing him for his favourite dramatist, and, during Ibsen's employment at that house, the following pieces by Scribe (sometimes with and sometimes without a collaborator) were presented there: *The Ladies' Battle* (*Bataille de Dames*), *The Guardian* (*Tutrice*), *The Ambitious Man* (*Ambitieux*), *Adrienne Lecouvreur*, *The Queen of Navarre's Tales* (*Contes de la Reine de Navarre*), *The Independent*

---

[1] *Op. cit.* p. 78.   [2] *Op. cit.* p. 126.
[3] Only with *The Vikings in Helgeland* (1858) do Ibsen's 'fables' become quite clear.
[4] Svensson, S., 'Brand och den Svenska Göticismen' in *Edda*, xxx (1930), p. 316. A controversy ensued: cf. *Edda*, xxxi (1931), pp. 81 and 98. It remains true that Ibsen knew *Frithjofs Saga* by Tegnér sufficiently well to name Ellida Wangel after the hero's ship, but Svensson's only convincing point seems to me to be the dependence of Gerd (in *Brand*) on Tegnér's Gerda (*Edda*, xxx, p. 343). In *Frithjofs Saga* Tegnér reconciled Christ and Odin in Balder rather as Ibsen did in *The Warrior's Barrow*, but both had the example of Œhlenschläger to work on.
[5] Kihlman, E., *Nordiska Profiler* (1935), pp. 231 ff., discusses many nineteenth-century French plays in connection with Ibsen, but mainly contents himself with pointing out parallels.

51

Man (*Indépendant*), *The Devil's Share* (*Part du Diable*), *A Glass of Water* (*Verre d'Eau*) and *A Fetter* (*Chaîne*).

Ibsen had come into contact with Scribe before—an early criticism[1] objecting to him on the odd ground of excess of realism—and at Bergen he must have been thoroughly familiarised with his technique, always the most interesting thing about him. That technique may be said usually to rest on a foundation of ignorance, misunderstanding and intrigue—in the sense that the action is guided to a goal of some difficulty by a person (the 'intriguer') who has certain important information which he utilises to gain his end, but of which those whom he meets are wholly or partially ignorant; these other personages are frequently played off, the one against the other, by the varying share of the intriguer's knowledge to which they are progressively admitted, and incidental complications proceed from the misunderstandings to which different degrees of participation in the secrets give rise. Sometimes, as in the case of Marguerite and Guattinara of *The Queen of Navarre's Tales*, two intriguers, with different purposes and different funds of recondite knowledge, are working against one another's designs, thereby greatly heightening the consequent misunderstandings.

Such, to speak in general terms, is the scheme of Ibsen's *Lady Inger*, in which, without taking anyone fully into her confidence, the high-born, patriotic chatelaine of Østraat employs her own wits and even her daughter's charms for ensuring the success of a popular rising to place Nils Stensson on the throne and drive out the Danes; in this intention she has to checkmate the Danish envoy Nils Lykke, a polished nobleman after the style of Bolingbroke in *A Glass of Water*, who is out to catch Nils Stensson and to make Lady Inger politically powerless henceforward by implicating her in the peasants' rising. At the outset, he has a piece of information unknown to anyone at Østraat—namely, that Nils Stensson is in the vicinity; and Fru Inger knows what nobody else there knows —namely that Nils Stensson is her own illegitimate son,[2] a fact which she passionately desires to keep a secret. This twofold mystery is complicated by the presence of a third stranger

---

[1] Cf. Koht, H., 'Henrik Ibsen i "Manden"', *ut cit.* p. 10.

[2] This was a piece of Ibsen's own invention; he also added the touch, curiously reminiscent of *Catiline*, that Lykke has previously seduced and abandoned the sister of Eline, who is seeking the malefactor, without knowing his identity, in order to wreak vengeance on him.

at Østraat, unexpected by either of the others, Olaf Skaktavl, and by the fact that Eline, whom her mother, Lady Inger, uses as a bait to 'play' Nils Lykke and assist in his undoing, falls in love with that practised seducer and (as it were) 'changes sides'.[1]

Nowhere else does Ibsen virtually construct an entire drama on the foundation upon which Scribe habitually relied. Yet his next tragedy, *The Vikings in Helgeland* (*Hærmændene paa Helgeland*, 1858), depends fundamentally on a deceit—the substitution of Sigurd for Gunnar not only in the fight with the polar bear outside Hjørdis's Icelandic bower, but also in the half-symbolical bridal night which he spent on her couch as his reward—, and the catastrophe is precipitated by the misunderstanding of a piece of benign mystification, when old Ørnulf sets off to rescue Hjørdis and Gunnar's little son and it is thought he has the intention of kidnapping the boy for a sinister end. In Bishop Nicholas of *The Pretenders* Ibsen painted the full-length portrait of a thorough intriguer, in its special dramaturgic meaning; and, in the vulgar sense of that word, Stensgaard of *The League of Youth* is, again, such an one.

The abiding interest of *The Pretenders* and *The League of Youth* resides not, however, in these characters' machinations—and the truth of this proposition is even truer of *The Pillars of Society*, where, in the past, Carsten Bernick undoubtedly proved successful in making use of knowledge denied to others and thereby gained his private ends. But a secret wrong committed long ago, thought forgotten except by such as profit from the oblivion and then disclosing itself with incalculable force, became an almost ubiquitous element in Ibsen's mature writing. To corroborate such an assertion, we need only call to mind Nora's forgery in *A Doll's House*, Alving's past life and misdeeds in *Ghosts*, all Rebecca West's dealings with the dead Fru Rosmer and Ellida Wangel's affair with the strange seaman (*The Lady from the Sea*), Borkman's discarding of Ella Rentheim, Rubek's of Irene (*When We Dead Awaken*); in fact, only *An Enemy of the People* is substantially free of this idiosyncrasy. (It will be recalled, though, that something of the kind was to be found underlying the short stories of Mauritz Hansen,[2] a most

[1] Lady Inger keeps her own particular secret too long and thereby brings about a tragedy more successfully than Scribe ever did.
[2] Cf. p. 36, above. *Datteren*, written long before, is included in the collected *Noveller* of the author (vol. VI, 1857, p. 1).

striking instance being afforded by the parallels between *The Daughter* (*Datteren*) and Ibsen's *Ghosts,* in both of which the child of a seduced servant-maid is employed in the seducer's family and feels an uncontrollable aversion from the limping old man whom she calls father and who has been married to her mother to save her reputation.)

A somewhat trivial concomitant of Scribe's technique goes by the name of the *qui-pro-quo,* a posture of things, due to the unequal distribution of information, in which one of the personages is believed by another either to be someone other than he is or to be referring to another subject than that to which in fact he is addressing himself. *Lady Inger* comprises, with its three strange visitors to Østraat, a good deal of such misunderstanding;[1] and *The Vikings in Helgeland* might be criticised as altogether erected over a grandiose *qui-pro-quo.* In his 'modern' plays Ibsen only once had recourse to the device: it is in *The League of Youth,* when friends lead Chamberlain Bratsberg into believing that Stensgaard's oration on the Seventeenth of May, actually directed against the venerable Chamberlain himself, was a tilt at the upstart Monsen family—a misunderstanding which conditions the whole future progress of the play.

The complicating factor of Mauritz Hansen disregarded, it may be properly asked whether Ibsen learned anything but inessentials like the *qui-pro-quo* from Scribe. Not everyone will agree that technical devices are mere trivialities, but, granting the point (without prejudice), one may answer to the innuendo: (1) that Ibsen's disposition to handle (as he had done already in *Catiline* and *Norma*) the situation of a man erotically attached to two women perhaps received a fillip from its elaboration at the hand of a master in *The Queen of Navarre's Tales, A Glass of Water, The Ladies' Battle,* indeed in most of the plays by Scribe included in the repertory at Bergen, and issued in the rivalry of Beate and Rebecca for Johannes Rosmer, the temptation of Halvard Solness, the positions of Borkman, Rubek (*When We Dead Awaken*), Alfred Allmers (*Little Eyolf*) and some others; (2) that in *A Fetter* he could find a most interesting

---

[1] *Olaf Liljekrans* has an unusually protracted *qui-pro-quo*; in Act II Kirsten proposes to settle the difficulty arising from Olaf's attachment to Alfhild by marrying the latter off to Hemming, but her delicacy makes her express herself to the interested parties so vaguely that Hemming believes she wants him to marry his beloved Ingeborg and Alfhild believes she wants her to marry her beloved Olaf, a misunderstanding which extends to the church-door.

variant of this situation,[1] the man having tired of his *liaison* with one of the women to the degree of finding her a galling clog upon his free movement, a situation which *mutatis mutandis* recurs in *Little Eyolf* and is not far round the corner in *The Master Builder* and *Rosmersholm*; (3) that in the amorous and, indeed, in most other relations too, Scribe represented the human female as more enterprising and effective than the male, an unconventional contrast on which the critics of Ibsen with *Rosmersholm*, *Hedda Gabler* and *Little Eyolf* mainly in their minds, are also apt to fasten.[2]

By far the most important lesson which Scribe had to teach the author of *Catiline* and *The Warrior's Barrow* is so elementary that generations thoroughly imbued with it may easily overlook the debt: namely, the necessity of maintaining at every moment of a play the specifically dramatic excitement of expectation, suspense and apprehension—the tension which, if it is to remain truly operative, must both be constantly varied and proceed from a clear apprehension of all the material facts disclosed. This was something which the playwrights of the Romantic Revival, bemused with poetry and ideas, had neglected, to their lasting detriment—in certain episodes and speeches of Œhlenschläger's plays, for example, dramatic tension falls away to nothing—but for which Scribe, as has been well said,[3] neglected all else, poetry, ideas, sentiment and characterisation. This lesson, reinforced by the Bergen public's obvious determination to be amused, or at least carried away when it visited the theatre, Ibsen never for a moment forgot, except in the two pieces which he expressly designated 'dramatic poems' (*Brand* and *Peer Gynt*) and in *Emperor and Galilean*, the failure of which may, indeed, with some plausibility be referred precisely to the disregard of Scribe's axiom.[4]

*   *   *   *

[1] In *The Feast at Solhaug* the situation of *The Ladies' Battle* is repeated; an older and a younger woman love the same man, who now cares for the younger alone, though once he was attracted to the elder; the women are relations.

[2] Scribe introduced nothing less than the *maîtresse femme* in *The Queen of Navarre's Tales*, *The Guardian*, *A Glass of Water* (and elsewhere); and such an one, in the guise of Hjørdis, confronts the inhibited males of *The Vikings in Helgeland*; her own inhibitions prevent Lady Inger from perfectly filling the part of a *maîtresse femme*.

[3] Doumic, R., *De Scribe à Ibsen* (n.d.), p. vii. Doumic does not discuss the question of Ibsen's possible indebtedness to Scribe.

[4] In their way the playwrights Augier and Dumas the younger also erected on Scribe's foundations a structure of social criticism, and, as they did so some time before Ibsen did and speedily enjoyed an international vogue, it is no vain under-

We must, lastly, turn our attention to two authors, who were Danes, like those discussed in Chapter III, but different from them in not being playwrights and in coming upon the scene too late to form part of the general literary background which Ibsen knew before he left Grimstad. They are Paludan-Müller and Schack.

With the great admiration which Ibsen undeniably felt for Frederik Paludan-Müller (1809–76) there probably mingled no inconsiderable adulterant of envy. Lacking the older man's equability of outlook and absorption in things of beauty for their own sake, he could not hope to vie with him in polish of phrase and impeccability of form. Yet Paludan-Müller, recluse though he became, was by no means ignorant of his contemporaries' lives and could turn a sharp eye on their telling idiosyncrasies. This awareness emerges clearly enough from his masterpiece, the narrative poem *Adam Homo* (1841–8), a curious blend, to the sensitive nostril, of Byron's *Don Juan* and Goethe's *Faust*, which undeniably pervaded those recesses of Ibsen's imagination from which *Peer Gynt* was to proceed. It is the poetic, varied and vivid account of a man's course from young manhood to the grave, with his final escape from damnation through a damsel of low degree, whom, when callow, he loved and abandoned; Adam Homo rises to public eminence, a profligate in his private life. So far the resemblance to *Faust* is close. His tale, on the other hand, is told in terms of modern society, by way of narrative in a varied *ottava rima* stanza and with many a mordant, satiric shaft directed both at his character and at the society which upholds him—in the style of *Don Juan*. But, at bottom, unlike Faust and Don Juan, to whom their creators gave something of their own greatness or distinction, their Danish brother bears no resemblance to Paludan-Müller,

taking of French critics to put Ibsen in their debt. *M. Poirier's Son-in-Law*, by Augier, was presented at Bergen while Ibsen was there. Though this is the only positive instance of direct contact, it is presumable that Ibsen had some fair knowledge of their work, all the more so as Georg Brandes's 'modern' campaign (to which we shall turn presently) virtually started out from them; but the conclusion is equally inescapable that no detail of Ibsen's work owes anything to the later French dramatists and that they gave him no immediate impulse of any sort. Ibsen told Brandes tartly that he only learned from them what to avoid (*Cosmopolis*, v, p. 112), though there is some superficial resemblance between *The League of Youth* and Augier's satires on politics and journalism, *The Brazen* (*Les Effrontés*) and *Giboyer's Son* (*Fils de Giboyer*). Ibsen's 'feminism' was independent of George Sand's. Hettner praised George Sand and Fru Ibsen admired her; but Ibsen himself, after wrestling for a time with *Consuelo*, gave her up.

being *l'homme moyen sensuel* of a very vulgar, if not contemptible, sort. Although the details of Peer Gynt's origin and career differ throughout from those of Adam Homo, Ibsen's dramatic poem repeats the three sets of components, which we may take leave to call Goethe's, Byron's and Paludan-Müller's, in similar proportions. In the process of composition it becomes, like *Adam Homo*, but unlike *Faust* or *Don Juan*, a lampoon, generally amusing, frequently savage and on occasion repellent, upon the average man—in this instance, on the average Norwegian—and, through him, upon the national character in certain of its aspects.

Only a bilious eye would see in *Peer Gynt* a mere copy of *Adam Homo*, deep though, without a doubt, the effect was which its perusal left on Ibsen, who, moreover (though to a somewhat less degree perhaps) was impressed by two other poems[1] from the same pen, *The Aeronaut and the Atheist* (*Luftskipperen og Atheisten*, 1852) and, especially, *Kalanus* (1854). The latter rehearses the story told by Plutarch of that Indian gymnosophist, the friend of King Alexander of Macedon, who, to attest the sovereignty of his will, committed his living body to the funeral-pyre he had deliberately raised and kindled for himself. *Kalanus* may be regarded as a poetic elaboration of one article in the moral teaching of Paludan-Müller's contemporary Kierkegaard (1813–55), about whom more will soon be said; and the religious conversion of the unbeliever (in *The Aeronaut and the Atheist*) by the terror that overtakes him in a balloon, though ironically managed, illustrates another of Kierkegaard's doctrines. An echo of the latter story may be picked up in the scene of the Strange Passenger in *Peer Gynt*[2]—the mysterious and unidentified travelling-companion who inaugurates Peer's preoccupation with his own soul's salvation—which is carried a stage farther in the following scene where Peer stands in actual danger and fear of his life.[3]

Aliment to Ibsen's imagination (to make no higher claim) was

[1] *Kalanus* is actually cast into dialogue, but does not appear to have been written with an eye to the stage.

[2] II, p. 385; Archer, IV, p. 202.

[3] A number of trifles which may owe their first inspiration to Paludan-Müller have been remarked—for instance (by Skard, E., in *Edda*, XXI, 1924, p. 90) the punishment of Furia in *Catiline*, which is identical with that meted out to a peccant priestess in *Vestalinden* (*The Vestal Virgin*). Andersen, V., in *Det Nittende Aarhundredes Første Halvdel* (1924), p. 521, draws attention to a certain metrical parallel between *Brand* and Paludan-Müller's *Ahasverus* (1854).

also conveyed from *The Fantastics* (*Phantasterne*, 1857), the novel of Hans Egede Schack (1820–59), which he knew and highly esteemed.[1] Its hero, Conrad, cultivates his imagination so persistently that, in the course of time, he is left with no life of his own, merely with day-dreams. Realising, however, that this unbalanced state will involve not merely his moral, but also his vital destruction, he clenches his evanescent hold on reality sufficiently to curb his phantasy and turn himself into a useful, if humdrum member of society; in other words, his feet are set on the path of Peer Gynt, with whom he shares several temperamental qualities, but he learns to know and to control himself as Peer Gynt never does. By means of extreme cases like those of his hero and one of his friends, Schack most vividly presented the antimony between phantasy and action, dream and deed (*Drøm og Daad*), which continually exercised Ibsen's mind—for one reason, because only where they were reconciled did he believe the individual's happiness to be possible. *Rosmersholm*, *John Gabriel Borkman*, *The Master Builder* (where the hero is almost ripe for the asylum to which Conrad's friend was consigned), all afford instances of a calamitous disequilibrium between phantasies and the world of reality; *The Lady of the Sea*, *per contra*, presents a case of disease and healing not unlike that of *The Fantastics*.

[1] Paulsen, J., *Mine Erindringer* (1900), p. 180.

CHAPTER SIX

THE NEWER NATIONAL ROMANTICISM

The Vikings in Helgeland (1858), *Love's Comedy* (1862),
The Pretenders (1863)

THE rapturous acclamation which greeted Skavlan's parody, *The Feast in the Mare's Nest*, set an abrupt period to that phase of the Norwegian national revival with which the Norske Theater at Bergen was principally associated. The more speciously picturesque and ingenuous findings of the pioneers who had enquired into orally transmitted fictions and other folk-lore, into the customs of the countryside and the condition of the peasantry[1] had been assembled to provide a theatrical entertainment which should evoke more laughter than thought, more ease than emotion and to which the labours of the scene-painter, the musical director and the dancing-master contributed as much as the poet and the dramatist. But if, with *The Feast at Solhaug*, Ibsen had achieved the acme of this diversion and so served Skavlan as his principal butt, his imagination was of its own motion turning into fresh channels under a twofold impulse. On the one hand his acquaintance with and (in 1858) eventual marriage to Susannah Thoresen gave, as he candidly acknowledged,[2] a new seriousness to his moral life, and on the other hand he was supplied with an artistic correlative to this by a more direct familiarity with the *Sagas* than he had hitherto enjoyed. (A living link between the two existed in the personality of Susannah Ibsen, who as a child cherished the belief that some day she would become Queen of Iceland and was animated by an infectious enthusiasm for her future subjects' heroic literature.)

The Sagas are prose narratives written in Old Icelandic during the Middle Ages and handle three sets of matter: (i) ancient mythology and religion common to the Teutonic peoples, (ii) the monarchies of Norway, and (iii) Icelandic

---

[1] The recently published investigations of the sociologist Eilert Sundt, particularly *Sædeligheds-Tilstanden i Norge* (*The State of Morals in Norway*) which came out in the critical year 1857, somewhat damped an ill-informed enthusiasm for the purity and simplicity of the countryside.   [2] *Breve*, I, p. 213.

59

family histories. The second of these classes Ibsen neglected, but, in accordance with the eclectic principle of *The Feast at Solhaug* and *Olaf Liljekrans*, out of the first and third sorts he made in his next play, *The Vikings in Helgeland* (*Hærmændene paa Helgeland*, 1858), a combination which was certainly ingenious, but which attracted some censure[1] at the time of its appearance. As was becoming usual with him, he conceived a remote and complicated history lying anterior to the action of his play, and for the most important feature of it—the substitution of one bridegroom for another—the legendary *Vølsunga-Saga* was drawn on, while *Njaals-Saga*, *Egil Skallagrimssons Saga* and, especially, *Laxsdøla-Saga*, of the Icelandic domestic group, furnished materials for the later developments.

Ibsen's indebtedness to Danish scholarship for his knowledge of the sagas has received notice in the previous chapter.[2] It is interesting to note that in his last play, *Kiartan and Gudrun*, Œhlenschläger had worked on the tragic quadrilateral situation between two men and two women which had been suggested to him by the *Laxsdøla-Saga*. But Ibsen had made striking progress beyond the tutelage of Œhlenschläger which is still so obvious in *The Warrior's Barrow*. He can scarcely have failed to know *Kiartan and Gudrun*, though nothing in *The Vikings in Helgeland* reveals such knowledge; even Œhlenschläger's preoccupation with the conversion of the heathen to Christianity (which again forms a prominent element in *Kiartan and Gudrun*) seems by now to have become an integral part of Ibsen's habitual ponderings.[3]

The greatest novelty in *The Vikings in Helgeland*, it seems at first glance, is one of form and style. Firmly resolved on a new departure, the author of *Olaf Liljekrans* originally proposed to make that plain by adopting a dramatic structure based on that of the ancients and by using the iambic trimeter as his vehicle. Herein he would have been repeating experiments of

---

[1] Bjørnson complained with some justice that personages of the age of Eric Bloodaxe are made to behave like those of the age of Sigurd, the slayer of the dragon-giant Fafner, that is to say impossibly, and Goldschmidt tempered his praise with a similar reservation (cf. Gran, I, p. 115 and Vasenius, V., *Henrik Ibsens Dramatiska Diktning i dess första Skede*, 1879, p. 155).

[2] He knew *Vølsunga-Saga* in C. C. Rafn's Danish version (1829).

[3] Sigurd's conversion (in *The Vikings in Helgeland*) seems to me quite in the spirit originally referable to Œhlenschläger's: I can nowise agree with Neckel, G., in *Jahresbericht der Schlesischen Gesellschaft*, IV (1910), p. 59, that "incompatibility between Christian and pagan was Ibsen's discovery".

Œhlenschläger,[1] and, in the event, he decided otherwise. The construction, indeed, while infinitely more ambitious (with four acts) than the older Viking play, *The Warrior's Barrow* (with one), exhibits a tauter construction than a *divertissement* like *The Feast at Solhaug*, without relying on intrigue and the other devices of the 'well-made' play to the extent that *Lady Inger* did. On the language of *The Vikings in Helgeland* that of the sagas (even though indirectly derived) left manifest traces the definition of which, however, would come improperly from a foreigner. He must rest satisfied with quoting a passage which strikes upon his unaccustomed ear as characteristic, with noting the approbation of most authorities[2] and with singling out from their number the evidence of Gerhard Gran, who says that "the diction is spare, without ornaments, the speeches as a rule are quite short, simple in construction—without long periods, quite without rhetoric and flowers of speech—almost without images; should an image occur from time to time, it is either taken direct from the *saga* or, at all events, is in the spirit of the *saga*—with an echo of the ancient circumlocutions".[3] As illustration this piece of dialogue has been selected:

Sigurd. Thou deemest my heart is bitter toward thee. 'Tis the last time, Hjørdis, that we shall have speech together; there is something that gnaws me like a sore sickness, and in this wise I cannot part from thee; thou must know me better.
Hjørdis. What wouldst thou?
Sigurd. Tell thee a saga.
Hjørdis. Is it sad?
Sigurd. Sad, as life itself.
Hjørdis. (Bitterly) What knowest thou of the sadness of life?
Sigurd. Judge when my saga is over.
Hjørdis. Then tell it me; I will work the while.
Sigurd. Once upon a time there were two young Vikings. . . .

[1] *Kiartan and Gudrun* has the iambic trimeter and *Earl Hakon* (*Hakon Jarl*) a chorus and the preservation of the 'three unities'.
[2] Koht, H., a stickler for Norwegian purity, evidently looks upon the style as somewhat of a bastard and deduces its paternity from Hauch's *Saga om Thorvald Vidførte* (I, p. 157); Carsten Hauch, though a Norwegian by birth, was identified with the culture of Copenhagen, where he held the professorship of aesthetics. At the time *The Vikings in Helgeland* came out a Danish critic thought the style the "only right one" for the matter (Rosenberg, C., in *Dansk Mannedsskrift*, VIII (1858), p. 490). Asbjørnsen (quoted by Woerner, R., *Henrik Ibsen*, I, 1900, p. 68) thought *The Vikings* the "purest" Norwegian work to date; that note ultimately faded away.
[3] Gran, I, p. 113. This last remark is inapplicable to the language proper. Traces of the saga style, according to some, may already be found in *Olaf Liljekrans*.

As for construction, *The Vikings in Helgeland* possesses a taut-ness and concentration comparable to these qualities in the style. Long as the drama is, theatrical producers have found it almost impossible to abridge it, and it exhibits more purely than *Lady Inger* did the author's mature technique of developing a highly charged situation from the slow disclosure of a doubtful or criminal deed perpetrated long ago and of making the tragic outcome depend upon it.

But perhaps the greatest benefit of all which accrued to Ibsen from his commerce with the sagas lay in the domain of charac-terisation, in which the Danish playwrights had little to teach and the diffuse and lyrical Œhlenschläger, for instance, had been weakest. The authors of the Icelandic family sagas dis-covered a keen interest in the variety and unexpected turns of human nature, made manifest in action and conflict—in the specifically dramatic aspects, that is to say—and untrammelled in the main by any moral code inimical to energy and passion.

Common to all the principal sources of *The Vikings in Helgeland* is the figure of a woman, unafraid, clear-sighted, resolute to put her intentions into practice, though they involve conduct which one of them, Gudrun of *Laxdøla-Saga*, summarises in the pithy sentence, "Worst was I towards him I loved most". Hjørdis, whose personality was plainly suggested by Gudrun, may not be in any respect as perfect a character[1] as those limned by Ibsen in his maturity, but in herself she is more interesting than any he had yet devised, even than Lady Inger, who on occasions seems limited by the claims of the intrigues amid which she is set; on Hjørdis and her personality the interest of *The Vikings in Helgeland* focuses and the essential trend of the action depends, as was later the case with Hedda Gabler, Ellida Wangel, Fru Alving and Nora Helmer. Opposed to her in character and the artistic arrangement of the figures is placed a woman of softer mettle, Sigurd's wife Dagny, as there were to her counterparts in Hauch's *Sisters at Kinnekullen* and, already, in more than one of Ibsen's earlier plays. From jealousy of Dagny and dissatisfaction with her own lot, Hjørdis foments a strife between her husband and Dagny's, even at the cost of destroying the man she most admires and, with him, herself—the situation almost exactly to be repeated in *Hedda*

---

[1] She inspired Edmund Gosse with horror (*Ibsen*, 1907, p. 74).

Gabler, which thus becomes in certain major respects a scion of the old Icelandic sagas.

The *maîtresse femme* of Scribe receives thus an unexpected reinforcement from the Amazons of the North. Even if, as has been said, the essential trend of the action depends on Hjørdis, the fact (among others) that she is the last to know the vital, explosive secret that mainly causes the catastrophe disqualifies her from ranking as an 'intriguer' in the Gallic manner. Something might, however, be said for giving the pleasant Kaare this appellation, as his secondary and somewhat complicated machinations have a way of obtruding themselves into the principal action at any moment when it threatens to come to a standstill.

*   *   *   *

If, as a man rather than an author, Ibsen ever succeeded in capturing the imagination of Europe, he did so for being a notorious recluse. The lady who described[1] the pharmacist's assistant as walking about Grimstad like a mystery sealed with seven seals was probably affected by this latter-day reputation; for, as has been seen, more intimate testimony relative to that period of his life draws another picture. But all agree that after his earliest residence in Christiania he was taciturn and retired, and, although he was not altogether unapproachable, no one who later was to meet him in Berchtesgaden, in Rome, in Sorrento or Munich or after his final return to Norway could truthfully lay claim to familiarity with him—not the flatulent Paulsen,[2] not excitable Laura Kieler (the prototype of Nora Helmer), not the thick-skinned barbarian Michael Georg Conrad.[3]

All the greater interest, therefore, attaches to those few years of his life, between 1857 and 1864, during which, on exchanging the position of assistant stage-manager at Bergen for that of artistic director at the Møllergate Theatre in Christiania and single blessedness for the married state, he formed a part of a generally recognised clique. In returning to the capital from provincial seclusion on the other hand, Ibsen ended a phase of his life made apparently enjoyable by some happiness and

---

[1] *Auct.* Jæger, H., *Life of Henrik Ibsen* (English translation 1890), p. 49.
[2] John Paulsen beats out some tenuous matter exceedingly fine in *Mine Erindringer* (1900) and *Mit Samliv med Ibsen* (2 vols. 1906–13).
[3] Conrad's very suspect reminiscences are incorporated in Lothar, R., *Henrik Ibsen* (2nd edition 1902), pp. 121 ff.

respect and entered upon one most wretched, in which he ran a grave risk of perishing in degradation and contempt. Not impossibly this combination of companionship and misery, as lamentable as fortuitous, recommended to him the habits and reputation of a hermit in later life.

In the earlier period of eighteen months which Ibsen had spent in Christiania his chief intimacy had been with Paul Botten Hansen.[1] During his friend's removal to Bergen, this remarkable man, a shop-boy of illegitimate birth, had become the editor of the *Illustrated News* (*Illustreret Nyhedsblad*) and advanced far on the way of eminence which ultimately led him (in 1857) to the librarianship of the chief public library in Norway, that of the university of Christiania. He was allowed to be the foremost bibliophile of the country, and his book-lined apartments at 28 Raadhusgade became the resort of all who wished to consult their contents or discuss them with their owner.

Those who were most assiduous in their attendance and felt their views to be most consonant with their host's formed an association on which was bestowed the sobriquet of 'Learned Holland'[2] (*Det Lærde Holland*). The appellation was suggested by a passage in Holberg's comedy of *Jacob von Tyboe*, in which a politically interested character exclaims: "Deuce take the Dutchman, he has his spies everywhere!"[3] and which the younger Daae applied to Botten Hansen on the occasion of a splendid find in the book-market. The association acknowledged no code of rules and had no fixed membership. From time to time it attracted frequenters, sometimes of a cast of mind (like Bjørnson's) markedly out of harmony with that of the majority and, for that reason, apt to fall away; but a nucleus consisting of Botten Hansen, Ibsen, Løkke,[4] Birkeland[5] and Daae[6] remained for some time constant, if not always by physical presence,

[1] 1824–69.
[2] A book has been devoted to this association, and I take pleasure in acknowledging a great debt to its industrious author, F. Ording (*Det Lærde Holland*, 1927). Both the association and the habitual meeting-place were called 'Holland' by its members.
[3] "Skam faae Hollænderen, han haver sine Spioner ude allevegne" (*Holbergs Comedier*, I, 1869, p. 567).
[4] Jakob Olaus Løkke (1829–81), schoolmaster and philologist, politically an extreme conservative.
[5] Michael Birkeland (1830–96), historian and keeper of the national records (*riksarkivar*); member of parliament, as a moderate conservative.
[6] Ludvig Daae (1834–1910), historian; succeeded Botten Hansen as university librarian (1869–76); professor at Christiania (1876–1910); he was an active opponent of *landsmaal*.

then at least in the sense of sodality. It has puzzled those who have given attention to the matter, that in this circle of friends Ibsen was known as 'Gert Westphaler', the name of that character[1] invented by Holberg whose meaningless chatter reduced,[2] it is said, all his fellow-barbers in Copenhagen to a most unnatural taciturnity. Perhaps the nickname was ironically given; but it seems more probable that, for once in his lifetime, he felt himself sufficiently free of all constraint to talk to his fellow-Dutchmen on all subjects, as well grave as trivial, to his heart's content.[3]

St John's Eve afforded an occasion for recording that in the ardour of youth Botten Hansen had wooed the muse of comedy; but, baulked of her favours, he had transferred his attentions. Except for Ibsen, no permanent member of this group distinguished himself in *belles-lettres* or strenuously attempted to do so. The fecund Bjørnson jeered[4] that they were a crowd of theoreticians and mockers, lacking all productivity. A politer and perhaps fairer verdict would pronounce them critics and scholars, the intellectual heirs of Welhaven,[5] as on Bjørnson's shoulders had fallen the mantle of Wergeland. In Botten Hansen to a wide and diversified culture was joined a genial liberality of mind. But the others of 'Learned Holland', particularly in their later lives, when first a shrewish wife and then premature death had removed Botten Hansen from them, became distinctly conservative in their outlook, and some of Ibsen's social dramas must have given them pain. Yet, if the radical nature of its criticism disconcerted, the pessimistic diagnosis often reassured them, and for long they cherished him as 'their' poet *par excellence*, the writer whom, apart from motives of affection, they admired for embodying their ideas. Not incomprehensibly the work by him of which they most strongly approved was *Emperor and Galilean*, with its classical subject, its rigorous attention to historical sources of information and its vast, but simple

---

[1] In the comedy of the same name.
[2] A remarkable proof, if a farther one were wanted, of the utility of drama.
[3] This is Ording's view (*op. cit.* p. 10); Paulsen declares (*Mine Erindringer*, p. 12) that the nickname was given to Ibsen in "his earliest youth" on account of his limitless garrulity. 'Learned Holland' perhaps revived in ironic intent an appellation once well merited.
[4] *Cit.* Gran, I, p. 104: "De ere en bande af theoretikere og spottere, men uden al produktivitet."
[5] Welhaven occasionally, it seems, patronised their circle.

and austere theme.[1] Conversely, it may be argued that,
especially in his middle career (when, besides this drama,
Brand, *Peer Gynt* and *The League of Youth* were composed), Ibsen
showed deference to an attitude of mind like that of his old
intimates of the Raadhusgade. During that period, the public
regarded him, by especial contrast with Bjørnson, as 'the conservative poet'. And that curious but persistent phenomenon,
according to which in many a play he apparently 'took back'
a great deal of what he had advanced previously, may have been
encouraged by the habit (so repugnant to a Bjørnson) of can-
vassing complex problems from all sides and by the reluctance to
over-state a case which he had the opportunity of acquiring in
the sofa-corner of 'Holland'.

*   *   *   *

However that may be, the more solid evidence of Ibsen's plays
suggests that a sentiment overtook him of contempt for what
he had written as theatrical poet of Bergen. It is not altogether
fantastical to presume that he speedily appreciated and
shared the opinion formed by men of gravity, taste and learning,
like his new familiars, and that he congratulated himself on his
initiative in undertaking, even before he could be swayed by
intimacy with them, the weightier subject of *The Vikings in
Helgeland*. If he felt any esteem for his former productions it
was for *Lady Inger*,[2] the only one of their number which he later
admitted to the canon of his Collected Works.[3] In *The Pretenders* (*Kongs-emnerne*, 1863) he turned again to Norwegian
history for his subject, and this time he consulted neither
the Sagas[4] nor the practice of poets, but the third volume of
The History of the Norwegian People[5] by P. A. Munch, the scholar
whose vagaries provided the symposia of Learned Holland with
a recurrent topic of conversation.

Even if no very noticeable element in *The Pretenders* can be
imputed merely to commerce with Learned Holland, yet, in

---

[1] Jæger (*ut cit.* p. 195) declares its style to be modelled on the Latin.

[2] Ibsen re-issued (and in great part re-wrote) *Catiline*, as we have seen. I have
no doubt in my mind that, but for 'Det Lærde Holland', he would have plumed
himself less on taking up this dull but eminently respectable subject.

[3] That canon (to which editors have extensively added since the author's death)
was first established by the *Samlede Værker* issued in 1898–1902.

[4] Though here too is discerned the style which Ibsen had distilled from them
in *The Vikings in Helgeland*.

[5] *Det Norske Folks Historie* (1852–63).

a way, Ibsen assumes also a more scholarly attitude to his material than he had done in *Lady Inger*. *There* an exciting drama and a vivid personality had, after the manner of Scribe, been thrust into a setting for which, almost fortuitously, there was some slight warranty in ancient fact; *here*, a moving and authentical chapter of the national annals is scrutinised with a poet's eye and interpreted to convey a lesson of wide historical application. 'Costume-play' was succeeded by historical drama in the philosophical sense that Hettner had distilled from the practice of Shakespeare.

The literary instigations of *The Pretenders*, however, proceeded from quarters that by now have become familiar: Œhlenschläger's *Earl Hakon* had dramatised the contrast between a monarch's sovereign genius and a nobleman's aspiring talent, which Ibsen elaborated in the rivalry of King Haakon Haakonson and Earl Skule; the third major figure, Bishop Nicholas, a scion of royalty likewise, fulfils many of the functions of one of Scribe's intriguers; and Shakespeare, whose Puck, though with halting steps, had walked again in *St John's Eve* and whose Hamlet may have prompted Lady Inger's hesitations, had, in *Macbeth*, set against the sterile, nerve-racked usurper (that Skule grew into) the unperturbed self-confidence of a young prince, the lawful and triumphant heir of Scotland (as Haakon Haakonson was that of Norway).

To these was added a greater, but also quite general stimulus, that imparted by the personality and literary labours of Bjørnstjerne Martinius Bjørnson (1832–1910). In the critical year 1857, when the simple-minded and rather facile national romanticism had, in its first phase, suffered an obvious check and the aspirations which it expressed were to all appearances baulked, Bjørnson advanced into the forefront of his countrymen's esteem by means of two works, which, together with Ibsen's *Vikings in Helgeland*, may be said to inaugurate the second, weightier phase of the new Norwegian literature. *Synnøve Sølbakken*[1] and *Between the Battles (Mellem Slagene)*[2] are by no abstruse or tortuous channel connected with the broad sentiments that had animated the new national art; the former, an

---

[1] The name of the heroine.
[2] By an odd coincidence, in *Limping Hulda (Halte-Hulda)* Bjørnson treated simultaneously with Ibsen the theme embodied in *The Vikings in Helgeland* and *Kiartan and Gudrun*.

idyllic tale of contemporary peasants, dwelt for preference on their virtues, amiability and happiness, and the latter, a drama in one act, inaugurated a series of plays from Norway's vigorous medieval history, setting forth the struggle for power between the factions of the 'Baglers' and 'Birkebejner', the very feud at issue in *The Pretenders*.

Bjørnson happily knew none of the hesitations that made the first fifteen years of his great contemporary's activities so dolorous and disappointing. He had discovered at once what he could do with great mastery and ease, and the people acclaimed a triumph so entirely consonant with their prejudices. He appeared before them, as they might have phrased it, in the guise of the man born to be king, invested with a radiance both as a public and as a private figure that charmed at the same time as it dazzled.[1]

Ibsen had made the personal, though not familiar, acquaintance of Bjørnson at the time of his first residence in Christiania,[2] but, as has been noted, first he and then, immediately after his own departure, Bjørnson had been engaged in Bergen, and when Bjørnson returned to Christiania in the autumn of 1859 it was, as it happened, for a stay of a few weeks only, after which he was travelling abroad for three years. But for a few and vividly remembered days in June 1863 both men took part in a Choral Festival[3] held at Bergen. On this joyous occasion both had won the applause of an enthusiastic concourse and, what is more, all Bjørnson's generosity of heart had been opened to his morose and afflicted brother-in-arms. There can be little doubt but that Ibsen's imagination, undamped by any touch of jealousy, caught fire at the clash of contrast both in temperament and fortunes between his friend and himself and that, with an *élan*[4] for which we vainly seek a parallel in

---

[1] I do not wish it to be thought that Bjørnson was invariably effulgent and acclaimed. He appeared as the scourge of his countrymen as often as did Ibsen. During the very festival at Bergen about to be remembered both his speeches and his private behaviour were often adjudged intolerable.

[2] It is a common belief, but erroneous, that the four outstanding *littérateurs* of their generation, Ibsen, Bjørnson, Vinje and Lie, simultaneously pressed the benches of Heiberg's 'cramming' establishment; actually Vinje was the only one of them to do so at the same time as Ibsen.

[3] *Sangerfest*; it was mainly an enterprise of the university-bred, and may have heightened Ibsen's academic self-consciousness in the same way that Det Lærde Holland did.

[4] He completed the composition of *The Pretenders* in less than three months after its conception.

the record of his creation, he embodied it in the tragic rivalry between King Haakon[1] and Earl Skule.

*   *   *   *

At an interval of some months *The Pretenders* had been preceded by *Love's Comedy* (*Kjærlighedens Komedie*, 1862), a piece which reveals a totally different spirit, but a similar diversity of received suggestions. Like *The Pretenders* and *The Vikings in Helgeland*, it represents an experiment in a more profound type of drama than any essayed in Bergen, corresponding to the heightened view of his poetic mission to which Ibsen's status as director of a theatre, married man and valued member of an intellectual circle had raised him. It is not argued that 'Learned Holland' suggested the theme or much material for *Love's Comedy* to him; but it is very likely that some of the aspects of Norwegian social life there canvassed occupied on due occasion the conversation of Botten Hansen and his friends; the play is, from first to last, instinct with a spirit of criticism for which Ibsen's earlier writing exhibits no true parallel and for which 'Learned Holland' was notorious; and, for all the brilliance of the verse with which it is conveyed, that criticism is mostly kept in the tone of persiflage such as a cultivated masculine company would readily bestow on its object and for which some of the self-revelation of the impostor Paulsen (in *St John's Eve*) alone gave some foretaste.[2]

Love's Comedy animadverts upon the trammels with which the volatile spirit of love is fettered by the customs attendant, and the effects ensuing, upon its legitimisation. These customs are the same under which the author presumably chafed during his betrothal, at Bergen, but for the only time in his plays of modern life he defines the place of action quite precisely "on the Drammen Road" in Christiania and, especially in the first edition,[3] there are specific references to life in the capital. It must not be assumed, however, that the pruderies and archnesses of courtship, the unction and platitude of matrimony were (or are) peculiar to Christiania, Bergen or Scandinavia in general,

---

[1] In a public speech delivered in Bergen at this time Bjørnson had referred to this king as Norway's best (Koht, 1, p. 258).

[2] It is true that with *Norma* Ibsen had showed an aptitude for this; but *Norma* cannot be called more than a squib, a parody throughout its short length.

[3] In deference to a Danish publisher and an international public they were largely obliterated afterwards, and the language was Danicised.

though they were more disgusting three generations ago than they are now and though they always tainted the free air of love more strongly on the continent than in these islands. It would be idle on this occasion to seek for the sources of Ibsen's fantasies in the works of Œhlenschläger or Shakespeare or Scribe, with their wholly different intentions, or, *a fortiori*, in the sagas, though, as it happens, the heroine takes her name, Svanhild, from the *Vølsunga-Saga* and, according to one interpretation, metaphorically suffers the fate of her namesake in tragic heroism and defeat. Heiberg, however, whose genius had presided at the birth of *St John's Eve*, had taught Ibsen that it is possible and diverting to speak truth with a smiling face, and the spirit of Heiberg, gay and keen, pervades the atmosphere of *Love's Comedy*. But the main literary source of inspiration is, without a doubt, Camilla Collett's novel of contemporary life, *The Sheriff's Daughters*.[1]

About Camilla Collett's agitated life little more need be said in this place than that, though the sister of Wergeland, she was also passionately enamoured of Welhaven; he, however, disdained her. Though her marriage to a very respectable civil servant (who early left her a widow) cannot properly be described as an unhappy one, her warm feelings for Welhaven never cooled, and they united with rankling disappointment at her failure to become his wife, a sense that she abundantly generalised when, on her sagacious husband's recommendation, she took up authorship.

The Sheriff's Daughters, which is almost contemporaneous with the novels of the Brontë sisters and shares certain sentimental and topical features with them, treats for its principal theme the frustrated love-romance of two high-mettled young people and the ultimate marriage of the heroine (by way of a *pis aller*) to an elderly archdeacon.[2] As the authoress sees the subject, both here and in others of her writings, it is a tragic one, which the unsteadiness of the hero and the understanding affection of the clergyman do not, in her estimation, effectively extenuate.

---

[1] *Amtmandens Døtre*, 1855.

[2] I thus inaccurately translate *provst*, the title of a dignitary in the Norwegian church who corresponds perhaps more closely to a rural dean in the Church of England. But as there seems to be no Norwegian equivalent to an archdeacon, the *provst*, as coming next below the bishop in the hierarchy, apparently enjoys greater honour than a rural dean as such.

Regardless of any considerations which might be urged from the masculine point of view, Fru Collett evidently believes marriage to be the prime aim of society and satisfactory marriage guaranteed by one thing only, the liberty of the bride to take unto herself the man on whom her unfettered choice has lighted. With *The Sheriff's Daughters* one highly important point in 'The Woman Question' was first argued, that of a girl's sentimental emancipation from parental tutelage and from the male prerogative of choice.

Quite probably Ibsen had not met Fru Collett at the time that *Love's Comedy* was written: the period of their fairly close acquaintanceship, which coincided with that of her more strident advocacy of women's rights and which certainly stimulated him to ponder them more deeply than hitherto he had done, was yet to come. But the conclusion is inescapable that the author of *Love's Comedy* had *The Sheriff's Daughters* well in mind and that, critical as his play is throughout, it is to be received among other things as a criticism of the novel. It would appear that Ibsen wished actually to advertise the connection between his play and *The Sheriff's Daughters*, since one of its rhetorical climaxes takes up the image in which Fru Collett had compared love with tea and most brilliantly enlarges upon it.[1] The outlines of the two plots are identical: a young man and a young woman fall mutually in love with an intensity as unusual as are their susceptibility, independence, emotional ardour and mental energy; their acquaintances, in the main represented as vastly inferior to them, harbour no sympathy with their infatuation; and the heroine ultimately enters upon a *mariage de raison* with a man blessed with understanding and a great maturity of years but no power either to experience or to arouse passion.

In so far as *Love's Comedy* implied a criticism of *The Sheriff's Daughters* that criticism must manifestly attach to the issue: *mariage de raison versus* love-match. Must the inference immediately be drawn that Ibsen, setting the dispute in a fresh light, advocated the former? Does Ibsen in effect congratulate his heroine on being quit of her romantic hero and acquiring a solid, if possibly humdrum husband? It would be rash to jump to this conclusion at once. Against it pleads perhaps most

---

[1] I, p. 332; Archer I, p. 386. Some of Ibsen's details ultimately come from *Chambers's Journal* (Ording, F., *Henrik Ibsen's "Kjærlighedens Komedie"*, 1914, p. 48).

strongly the heroine's name Svanhild. Her prototype in legend suffered the terrible fate of being trampled to death by wild horses, and in the first draft of Ibsen's play that event is directly alluded to, when her lover, Falk, remarks "Svanhild, as she now is, must be trodden underfoot, stamped upon, crushed under the hooves".[1] This first draft, written in prose, apparently never advanced beyond the first act, but it bore the heroine's name for its title and in the passage quoted clearly foreshadows for her an end as a martyr.

More abundant evidence supports the other side of the argument. All the other couples presented in the play, married or quite securely affianced, have come together through love of a more or less passionate nature. One and all they cut ridiculous and wretched, if sometimes pitiable figures: Frøken Skjære and her Styver, but notably the deuteragonist Lind, that earnest theologian who, upon his engagement to Svanhild's sister Anna, is precipitately prevailed on to abandon his perilous project of emigrating as a chaplain in favour of a teaching appointment in a young ladies' seminary, and the prime figure of fun, Pastor Straamand, once among the brightest students of his generation, now a platitudinous, uxorious country parson with a progeny of twelve girls. Valuable supporting evidence as they might afford, the cause at issue is emphatically that of Svanhild. The really significant feature in it is the circumstance that she is given a choice—and we may assume that it is a free choice: she may either marry Falk or she may marry elderly Guldstad (who pretends to no passion for her), or she may refrain from marrying either in fairly confident hopes of a more satisfactory third—for she is not placed, like the daughters of Camilla Collett's remote and unenterprising sheriff, where the likelihood of farther courtship is negligible, but in her mother's lodging-house, to which the most eligible young men constantly resort. She has her choice and she deliberately exercises it in favour of a man whom she does not love—in fact, she still loves another—and who has made his unromantic sentiments towards her and towards marriage unambiguously clear. By implication, thus, Ibsen goes half the way with the authoress of *The Sheriff's Daughters*, but then parts company with her: a girl should be allowed her choice, but she need not exercise it in favour of 'the man of her heart'.

---

[1] My translation from *Efterladte Skrifter*, I, p. 459.

The point, however, is not thus completely disposed of. If Ibsen should drop any hint that Svanhild decides mistakenly, disastrously, then he and Fru Collett would be in substantial agreement. But there is no such indication. The play is labelled a comedy, its whole tenour justifies a presumption of partial disagreement with *The Sheriff's Daughters*, the passage relative to the legendary Svanhild's fate has been suppressed, the satire of love-matches encourages a belief that matches of another sort will be less preposterous. In brief, Ibsen must be held to have given his vote for *mariage de raison*, provided always that it is freely entered upon by both parties.

Hitherto, in natural pursuit of the trail laid by Camilla Collett, we have directed our attention to the distaff-side. Transference to a masculine viewpoint brings another set of considerations into view.[1] It is the hero, Falk, his position in the play and in Ibsen's esteem that perhaps have caused the greatest uncertainty about the interpretation of *Love's Comedy*. He seems plainly to be the kind of young man with whom the author sympathises. Not only is he ardent in feeling and keen in intellect, but his emotions are yoked to his thoughts and his mind is observant and critical; at first resolved to be a poet, he later selects things rather than words for his tools. Why does he not receive the customary reward of comedy? Is it solely because (in agreement with Fru Collett) Ibsen believed that women should be the supreme disposers in matrimonial affairs and because (more originally) he let his admirable, but not untypical heroine be convinced by the common-sense of a Guldstad? Is the fault wholly Svanhild's?

Not altogether. A distinction must be made between the man and the lover. As the former, Falk possesses high merits, but as a lover he is completely egoistic: as to his contemporary Wilfred Pole, in Meredith's *Emilia in England* (*Sandra Belloni*), his mistress is chiefly to serve him as the evoker of exquisite sensations.[2] She—and not only she—is aware that the exquisiteness of such sensations is equalled only by their evanescence: they afford no ground for any durable partnership.

If on no other shoal, then, the love of Falk and Svanhild

---

[1] It may be held that the weakness of the play, its genuine ambiguity, is due to precisely this 'transference' (as from the draft to the revised text), coupled with the transference from tragedy to comedy.

[2] We may assume that the sensations of a poet possess a higher value than those of a cornet in the cavalry.

strands on the former's egoism, his egoism as a lover. Elsewhere, however, his egoism is not condemned, but the reverse. Even Svanhild enthusiastically agrees that in pursuit of what in Danish and Norwegian is designated his '*kald*', his call or mission, a man, whether he be a poet or anything else, should have leave to be altogether ruthless. There are two things to be observed of the Ibsenian 'call': it is self-imposed, presented to a person's conscious volition by the profound urgings of his own conscience, and it wreaks its ruthlessness as much on him who is possessed by it as on others. Falk appreciates this; for his departure does not mar the end of the comedy: though he has lost his dearest treasure before fully gaining it, he goes off on his walking-tour to the highlands, cheerfully.

It would be possible, therefore, to add a second proviso to the thesis which *Love's Comedy* apparently upholds: a *mariage de raison* is preferable, provided it be entered upon by mutual consent and provided that the alternative is a passionate union with someone possessed of a mission! The minor cases in a negative manner support such an amendment: young Straamand evidently had a *kald* very different to that which in middle age he tries to equate with it—a ministerial 'call' to the first vacant country-parish; Lind sinks into insignificance on renouncing his evangelising ambition, and in him and Anna the lamentable history of the Straamands will doubtlessly repeat itself.

An examination of Ibsen's later work does not permit us to declare with certainty that the theme of *Love's Comedy* represents his settled conviction. It is remarkable that his plays scarcely trench on the modern playwright's standing dish, courtship. Maja and Ulfhejm go off with one another in *When We Dead Awaken*, as do Erhart and Fanny Wilton in *John Gabriel Borkman*; but the *pourparlers* are all conducted off the stage, and no protestations of love are made in the course of the action. The closest approximation, perhaps, to an ordinary wooing is the double approach made to Boletta Wangel by young Lyngstrand of the one part and middle-aged Arnholm of the other in *The Lady from the Sea*, where the younger sister's derision seems to do very fair justice to the situation. Even when Ibsen fairly sets before the public what they would at once classify as 'lovers' like Rosmer and Rebecca West (in *Rosmersholm*) or Solness and Hilda Wangel (in *The Master Builder*), not only do

Rebecca's sins and Solness's obsessions quite eclipse the passion, but the passionate relationship (such as it is)[1] scarcely seems of this earth; and if, as with Nora and Thorvald Helmer, it is a normal, healthy one, it cannot be described as particularly satisfactory. He who treads this delicate ground may go a step farther and voice the suspicion that Ibsen contemplated the complete union of the sexes with the abhorrence clearly evidenced in Alfred Allmers *vis-à-vis* his voluptuous wife Rita and in Johannes Rosmer's shuddering recollection of his perfervid Beata.[2] But Ibsen did not believe that what he disliked did not exist: the whole of *Ghosts*, to take no farther example, is built on a mass of adultery, fornication, pimping and incest.[3]

* * * *

Certainly we cannot say that Ibsen showed himself an apostle of sexual passion. He attributed to it no ennobling or liberating, no redeeming or even invigorating virtue, such as it was a commonplace for the minor authors of the Romantic generation to do—a belief for which they had illustrious preceptors in a Victor Hugo, a Shelley, an Œhlenschläger and a Goethe. With him no man is a great man because he is a great lover, no woman redeemed through the exercise of her functions as a concubine. He would fain disregard those things in them and fasten the attention to more incorporal, as more important, urges.

It would seem then that in his treatment of love between the sexes Ibsen had turned against the prevailing tide of Romantic notions, as in France the *École de Bon Sens*[4] was doing simultaneously, but as no imaginative writer of the North had yet thought of doing. But some very weighty reservations must be made—weightier than the curious case of Solvejg and Peer Gynt, about which no more need be advanced in this place than the not insignificant observation that their union was never consummated. The first is that though Ibsen held no

---

[1] I say "such as it is", because it is arguable that Hilda is nothing to Solness but an audience.

[2] Beata seems to have been sexually abnormal; the suggestion that she was in love with Rebecca is substantiated by the latter's residence in Rosmersholm. It is a singular circumstance that when only children die, to their parents' distress, no one in Ibsen's plays thinks of their replacement in the normal manner (e.g. in *Brand* and *Little Eyolf*).

[3] The idea of incest between brother and sister, which recurs in *Little Eyolf*, may have come to Ibsen from Mauritz Hansen's *Othar af Bretagne* (cf. Collin, C., in *Tilskueren*, 1906, p. 605). It is, of course, a very common poetic *motif*.

[4] Augier and the younger Dumas are reckoned as members of it.

brief for a Haidée or a Marion Delorme he repeatedly brought into his plays, with evident approval, the Egeria and the Valkyrie, who, attached to her hero by bonds of undeniable affection on both sides, rouses (or tries to rouse) him to great endeavour. Of the former we have the humble example of Thea in *Hedda Gabler*, of the latter a perfectly plain, an express instance in Hjørdis of *The Vikings in Helgeland* and a representative, fully elaborated in terms of the present day, in Rebecca West.[1] Something will be said in connection with this when Ibsen's position in the feminist movement comes under review, and we turn to the second reservation. Whatever his attitude towards its physical manifestations (which, however, he nowhere ascetically prohibits), Ibsen was as deeply persuaded as the most hot-blooded Romantic before him, not merely of the importance of love in itself, but of its indefeasible rights. His later plays,[2] for instance, it is almost a commonplace to remark, are for preference plays about great sinners—and the great sins which Borkman and Rubek have committed are not fraudulent appropriation of trust funds or the caricaturing of their fellows, but sins against love, in wilfully blasting their own primal erotic promptings or those of the women with whom they were in close relations. Perhaps Solness comes into the same category.[3]

One may put the matter baldly then and, in doing so, fairly accurately 'place' Ibsen in the current of literary thought on the topic: love, in his view, is very important and to deny it may be unpardonable, but it should never become an end in itself, and there are many more important things, which, in favourable circumstances, it may help to an incalculable extent, while, in unfavourable circumstances, they may even conflict with it—the situation presented in *Love's Comedy*. Of the varieties of love, provided it be genuine and understanding, the affection of wont and common interests, such as that which Dr Stockmann and his wife enjoy and to which Rita and Alfred Allmers[4] evidently look forward, seems to be the most satisfactory. And there is nothing in the range of Ibsen's imaginings

[1] The Valkyrie, it will be remembered, presages death. Under this aspect, Hilda Wangel (of *The Master Builder*) can be called a Valkyrie.

[2] Bernick's past relations to Lona in *Pillars of Society* give a foretaste.

[3] Signora Duse, the actress, believed that Hedda Gabler did too, and she interpreted the part accordingly; but I can find no justification for the theory.

[4] I should like to add Fru Sørby and the elder Werle, whom critics have hideously abused.

to suggest that there is any surer way of attaining to this admirable condition than through the kind of marriage which Guldstad advocates and Svanhild Halm embarks upon with open eyes.

Since the present chapter has of necessity contemplated one of its favourite tenets, it may not be out of order here to establish with rather more circumstance Ibsen's position in that general movement of literature which goes by the name of Romanticism.

To the innumerable definitions of that term it is not proposed to add one more, and perhaps for the purpose in view the mention of a few much used phrases and words will suffice: the 'Romantic' connoted the evocation of a sense of the mysterious both by the choice of recondite subjects and an insistence on profundity in ordinary objects and occurrences; a cult of the extraordinary individual, the genius, and of each person's potential or real individuality as such and of the unique thing, the ideal (confused with the Hegelian 'idea'); the preference of aspiration to achievement, of dreaming to acting, of the imperfect and great to the perfect and small, of the extreme to the norm, of impulse to deliberation, of longing to satisfaction, of faith to demonstration, of poetry to prose, of colour to line, of nature to civilisation and society.

In connection with the violent, grandiosely inspired, formless and tasteless genius of Wergeland something has been said to indicate how well Norwegian Romanticism concurred with the general European movement. The poverty of the country in every particular and its recent history both tended to accentuate what might be called the Rousseauistic aspects of Romanticism— the contemplation, on the one hand, of the virtuous simplicity of the peasants and, on the other hand, of a remote past untinged by the sophistication and vice of developed societies.

That this tendency led to the identification of culture with depravity, of taste with insincerity, of the rude with the good, Welhaven had reprehended. Ibsen was in general agreement with him, and, in fact, much of his own development seems to amount to no more than a continuation of Welhaven's recalcitrance. He turned, as the reader will shortly have an opportunity of judging, with especial ferocity against peasants and all that, in the life of the nation, peasants represented, and, for a particular reason, he broke the spell which its past history had cast upon him. No one could be more acutely aware than he was of the danger of dreaming when it became an anodyne or a substitute for action; perhaps his greatest conscious efforts were lavished on the perfection of a perspicuous technique in the extremely confined and exacting limits of the dramatic form; he ultimately rejected poetry entirely in favour of prose; and the whole of his mature work can be plausibly construed as a series of devastating attacks upon ideals.

But Ibsen was no materialist in any definition of the term, with the distinguishing tenets of *le naturalisme* he was utterly at variance, classical art made no appeal to him whatever.[1] If he directed the full force of his critical intelligence and his consummate workmanship against ideals, it was to subserve a higher and more comprehensive ideal, that of freedom, freedom to develop the human personality to the limit of its capabilities. Not only in this supreme striving of his did he betray the soil in which, so to speak, his moral being had its roots, but also in the countless small touches—his use, for instance, of lighting and of music—with which he diffused even over apparently prosaic subjects an atmosphere of mystery and of what for want of a better term we must designate poetry: the neurotic wife of a country doctor becomes a 'Lady from the Sea', the squalid studio of a third-rate photographer is shown as the ante-room to fairyland; has anything in the play of *Rosmersholm* a greater reality than the spectral White Horses that finish it off?

No important reservations then need be made in declaring Ibsen to be a typical, if perhaps the greatest, representative of that age of Poetic Realism which followed on that of the great Romantic Revival. With all the incalculably momentous differences which distinguish all genius, he was yet at one with Dickens, Browning, Turgeniev, Hebbel, with Balzac and De Coster. The most demonstrable proof of this assertion lies in the two great dramatic poems that were to succeed *The Pretenders* and *Love's Comedy*, in *Brand* and *Peer Gynt*.

---

[1] Milan Cathedral seems to have been the artifact which he admired most in Italy and, after that, the products in painting, sculpture and architecture of the *baroque*.

CHAPTER SEVEN

IBSEN AND KIERKEGAARD

Brand (1866)

Søren aabye kierkegaard, though born as far back as 1813, has only become familiar to the English-speaking world in quite recent years. Northern Europe, however, at once recognised the Danish thinker's originality and fervently discussed his philosophical and religious doctrines while he was still adding to them; and these had passed into general currency very soon after his premature death in 1854. "The philosopher's thought", a French critic has observed,[1] "has impregnated the Norwegian atmosphere to a singular degree." This seems by no means remarkable when the great and enduring effect of Hauge's[2] stern pietism is remembered.

Sixteen years later, in 1870, when Kierkegaard's name was being bandied about with that of Brand, the latter's creator declared[3] that he "had read very little and understood even less" of Kierkegaard's writings. We need not take this disclaimer any more seriously than others of a like nature; certainly it is no bar to an investigation into the relations of Kierkegaard's and Ibsen's notions, which a consideration of *Love's Comedy*, *Brand* and *Peer Gynt* has forced upon every critic possessing some knowledge of *Either-Or*, *The Concept Fear*, *Stages on Life's Way* or *Sickness unto Death*.[4]

We may concede from the outset that, even if some of Ibsen's ideas should appear to have been Kierkegaard's before they were his, it by no means follows that the dramatist worked them straight into his plays from the moralist's books. There is, however, pretty good evidence that he had actually read some of the earlier volumes, borrowing them (it seems) from a lady of British extraction, Jomfru Crawfurd, who had befriended him

[1] Chesnais, P. G. de la, in *Edda*, xxxiv, p. 363.
[2] See p. 46, above.
[3] *Breve*, i, p. 214 ("læst meget lidet og forstaaet endnu mindre").
[4] *Enten-Eller* (1843), *Begrebet Angest* (1844), *Stadier paa Livets Vei* (1845), *Sygdommen til Døden* (1849).

at Grimstad.[1] At second hand he must have absorbed a great deal of the same sort; with the revivalist preacher Lammers, who exercised his ministry in Ibsen's native town,[2] whose doctrines contributed to alienate him from the rest of his family and on whom Kierkegaard had exerted a considerable influence, he seems to have been personally acquainted; Magdalene Thoresen, his wife's step-mother and a Dane by birth, was an enthusiastic disciple[3] of Kierkegaard, and it may be conjectured with the greatest plausibility that the latter's ideas and eccentric personality formed a topic of conversation in the literary *salon* into which her step-daughter's wooer was introduced; nor is it credible that this should not have been the case too in the almost daily colloquies of 'Learned Holland'.

The ideas of Kierkegaard which most forcibly struck his contemporaries and made them often rank him as the 'idealist' *par excellence* appear to have been the following: (i) the rigid delimitation of three moral spheres, as the aesthetic, the ethical and the religious stages or *stadia*, and the denial of any valid compromise or synthesis between them; (ii) the inordinately stern conception which admitted as 'Christian' nothing less than 'Christ-like' and held the profession of Christianity not merely to imply a readiness to suffer the fate of its founder, but to involve actual martyrdom, so that, in effect, a man only becomes a Christian by ceasing (in carnal terms) to exist, a condition which might be called the Christian paradox[4] in its most extreme form; (iii) concomitant with this, a devastating contempt for the modern clergy as being no Christians according to the definition, but odiously hypocritical civil servants;[5] and (iv) the paramount power and importance of the human will and of the free choice which is granted the individual, by his sole exertion, to abide in any of the three *stadia* mentioned or, alternatively, to pass from one of them to another.

[1] Due, C., *Erindringer fra Henrik Ibsens Ungdomsaar* (1909), p. 40, says that he, Ibsen and Schulerud read at any rate *Either-Or* and *The Acts of Love* (*Kjærlighedens Gjerninger*). Koht, 1, p. 40, suggests that they were borrowed from Jfr. Crawfurd.

[2] Not, to be sure, until 1849, after which date he revisited it but twice, for a brief stay either time.

[3] Cf. a letter from her to Frk. Wiehe in *Breve fra Magdalene Thoresen* (ed. Clausen, J. and Rist, P. F., 1919), p. 36.

[4] Viz. that triumph comes through defeat, that defeat is triumph. Peer Gynt accurately phrases this paradox: At være sig selv, er: sig selv at døde (II, p. 411; Archer, IV, p. 252).

[5] The organisation of the Lutheran church in Denmark (to which Kierkegaard belonged) was the same as in Norway.

Ideas such as these—and others probably derived from the same source—figure prominently already in *Love's Comedy*,[1] to give it much of that Aristophanic stiffening which Hettner had declared so desirable for the comedy of the future.

Svanhild's two suitors, for instance, correspond by no means remotely to the aesthete of *Either-Or* and his ethical correlative. Falk might be described as mired in the aesthetic *stadium*, while Guldstad has advanced[2] (for Kierkegaard regards it as a promotion) to the ethical. The latter's position is clear:

> And marriage? Why, it is a very sea
> Of claims and calls, of taxing and exaction,[3] . . .
> It is the feeling of the blessedness
> Of service . . .
> The joy of mutual self-sacrifice,
> Of keeping watch lest any stone distress. . . .[4]

Seen from the Kierkegaardian, as from other angles, the position of Guldstad's opponent is more indeterminate. But it is a fact that he *is* an opponent and that the ground of opposition between them lies mostly in the realm of ideas. He thus may rank as the 'aesthete', by contrast with the 'moral man', and the argument, though obscured, is not controverted by the appearance of a certain 'conversion' at the end. For when he cries out

> I or the Lie, one of us must yield,[5]

he may be announcing an ethical campaign, but no one knows whether he has it in him to carry it through; and the resolution

> My poetry shall be lived[6] [i.e. not written]

may mean no more than that he proposes, as the phrase went later, to become 'an artist in life', a meaning which perhaps

---

[1] Kierkegaard had poked fun at betrothals in *A Seducer's Diary* (*Forførerens Dagbog*).
[2] Guldstad insists that he was once like Falk:

> "But this hair grey-sprinkled
> Once fluttered brown in spring-time, and this brow,
> Which daily occupation moistens now
> With sweat of labour, was not always wrinkled."
>
> (Archer, I, p. 436; I, p. 350.)

[3] Such "married lives" Falk calls "All servitude, captivity, and gyves" (I, p. 293; Archer, I, p. 325).
[4] I, pp. 352 and 354; Archer, I, pp. 441 and 444.
[5] I, p. 332; Archer, I, p. 405.
[6] "Mit digt skal *leves*" (I, p. 332, italics in the original); "My verse shall live" (Archer, I, p. 405).

receives confirmation when he begins the new life on nothing more useful or ethical than a musical walking-tour.[1] In his final withdrawal from the scene we may faintly discern a counterpart to the great Christian paradox which was not unknown to older casuists, those of the Courts of Love: by losing his lady, Falk really merited her.[2]

The cleric whose large paunch and numerous offspring show him to have compromised very completely with the flesh has repeatedly been delineated as a figure of satire. But Pastor Straamand bears the marks of Kierkegaard's brush. A passage, for instance, which goes ill into English, plays with the double meaning of the word *offer* ('sacrifice' and 'offering');[3] when Straamand first takes it into his mouth, Falk assumes that he is speaking of the great Christian virtue of self-sacrifice, but his interlocutor makes it clear that what he aims at is the equivalent to our 'Easter-offerings':

> In virtue of his post
> The Offering is not what he has to *bring*
> But what he has to *get*.[4]

In his learned dissertation on *Søren Kierkegaard and Norway*,[5] H. Beyer draws attention to two farther approximations between the ideas of Kierkegaard and those to be found in *Love's Comedy*, differing from those just discussed because they might be said to belong to a more widely distributed Romantic stock-in-trade. They are the theory to which Falk subscribes and which he impresses on Svanhild, that the most precious part of love is the subsequent memory (*erindring*) of it[6], and the belief, of some comfort to him in his disappointment, that sorrow benefits the poetic activities.

The bard or *skald* Jatgeir says in *The Pretenders*, "The gift of

---

[1] It is not inapposite to remark that Ibsen's curious poem, 'On the Moors' ('Paa Vidderne', 1859, VI, p. 355) shows that he could identify a life in the wilds with pure aestheticism, by contrast, for instance, with the duties and obligations which social life in the Christiania of *Love's Comedy* involves.

[2] Of course, if Falk is to be regarded as having definitely entered the ethical *stadium* at the end of the play, the reasons for Svanhild's rejection of him are much diminished; a belief of this sort perhaps accounts for some of the uneasiness about it.

[3] German papists use the cognate word *opfer* in these two senses also.

[4] I, p. 314; Archer, I, p. 367. Just before there is a similar play on the word 'kaldet' (='call').

[5] *Søren Kierkegaard og Norge* (1924); the relevant passages are p. 121 (where Kierkegaard's *Værker*, I, p. 17 is quoted) and p. 139 (which refers to *Enten-Eller*, I).

[6] I, p. 358; Archer, I, p. 450.

sorrow came to me, and I was a *skald*".[1] But, otherwise, these last points of resemblance differ from the others also in disappearing from Ibsen's later work. The contempt for the official clergy remained, however, as the Archdeacon of *Brand*, several figures in *Emperor and Galilean*, Molvik of *The Wild Duck* and, in particular, Pastor Manders of *Ghosts* attest. The relation of the aesthetic to the other values of life, to life itself, was nothing less than an absorbing theme throughout the whole of Ibsen's life, and, indeed, almost all his later work touches upon it in one form or another;[2] of *The Master Builder*, *When We Dead Awaken*, perhaps even of *Hedda Gabler*, we may say that it constitutes the subject of the whole work of art. If Ibsen never solves the problems which it raises—or, rather, if he never provides a humanly satisfactory solution to it—the fact may testify to the sharpness of the distinction between the aesthetic, the ethical and the religious which Kierkegaard's moral earnestness and literary brilliance had impressed on such wide circles among his own and Ibsen's contemporaries.

*   *   *   *

If ideas derived from Kierkegaard or bred in an ambience which by its nature proved especially propitious to their propagation are found permeating the comparatively airy texture of *Love's Comedy*, it is natural to seek them in the work which next followed from the author's pen, in *Brand*[3] (1866). The tone of the whole is more solemn, the issues at stake are more considerable than the identity of a young girl's future partner in life; moreover, the principal character and his notions were in good measure copied from Christopher Arnt Bruun,[4] the virile young parson with whom Ibsen had much intercourse during the days when the subject of his new work was most actively fermenting in his brain, and Bruun, with several others of their acquaintance at this time, was a very ardent propagandist for Kierkegaard's doctrines.

---

[1] II, p. 76; Archer, II, p. 260. Cf. Heine's lines:
"Aus meinen grossen Schmerzen
Mach' ich die kleinen Lieder."

[2] *The League of Youth* and *The Pillars of Society* perhaps have least of it.

[3] *Brand* was first drafted in an epical form, much less 'Kierkegaardian' in its bias than the drama.

[4] Ignorant persons have thought Brand a portrait of Kierkegaard himself; Ibsen's denial (*Breve*, I, p. 214) is really superfluous.

6-2

As was habitually to happen, the action of *Brand* and what may be deduced from it became a subject of acrimonious dispute. But all commentators are agreed on at any rate one thing: it delineates the effects of a powerful, not to say excessively developed, will. That prevailing characteristic in the hero emerges from the first scene of the play, in which he pursues the mountain path he has intended to take, in the face of dangers from precipice and glacier before which men more familiar with physical hardship recoil; a parallel, extended almost to the infinite, presents itself a few hours later when at the call of pastoral duty he pits himself against the active, not the passive, dangers of nature and launches a boat on to the storm-lashed firth where no other man will join him. Brand's will, it has been seen, is always allied to the duty he prescribes to himself and which by reason of that fact he is determined to perform at all costs.

His duty commands him to stay in his native parish, so as to be near his hardened mother when the time shall come for the final absolution of her sins and, later, in order to impart to the parishioners the ministrations they demand of him, even though continuance in that clime causes the death of his infant son Alf and, indirectly, of his beloved wife; it urges him to pull down the old church and build a new one at his own expense; then to exclude the congregation from it and the man-made religion which it represents in order to lead them up into a kind of promised land amid the upland wilds, where they fall away, stone and abandon him. Brand, conscious of what is right at all times, unswervingly proceeds to do it. His attitude of mind thus represents the ethical *stadium*, and, lest any doubt should remain on that score, the second scene confronts him with another character, the artist Einar,[1] for whom the enjoyment of the senses is all and who for that reason remains at the aesthetic stage of *Enten-Eller*, that Either-Or to which Brand gives the variant 'All or Nothing'.[2]

Brand's clerical status and pastoral activities have led several to suppose that he should be regarded as a representative not of the ethical *stadium*, but rather of the religious. The best support

[1] As has been mentioned, Einar reappears in Act V, no longer a foil to Brand, but, 'converted', a most disgusting caricature of him.
[2] This alternative is not actually presented by Kierkegaard, but it is a rider on his rigorism, perfectly consonant with the spirit of his teaching.

for an argument in this sense comes from the very striking parallel between the death of the child Alf (whose life his father could have saved) and the supreme instance of religious behaviour which Kierkegaard adduced, the intended sacrifice of Isaac,[1] when at God's express command his servant Abraham deliberately set out to commit an 'unethical' act under conditions which the Almighty alone could mitigate by a mysterious compromise. But it may be observed that none of Brand's actions is commanded by God, that he is not represented as a mystic in communion with the unseen world and that, if a voice from that world makes itself heard in Ibsen's poem, it nowise expresses approval of what Brand has conceived as his duty.[2] Ibsen himself protested[3] against any religious interpretation, declaring he could have made *Brand*'s 'syllogism' equally well for a sculptor or a politician; and most contemporary criticism, which had a very keen nose for distinctions of this kind, agreed that he had made a contribution to ethical debate, not religious. But, if (to speak very loosely) God and 'the religious' cannot be made responsible for the human and dramatic tragedy of Brand, it is worth remarking that the God who has his allegiance and in whose name he formulates the articles of his ethical duty, is very much the stern Jehovah of Kierkegaard's paradox— "whom he loveth, he chasteneth".[4]

Regarding the end of *Brand*, with its supernatural Voice calling "through the crashing thunder"

He is the God of Love,

and the inferences that ingenuity can extract therefrom, almost as many varying opinions have been advanced as there have been critics concerned to give them.[5] This is the place neither to canvass them nor to add to their number. But it is difficult to avoid the conclusion that the last scene

---

[1] In the course of the play Ibsen actually refers to the biblical incident (II, p. 174, "Isaachs Rædsel", Archer, III, p. 97).

[2] The Voice heard above the landslide that finally annihilates the hero, crying "Han er *Deus Caritatis*" may be nothing more than a subjective hallucination.

[3] Letter to Georg Brandes of 26 June 1869 (*Breve*, I, p. 188).

[4] Early in the play (II, p. 129; Archer, III, p. 22) Brand says he scarcely knows whether he is a Christian or not: the same, I fancy, Ibsen would have said of himself. He never approached what Kirkegaard calls the religious *stadium*. He reverenced the person of Jesus Christ but his love of the Bible seems mainly to have been literary.

[5] The whole subject is summarised by Kinck, B. M., 'Dramæt "Brand" Opfatninger og Tolkninger', in *Edda*, xxx (1930), pp. 81 ff.

comprises a hostile criticism, if not of Kierkegaard, then at least of some of his most cherished tenets. The words of the Invisible Choir which Brand hears

> Never shalt thou win this spirit;
> Thou in mortal flesh wast born:
> Spurn his bidding or revere it;
> Equally thou art forlorn.[1]

suggest that Kierkegaard's specifically religious message to his brethren implies an impossibility: man cannot become a Christian in his sense, it is not for him to attain the Christian, Christlike martyrdom which alone is valid, for the mere reason that he is man and Christ is god. And a similar condemnation of the doctrine of the supremacy of the will seems implied.[2] The play can scarcely be otherwise described than as a *tragedy* of the will. 'Faith will move mountains'—well and good. Here, in the literal sense, the mountain does move,[3] only to kill this apostle of faith in will.[4]

If, in one sense, then, *Brand* might be called 'the Kierkegaardian Tragedy', it is possible to see it as Kierkegaardian tragedy also from another point of view: not as the tragic fate of one imbued with Kierkegaard's ideas, but as a tragedy made in accordance with the aesthetic notions of the thinker from Copenhagen. The contention was ably argued by M. A. Stobart in *The Fortnightly Review*.[5] In *A Seducer's Diary* Kierkegaard draws a distinction between two kinds of tragic guilt: that which the hero incurs voluntarily, on his own account, and which Kierkegaard denominates 'ethical', since it is the effect of deliberate choice; and that which is forced upon the hero by circumstance or by inheritance and which Kierkegaard calls 'aesthetic', because it is guilt only for the purposes of the play;

---

[1] II, p. 269; Archer, III, p. 248.

[2] Möhring, W., 'Ibsens Abkehr von Kierkegaard' in *Edda*, XXVIII, pp. 43 ff., believes (p. 45) that Ibsen turned against the Kierkegaardian ideas and himself lost sympathy with his hero *while* he was finishing the play. The 'epic' fragment gives no help on this point.

[3] It is reported (Chesnais, P. G. de la, in *Edda*, XXXIV, 1934, p. 367) that the missionary, H. C. Knudsen, whom Ibsen must have known, perished in an avalanche; the incident may have hit his saturnine fancy.

[4] Even if the extreme view be taken that the last words represent the plenary pardon by the supreme being capable of according such pardon, pardon can only be given for wrongdoing and Brand the man is forgiven for the wrong of acting on 'Brandian' principles.

[5] 'New Lights on Ibsen's "Brand"', *Fortnightly Review*, new series, LXVI (1899), p. 233. The 'new lights' of the title all come from Kierkegaard, then unknown in Great Britain.

he goes on to declare that true tragedy holds a balance between these two kinds of guilt, or, in other words, that both these elements should be equally present in it. In adducing *Antigone*, the favourite tragedy of his enemy Hegel (as of many others), to illustrate his tenet, Kierkegaard apparently disclaims any intention of novelty, and we might allow Ibsen to have reached some similar conclusion independently of him, were it not for the business connected with Brand's mother, which, if it be a mere episode to illustrate the hero's steadfastness, is given a prominence that seems excessive in so economical a craftsman. For the manner after which, in well-nigh legal or mercantile terms,[1] her son 'takes over' the debt incurred by his parent through her avaricious clinging to worldly possessions suggests that Ibsen was patently saddling his hero with an 'aesthetic' guilt also to counterweigh the 'ethical guilt' imputed to him on the strength of his behaviour to wife and son.

The conjunction of 'ethical' and 'aesthetic' guilt is somewhat mechanically made in *Brand*. It is worth while to investigate whether something of the same sort is attempted or carried out more happily in Ibsen's later plays. "Tragic guilt", Kierkegaard had declared, "is more than merely subjective guilt, it is hereditary guilt (*Arveskyld*)", and the idea of hereditary guilt is certainly not absent from Ibsen's conceptions. The first effective defence of the abhorrent *Ghosts* was put forward[2] on the ground that it perpetuated a practice of the Greeks. But, again, if too much stress is laid on this factor, in other words, if the play of *Ghosts* is seen as the tragedy of Oswald,[3] rather than of his mother, the 'balance' which Kierkegaard enjoined can again only be established in a mechanical way, since the 'subjective' or 'aesthetic' tragedy, that resulting from personal choice, is not that of the young man at all, but of Fru Alving.

No other play presents so good a case for the imputation of 'ethical' or 'hereditary' guilt. But Ibsen toyed elsewhere at least with the idea of 'hereditary destiny' (if the phrase be allowed). Thorvald Helmer definitely accuses his peccant wife of being her frivolous father's daughter; that self-imposed

---

[1] As her heir, he is to expend the exact amount of her fortune on a new church, for instance.

[2] By Schjøtt, P. O., in the first number of *Nyt Tidsskrift* (1882).

[3] As, in fact, it very commonly was at the time of its first publication.

mission in the name of which Gregers Werle spreads so much misfortune must in some measure be referred to his mother's puritanical self-righteousness; Hedda Gabler perhaps would have not chosen her particular 'way out' had she not been a general's daughter;[1] and little Eyolf has become a cripple, with all that follows from it, through his parents' negligence. All these propositions may be true enough, but none of them seems particularly relevant to the main point at issue in each particular case. Whatever tragedy there is in *The Wild Duck* would be no less effective if nothing were known about Gregers Werle's mother.[2]

It would seem then that if, in composing *Brand*, Ibsen intended it to embody the particular tragic theory of Kierkegaard just discussed, he found it unsatisfactory as a guiding motive and, if for anything, admitted thereafter vague recollections of it only to give to his 'aesthetic' tragedies a colouring which may be effective, but is applied in the main merely to secondary features; there is however no need to refer such colouring to conscious or unconscious memory of the Danish theorist.

Does a like diminution reveal itself also in the ethical elements which the plays of Ibsen have in common with the speculations of Kierkegaard? The next play after *Brand*, *Peer Gynt* (1867), as it has become a commonplace to remark, forms the reverse to which its predecessor is the obverse. If *Brand* had unfolded the catastrophic career of the extremist, in *Peer Gynt* are depicted the serious, the ethically dangerous, consequences of complying with that spirit of compromise[3] which Pastor Brand put behind him for an abomination, just as Kierkegaard had done; and, if it was just to designate *Brand* as a Kierkegaardian tragedy, it would not be very far beside the mark to see in *Peer Gynt* the tragic consequences of not being a Kierkegaardian. Peer Gynt is obviously one whom Kierkegaard would think a base creature for remaining unmoved in the 'aesthetic *stadium*', carefully "going round about" when an opportunity presents itself to qualify for the 'ethical *stadium*', but at the same time his belated attempt to pose as a man of weight and culture lands

[1] In one of the notes he made while pondering on the subject (Archer, XII, p. 383) Ibsen laid stress on the fact that she came of degenerate stock too.

[2] In fact, there might be more tragedy, because more pity for Gregers; as it is, we are left with the conviction that his attitude to his father and, consequently, to society, was mainly conditioned by an unpleasant woman's warped fancies.

[3] "Akkordens Aand" (II, p. 273; Archer, III, p. 256).

him into complete failure, in fact into a lunatic asylum; he sets no true mission before himself, and an exertion of will for the purpose of achieving a mission never comes into question. His career is not distinguished. The observer of its inglorious episodes might jump to the conclusion that he has before him a tragedy even more Kierkegaardian than *the* Kierkegaardian tragedy *Brand*. But it would be a rash conclusion. Some critics have found it hard to fit Ibsen's implied philosophy at any stage into Kierkegaard's categories; and none of the material is perhaps more recalcitrant to such treatment than *Peer Gynt*, with its lack of plot and with its satirical treatment of religion, philosophy, the supernatural and life after death. Heiberg could not stomach the relentless rigour of Kierkegaard, and it is the airy spirit of his 'apocalyptic comedy', *A Soul After Death*—a piece of which Ibsen highly approved[1]—, that plays over the darkest scenes of *Peer Gynt*. Kierkegaard's would have implied complete condemnation; and it is more than doubtful whether *Peer Gynt* is a tragedy at all.[2]

Yet the dissociation must not be carried too far. The kernel of the thought implied in *Peer Gynt* is not only a Kierkegaardian notion, but even phrased in the language of Kierkegaard. Over and over again, the Danish moralist insisted on the vital importance for every man to "be himself" ("være sig selv"); *Peer Gynt* rehearses the biography of a man who rejects this principle in favour of that enunciated by the Old Man of Dovre, a monster, almost a devil: "Troll, to thyself be—enough!"[3] ("Trold, vær dig selv—nok!"), with the deliberate addition

> . . . "Enough", that most potent and sundering
> Word, must be graven upon your escutcheon.[4]

Peer Gynt certainly adopts the *trolds*' slogan, not Kierkegaard's, and everything in his life that is blameworthy or preposterous can be referred to it.

[1] Paulsen, J., *Samliv med Ibsen*, I (1906), p. 44.
[2] The common view is that the hero is 'redeemed' at the close; if he is not, then it seems almost unavoidable to assume that the Button-Moulder will have him in the end, i.e. that as an individual entity he will just cease to exist.
[3] II, p. 313. Archer, IV, p. 71.
[4] Beyer (*op. cit.* p. 175) draws attention to this parallel between Kierkegaard's: "The great thing is not to be this or the other, but to be oneself, and of that every human is capable, if only he wills it", and Ibsen's: "It is a question not of willing this or that, but of willing what one absolutely must, because one is oneself and cannot help it." The latter remark occurs in *Breve*, I, p. 208.

Before dismissing this drama, however, we must dwell for a moment on the incident of the Strange Passenger, whom, in Act V, Peer suddenly encounters on the doomed vessel that is conveying his aged body back to Norway. Kierkegaard looked on Fear as a sovereign specific in the therapeutics of the soul, and the Strange Passenger has sometimes been taken for Fear personified. Ibsen hotly denied the identification[1] and described the scene, as he did others of an episodic nature,[2] merely as a 'caprice'; but, as probably often had happened in cases when he proffered a *démenti*, a very deep-rooted conception may have passed altogether out of his conscious recollection of its origin. It is undeniable that the slow and halting process of Peer Gynt's conversion, at his latter end, to a more serious view of his life and of his own insufficiency begins with this scene.

The exertion of will-power for the purpose of achieving individual profit according to a fixed scale of values, in the manner that Kierkegaard enjoined, would naturally induce many of those who accepted his guidance to phrase their moral activities as obedience to the 'demands of the ideal'. Other doctrines could have the same effect, and we would do wrong to over-emphasise the point in connection with Kierkegaard's influence on Ibsen. We may, however, observe that the personages in Ibsen's later plays who use such a phrase and consider themselves as acting up to its implications, cut a somewhat pitiful figure; they certainly do not appear to enjoy the author's approval, and even they who hesitate to construe *Brand* as a hostile criticism of Kierkegaardian tenets can scarcely ignore the ridicule of idealism in the author's later work.

Hilmar Tønnesen of *Pillars of Society* sees himself as almost unaided 'holding aloft the banner of the ideal'—and is revealed as a phrase-making romanticist of the cheapest sort, lacking everything that could properly be called either reflection or principle or insight, and his frivolous incitations are an im-

[1] *Breve*, I, p. 159. Eitrem, H., 'Den fremmede Passager i "Peer Gynt"' in *Edda*, XIV (1921) suggests that Ibsen took some minor ideas from V. A. Thisted's *Breve fra Helvede* (*Letters from Hell*, 1866), which was partly inspired by *Brand*, partly by Heiberg's *Soul after Death*. According to Thisted, certain souls, on ticket-of-leave from hell, are permitted to deal with mortals, and the Strange Passenger may be one of them.

[2] "Those apparently capricious and wanton scenes in which Ibsen not rarely hides his deepest teaching" (Wicksteed, P. H., *Four Lectures on Henrik Ibsen*, 1892, p. 48).

mediate cause of his young nephew's attempt to sail for America as a stowaway on the unseaworthy *Indian Girl*.

In *Pillars of Society* a tragedy is averted. But Gregers Werle's devotion (in *The Wild Duck*) to the 'ideal' goes much deeper than Hilmar Tønnesen's, it cannot be justly designated as frivolous, and the consequences of it precipitate a genuine catastrophe. In the belief that his friend's marriage (like all other marriages) should imply absolute candour between the spouses and unclouded knowledge of all the conditions of their union—a belief which on the loftiest grounds should be un-exceptionable—Gregers Werle convinces Hjalmar Ekdal that the latter's wife was a fallen woman before he became engaged to her and that the daughter Hedvig, whom he believed to be theirs, in reality is the consequence of his wife's *liaison* with her former employer. Hjalmar Ekdal's reaction to the information breaks Hedvig's heart, and the 'idealist', once more intruding, brings about her death by suicide when he puts into her head the notion of propitiatory self-sacrifice—once more, a notion to which, as a general principle, many severe moralists would raise no objection. But that the competence of the severe moralist does not extend indefinitely, that the doctrine which he supports has no universal validity, becomes plain in the catastrophic outcome and is almost formulated by Dr Relling's words in the last moments of the play:

Oh, life would be quite tolerable, after all, if only we could be rid of the confounded duns that keep on pestering us, in our poverty, with the claim of the ideal.[1]

Pillars of Society and *The Wild Duck* have perhaps diverted attention somewhat away from Kierkegaard. In *The Master Builder* the approximation, on the other hand, is rather nearer. Hilda Wangel in that play, is in a certain sense, a more over-strained idealist even than Gregers Werle, in fact she may be looked on as mentally unsound, and her demand "Do the *impossible* once again!"[2] has a true Kierkegaardian ring about it (though there is not the smallest grounds for supposing that the young lady knew anything of *Either-Or* or its companion-volumes). She imposes her command upon the reluctant will of Halvard Solness, who thereupon, at her instigation, subject

---

[1] v, p. 106; Archer, VIII, p. 400.
[2] VI, p. 81; Archer, X, p. 356.

to vertigo though he is, climbs to the top of a newly built tower in order to decorate it with a garland, loses his balance and falls dead to the ground. He is a victim to another's uncompromising 'idealism' just as Hedvig Ekdal was.[1]

Under the influence of doctrines which will be considered later, but mainly perhaps on the pragmatic failure of the experiment in Kierkegaardian morals which he conducted in *Brand*, Ibsen thus turned away first from the rigour of Kierkegaard's idealism and subsequently from other forms as well. That it was hostile to life was a circumstance that did not vex the ex-theologian with his eyes fixed on the eternal and absolute; but to Ibsen as to his Relling it came to be a material consideration. Life and the 'joy of life' which gave Fru Alving so much food for thought had to be reconciled. *Emperor and Galilean* turns almost exclusively on this reconciliation. A sensitive and knowledgeable reader of the last-named drama when it first came out, Jens Peter Jacobsen, the author of *Fru Marie Grubbe* and *Niels Lyhne*, at once scented that what the apostate Julian was aiming to reconcile with hedonism or to supersede was the spirit that informed Brand: alluding to his pedantry, "Julian", Jacobsen writes, "is a Norwegian-German, who has read his Søren Kierkegaard".[2]

This is not the only instance of a retention of Kierkegaardian tenets after they have been discarded as a rule of life. Beyer draws attention[3] to the fact that Bernick makes, in *Pillars of Society*, the same discovery as Judge Wilhelm, the representative of the 'ethical' in *Either-Or*, namely that to serve others is to realise himself,[4] and it has been held that the 'helpers and servers' in whom Solness believes are the self-same 'dark powers' (*dunkle Magter*) in the human personality to which Kierkegaard refers. This is very doubtful.[5] On the other hand, the basis of Dr Stockmann's character—his belief that the

---

[1] The intransigeance with which Rosmer provokes Rebecca West to the self-immolation which involves his own could be similarly criticised: but any notion that if the two lovers had retired for a little to think things over they might have lived happily ever after is not only philistine, but unsupported by anything that Ibsen wrote or implied.

[2] Beyer, *op. cit.* p. 171.

[3] *Op. cit.* p. 167.

[4] It is very doubtful whether this idea occurs again, even in *Little Eyolf*.

[5] Beyer (*op. cit.* pp. 165 ff. and 175 ff.) lists a number of minor parallels between Kierkegaard and Ibsen of which it is impossible to say whether they are accidental or not.

individual, convinced of the justice of his 'mission' and of his indefeasible right to enforce it in the teeth of the majority, not only always has right on his side, but is also the strongest—that is Kierkegaard's too, with his "Truth is in the minority" and "A single individual is the highest power".[1] Like Stockmann's too, Rosmer's and Allmers's are *animae naturaliter Kierkegaardianae*. And that great and tragic quest of all Ibsen's greatest creations to realise themselves, to discover their mission, to free their minds and bodies from all the trammels which could prevent that realised self from doing what the mission imposes on them, is one which Kierkegaard would have hailed as pulsing with the heart of his doctrine, and is also conceived in forms which would have been other but for that doctrine.

[1] Quoted by Beyer, *op. cit.* p. 182.

CHAPTER EIGHT

IBSEN AND SCANDINAVIANISM

Peer Gynt (1867)

THE intransigeance of Parson Brand and the sympathy accorded
to him almost throughout his dramatic course are in very great
measure due to Ibsen's contemplation of the opposite cast of
mind, one in which rigour and conviction seemed to him to be
notably deficient. When he had discharged his venom against
it, he felt, as he frequently came to do in analogous circumstances, that he had over-stated his case, and in *Peer Gynt* he
could let fancy and laughter play where little had been heard
in *Brand* but the crack of the whip and the exhortation to repent.
Ibsen believed the state of mind in question to be a specifically
Norwegian characteristic, which a demonstrable series of events
had exposed before the whole world. It becomes our task now
to outline this series of events, to describe Ibsen's position relative to it and to his fellow-countrymen as revealed at the time
and to indicate the effects in *Brand* and its successors.

*   *   *   *

The scattered interest roused in Scandinavian Europe by the
revolutions of 1848, as was remarked in our first chapter,
speedily concentrated on one of their major consequences, the
first war between Denmark and the German powers for the
control of the Duchies of Slesvig, Holstein and Lauenburg,
which lie on the neck of the Jutland peninsula. From the first,
Oscar I, King of Sweden and Norway from 1844 to 1859, took
the view that this struggle was a more than local affair; the
martial preparations which gave force to his opinions, combined with the diplomacy of Palmerston and other foreign
statesmen, and more particularly with the prowess of the Danes
in the field, brought the campaign to a conclusion eminently
satisfactory to the latter. But the son of Bernadotte had been
able to rely on support at home that was only reluctant and
partial; and the *Storthing*, in placing at his disposal the Norwegian armed forces and certain credits for maintaining them

94

on a war footing,[1] had gone out of their way to declare that their vote implied no *rapprochement* to the hereditary enemy, Denmark.

The policy which envisaged common action on the part of the states of Denmark, Norway and Sweden and the creation of conditions both moral and material which would further such a policy went by the name of 'Scandinavianism'. Its most enthusiastic supporters were the students' clubs in the four Northern Universities of Christiania, Copenhagen, Lund and Upsala; and it must be borne in mind that, much more so than in the Union Societies of Cambridge and Oxford, certain older members of these clubs, even professors, continue to exercise a preponderant influence after they have graduated (or at least attained the necessary standing of seniority to qualify for their degrees). An outstanding advocate of such 'student' Scandinavianism, thus, was Carl Parmo Ploug, the Danish author and for forty years editor of the daily newspaper *Fædrelandet*, who was thirty-four years of age when the first Slesvig war broke out. The movement was greatly aided, if indeed it was not engendered, by the periodically convoked congresses to which two or more of the Northern Universities sent delegates[2] and which, like most 'youth movements', enjoyed considerable favour by reason of the opportunities provided for cheap travel and facile debauchery.

Although regarded with a jealous eye by responsible statesmen, these student congresses were eventually patronised by the Swedish Royal House, whose own Scandinavian proclivities were enhanced by the events of the Crimean war (1853–6). Sir Charles Napier's expedition to the Baltic in 1854 revealed to King Oscar how important a part in European politics a strong Northern state could still play, and the requisite strength might be accumulated if he could induce the Scandinavian states to act as one. The imminent extinction of the Danish dynasty[3] moved a second Union of Calmar[4] into the realms of possibility, and the proposal was actually made in 1857 of a kind of *tontine* to be entered into by the house of Oldenburg and the house of Bernadotte.

[1] Norwegian and Swedish troops were moved to northern Jutland in 1849.
[2] The earliest at which all four were represented was held in Copenhagen in 1845.
[3] King Frederik VII, the last of his line, died in 1863.
[4] Which in 1397 combined the crowns of Denmark, Norway and Sweden.

No doubt, the hope of winning back Finland, which Sweden had been obliged to cede to the Russians in 1809, gained some Swedish adherents to the cause of Scandinavianism during the Crimean war, but enmity towards Russia proved a double-edged weapon. For to others a greater danger seemed to be threatening Sweden and Norway from the east than ever could be apprehended from the south; they believed that any experiment in the direction of a closer union of the three Scandinavian powers would be construed by Russia as a threat, to be visited upon them by condign action before the alliance had time to yield the increase of strength anticipated. Such a consequence held particular terrors for the rural population of the vast Northern provinces of Sweden and Norway, in any event averse to the loss of man-power which war and its preparations entailed; and most of the royal ministers in these two countries took the view that the disadvantages of a union or alliance would outweigh the benefits. The opposition to Scandinavianism was formed by the two cabinets, by most of the members of the Norwegian *Storthing* and the Swedish *Riksdag*, together with their numerous understrappers in the press, by the peasantry and by the mercantile part of the community, always anxious to avoid any appearance of truculence. On the other hand, it enjoyed the favour of the Swedish court, of the very vocal student bodies and their journalistic organs and of some of the younger civil servants, professional men and politicians who still retained a connection with the student-clubs and also cherished no affection for the large peasants' parties in the legislative assemblies. It is natural that in Denmark, where the menace from abroad was most immediately terrible, proposals for a defensive alliance should seem most desirable and scruples about it most frivolous.

This was, in broad terms, the posture of affairs when the question of 'the Duchies' again became urgent in the early 'sixties. There was an almost proverbial number of complications, some of which were *sequelae* of a most unfortunate crisis relative to the office of viceroy in Norway; suffice it in this place to say of the latter that it had lowered the prestige of the new king Charles XV[1] in both his kingdoms and had reawakened the reciprocal suspicions of their inhabitants which had slowly been diminishing in the preceding half-century.

[1] Who reigned from 1859 to 1872.

The Scandinavian sentiment was, it will have been inferred, an unreliable and dangerous support for any major policy. Nevertheless, as on various earlier occasions, a resolution of the Christiania students' club in December 1863, when German armies were again preparing an invasion, reaffirmed a determination to take up arms for the threatened 'brothers' on the southern frontier, and the resolution roused much local fervour. But when the *Storthing* reassembled in the following March, after the Prussian and Austrian armies had made good progress in their victorious march northwards, the emotional thermometer fell abruptly; the chagrined king must have realised that the climb-down to which he had had to stoop had been well advised. Finally the Norwegian parliament passed a vote, once more putting the armed forces with the necessary credits at the disposal of the crown for the defence of Denmark proper,[1] but it attached to it the proviso that at least one of the great western powers (i.e. Britain or France) joined the alliance and it reaffirmed its objection to any alliance of a permanent nature with Denmark. France and Britain made no move, Charles XV was reduced to impotence, the Danes, dislodged from their old rampart on the Dannevirke and their newer trenches at Dybbøl, were utterly defeated on land and the Duchies detached from their crown.

*   *   *   *

Among the political verse of 1848 and 1849 which almost inaugurated Ibsen's poetical career there figures an appeal "to the Norwegian and Swedish brothers", bearing the significant title 'Scandinavians, Awake!'[2] The peril threatening Denmark from the South, from the German violators (*voldsmænd*), stimulates the writer; he counsels resistance on the part of "that fraternal spirit of the North which knits Norwegian and Swede and Dane together". In this strain he proceeds for forty-eight stanzas (now of four, now of three lines each), very familiarly appealing to "Du, Oskar!", asking whether Norway shall sully with a faithless deed the fair dawn of her young freedom and enquiring of the Swedish brothers why they hesitate to speed over the waves of the Sound. The end runs:

---

[1] I.e. not Holstein.
[2] *Efterladte Skrifter*, i, p. 31; the translations from this piece are my own.

Ye noble sons of Norway,
Ye valiant Swedish brothers! Wake at last!
Hear yet the sound of battle roar from Denmark!
Soon will the leaf of Fate's decrees be turned.

Remember Slesvig from the long-departed days,
The fair branch of the Northlands' giant oak,
—Soon maybe of Denmark will no more be left
Than honour, as a cromlech of the past.

Perpend, posterity will judge our acts.
Forget we not the heart's supreme dictate
Nor snap the North's fair brother-bond.

So boldly work with word, with script, with sword,
Obey the voice of honour, duty, sense,
Loving stretch out a brother's hand to a brother race.

Nine years later, in a set of verses to the memory of Berna-dotte ('Til Carl Johans Minde'),[1] Ibsen rather comically hails the Pau attorney's son as "the first Scandinavian of the century" ("Seklets første Skandinav"), glorifies his 'Alexander's Progress' as a heritage common to all the peoples of the North and calls for the banishment of discord and for a sworn brother-hood based on freedom ("Fosterlag paa Frihed bygget").

Ibsen was thus naturally predisposed to burst into renewed ardour when Scandinavianism once more became a burning issue in the 'sixties. Other factors contributed. It is by no means an uncommon phenomenon that the most devoted par-tisans of a cause are those who only just come within its sphere of attraction. We saw that, in a strict definition, Ibsen could scarcely count as a member of the university. He took part in none of the international students' congresses. But it was always his pleasure to identify himself with academic activities, and the prominent position which he was accorded in "Det Lærde Holland" greatly raised his self-esteem as one of the intellectual *élite* of his country. These men with whom he associated were not only (as we have noted) critics and scholars, but to a man convinced 'Scandinavians' also, and their attitude to the cause contributed something to such prestige as it enjoyed in Norway.

The Choral Festival at Bergen in the early summer of 1863, in which Ibsen joined, may be accounted a contributory factor; it was not one of the international student congresses; but the

---

[1] *Efterladte Skrifter*, i, p. 148.

98

members of Christiania University were strongly represented, Ibsen travelled to Bergen as one of them, and he felt his comradeship confirmed even more strongly as this excursion proved one of the supremely enjoyable moments of his life. He felt around him the same, possibly factitious, but certainly heady enthusiasm which had provoked foolish oaths of mutual succour at Upsala and Christiania and he came to cherish too sanguine a belief in their effectiveness towards aiding a cause which was now constantly in his mind. By no very great stretch of his capacious imagination he could feel himself a Scandinavian amid Scandinavians.

It has been remarked how in the fever of this excitement and under the spur of the sharp contrast which he saw between himself and his own lot on the one side and Bjørnson, the radiant and friendly, on the other, he had conceived the drama of Earl Skule and King Haakon, *The Pretenders*, and the theme of the play was, we observed, the triumph of the natural leader over the doubting malcontent. What stamps Haakon as the true king of Norway is his Royal Idea or Thought (*Kongetanke*), the conception (which he strove to realise) of Norway as a nation, instead of a forcibly unified state. There can be little doubt that what gave heat to this conception of the poet's and what at the same time he hoped to propagate with his ardour was another Royal Idea or Thought, appropriate to the nineteenth century as the other had been to the fourteenth; and this Thought was nothing else than the Scandinavianism under discussion, the unification of Norway, Sweden and Denmark as a sworn brotherhood based on Freedom and directed by Charles XV of Sweden.

Ibsen's disappointment at the outcome of events in the spring of 1864 proved correspondingly bitter; and it was exasperated and complicated by a great variety of considerations. The Royal Thought which he had hoped to promulgate from the stage he felt to be quite peculiarly his own—the one great positive programme to which he irrevocably dedicated himself; and when others, both those near to him and those farther off, remained inactive either because they objected to the idea as visionary or because they despaired of carrying with them the requisite number of their fellows to make it effective, it seemed to him a personal grievance, even an insult, as well as a major national misfortune.

7-2

Inextricably tied up with this sentiment was another which is harder to appreciate. Ibsen believed that, in refusing to fly to the succour of their brothers[1] at the Dannevirke and in the trenches of Dybbøl, his fellow-countrymen had made themselves guilty, not merely of cowardice[2] (an understandable notion), but also of disloyalty, of treachery. He felt and spoke as if they had broken their pledged word. But the Norwegian people had never given their word; their accredited representatives in the *Storthing* and their leaders in the government (if it be proper to call them their leaders) had made no promise whatever, except of a conditional character. The condition had been published with a candour that was brutal or pitiable according to taste; it had not been fulfilled; neither France nor Britain had shown any disposition to come into an anti-German alliance, and no breach of troth could properly be alleged against the Norwegians. (Perhaps the feeling that the Norwegians *ought* to have pledged themselves and had fallen away from the pledge which they ought to have, but had not, given aggravated Ibsen's anger against his fellow-countrymen—the phenomenon, though irrational, is not uncommon; many Englishmen experience it against the Irish.)

However, one part of the community *had* made pledges, and, though some of its members honoured them of their own free will, the majority did not. That was the academic society with which Ibsen had identified himself. Unjust though it might be to extend it to the rest of the nation, Ibsen might with some show of right impute guilt to *these*, who, without much warranty, had spoken in their country's name and had promised what, with insignificant exceptions, they either could not or would not perform. And if they, as a fraction of the community, could be justly saddled with guilt, so he as a fraction of that fraction might be accused with equal justice. There can be no doubt that the events of 1864 proved a dreadful humiliation to Ibsen, and there was one way of braving it out. But Ibsen did not don a volunteer's uniform and join the forlorn hope at Dybbøl, as the chief model for Brand had done. "We poets have other tasks", he replied when Bruun in his blunt way put

[1] There was a section of public opinion in Norway which on ethnological grounds denied all kinship with Swedes or Danes.
[2] Nearly twenty years later Ibsen held the Norwegians to be the most cowardly of people (Koht, II, p. 211).

the point directly to him.[1] Speciously, the answer might serve well enough, but no one realised the speciousness of it more acutely than the speaker. The fury, increased by its irrationality, which Ibsen felt against the Norwegians for repudiating *his* cherished ideal turned also into his own entrails. The cathartic effect which we may suppose that he promised himself from *The Pretenders* proved only of the shortest duration. He had hoped thereby to purify the sentiments which he had harboured for an indifferent and hostile environment. The events of the weeks immediately succeeding rendered that hope vain; indeed, they left something in the nature of a permanent lesion.[2]

Ibsen's sense of personal responsibility and guilt is expressed in 'Till de Medskyldige'.[3] This poem of seventy-two lines survives in two substantially similar versions, of which the earliest is to be found in the first volume of the *Efterladte Skrifter* and the revised form as Prologue to the epical *Brand*.[4] The author begins in the deepest dejection. He apostrophises his fellow-countrymen of the "poverty-stricken land in the North",[5] where the body is barred from sun and sound exercise and the wings of the spirit are in still worse plight; then goes on to hint that this may prove his last lay "as Norway's singer", since "no singer sings another song, once the dirge has been chanted over his people's coffin". The people are deadly sick, he alleges, their offence has been to cherish a past that is dead and rotten, as, according to story, King Harold clave to the corpse of his Snefrid. The poets are implicated more than any. "The common weight of guilt does not crush all, with tenfold heaviness it threatens them who first put themselves forward in the host; but a hundredfold thy poets sinned!" For, he goes on to

[1] "Vi diktere har andre opgaver" (*cit.* Koht, I, p. 312). Perhaps Ibsen comforted himself with the pronouncements of a god in Œhlenschläger's tragedy: "Ha, Balder, courage goes to singing as much as to fighting" ("Ha, Balder, til at synge hører mod, som til / At stride", *Balder hin gode*).

[2] It had its beneficial aspect in making Ibsen more than ever convinced that his mission was what he felt it to be, not what 'the folks at home' expected of him. He was never seduced into repeating a success.

[3] There is no single English word which conveys adequately either the sense or the significance of this word. "To the fellow-culprits" does it feebly. In the term "Medskyldig" Ibsen probably not merely confesses his own guilt, together with that of his fellow-countrymen, but conveys at the same time also that he and they are to be accounted *accomplices* in the ruin of Denmark.

[4] *Efterladte Skrifter*, I, p. 205, and II, p. 3, respectively.

[5] Rather touchingly, Ibsen, writing the revised version in exile, altered the first line from the sense given to "My folk, my fair country, my home in the North...".

declare: "We have toyed and flirted (*bolet*)[1] with an extinct generation, have rouged the cheeks of a mightier age's corpse, have adorned every beam and wall in the hall of memory with a giant's panoply, to give joy to dwarfs. In the night of to-day resounded the song of the day that is past—all was feasting and drunkenness; none was minded to enquire if on the inherited hoard he may rightly lay hands who lacks the thews to raise it." As a poet, a 'skald', vocal amid feasting and ebriety in the occasional poetry turned out by him, but especially remembering *The Vikings in Helgeland* and *The Warrior's Barrow*, *The Pretenders* and *Lady Inger*, perhaps also *The Feast at Solhaug* and *Olaf Liljekrans*, he knows himself to bear a peculiar blame for the toying and flirting. There will be no more of that, he vows. Henceforward he will steal into the misty twilight of the present world, which will spread a veil over his shame and oblivion over sorrow.

*   *   *   *

Even when feeling so guiltily his own responsibility in the national humiliation, Ibsen significantly neither published this confession of it nor reverted to the subject in his versifying. His was not the wish to win notoriety by public self-flagellation. "We poets have other tasks" was probably his sentiment here too. It is the broad buttocks of his fellows that he now proceeds diligently to belabour, though he finds bitter things to publish about Germany and Prussian militarism (in the 'Balloon-Letter to a Swedish Lady')[2] and in the pertinent reminder to the world at large on the occasion of Abraham Lincoln's death[3] that the bloody violence which triumphed at Dybbøl and sent a bullet into the American president's heart was the foundation on which the international structure of society rested.

The chastisement of his fellow-countrymen to which Ibsen now gave himself was administered in lyrical verse, in *Brand*, in *Peer Gynt* and in the subsequent prose plays, notably *The League of Youth*.

The shortest, cruellest and most stinging reproof was that conveyed in the colloquially phrased little poem, 'The Basis

[1] More like the 'whoring' of the Biblical Israelites, who went a-whoring with their own inventions.

[2] 'Ballonbrev til en svensk Dame' (vi, p. 376). Ibsen sent off the poem from Dresden in December 1870, surrounded by hostile Germans, just as simultaneously the beleaguered Parisians were despatching their correspondence by balloon.

[3] 'Abraham Lincolns Mord' (vi, p. 369).

of Faith' ('Troens Grund').[1] The poet feigns that he is sailing on a steamship across the Cattegat just after the fall of Dybbøl. His attention is drawn to a grey-haired lady, for whom her fellow-passengers are expressing a lively concern, since she is the mother of an only son. All will be well, despite of wars, with her son, she says. The poet is filled with admiration for the magnitude of this simple faith. Whence does it spring? The answer is: the son is a soldier "in our Norwegian army".[2] Nothing will ever hurt *him*.

The consideration of *Brand*, in the chapter before this, concentrated on the hero, the theme of the play being his struggle with himself, his mission, his God. The incidents and other passages serve to make concrete this moral issue and possess only an ancillary significance. But in some of its most dramatic moments Brand's struggle assumes the guise of a contest between the pastor and his flock, the individual and the multitude, and it is upon this aspect that we must now fasten our attention.

With whatever degree of severity Ibsen may condemn Pastor Brand in the essential aspect of the play, in the secondary, outward action he clearly fills the *beau rôle*. The present task will be to determine what Ibsen specifically has to allege in condemnation of his many-headed antagonist. A most obvious characteristic is fickleness. Bit by bit Brand's integrity gains him the adhesion of the parish until a day comes when the chairman of the council, an expert in such matters, informs him that he commands the majority; he then carries them so far with him that, on the day of public holiday set aside for the consecration of the new church, they accept his reasons for keeping it shut and follow him into a new Promised Land above the village to receive his gospel. There, however, the enthusiasm has run its course; the congregation desert and even injure their monitor.

The effective cause of this revulsion is the report[3] that a gigantic shoal of herring has been sighted just outside the firth—a most manifest materialism, a devotion to the belly, rendered pardonable by the extraordinary poverty of the district in which the action lies. The refusal of the men in Act II to form a boat's crew for Brand in the tempest may possibly be construed as a complaint against them as grave as that of incon-

---

[1] vi, p. 337. The poem was not published till 1871.
[2] "Sønnen var krigsmand i vor norske hær."
[3] False and fraudulent, as it happens.

stancy and greed, but in one passage[1] (which he later cancelled however) Ibsen exculpated them: on Brand's being brought to observe how small were most of the graves in the burial-ground, a man reminds him that, for the most part, only women and children find their sepulture on land; the men rest in the deep.

Yet, if Ibsen might go some way to acquit the ordinary men and women, the more bitter is his censure of their 'betters', the constituted authorities:—the prefatory poem, it will be recollected, attributed to them a tenfold blame. In *Brand* they are represented by the *foged* or chairman of the parish council,[2] the *provst* or archdeacon,[3] the schoolmaster (who has been a member of parliament) and the parish clerk. The first of these is exhibited, though certainly as a man of ability and some culture, even a hero in the execution of his duty,[4] as a mere administrator. He has neither succour nor comfort nor even thought for anyone not in his own district:

> I do my duty with precision,—
> But always in my own Division;[5]

no visionary ideal visits his sleeping or his waking dreams; his grand scheme is of a large central establishment (what would to-day be called a civic centre), which shall be council-chamber, assembly-hall, hospital, lock-up and (if funds allow) also lunatic asylum under one roof.[6] Were an institution of this sort provided, he would feel his responsibility for the *administrés* fully satisfied. The *provst* is conceived in perfectly Kierkegaardian terms: he is an unctuous windbag, over-intent on the loaves and fishes, who quite cynically describes the functions of the established church as follows:

> For to the state, religion is
> The power that lifts and purifies,
> The stronghold where its safety lies,

[1] *Efterladte Skrifter*, II, p. 56.

[2] It was noted in Chapter II above how in Norway (as in most continental countries) the chief executive officer, urban or rural, is a stipendiary nominee of the central government. In country districts it is the *foged*. Lest I be accused of ignoring a vital distinction in local government, I observe that the inhabitants in Northern Norway are so thinly spread, the parishes for that reason so vast, that the territory subject to a parish council may well exceed by much the average English urban district or rural district.

[3] On the status of *provst* see p. 70 n., above. Herford, whose translation is comprised in Archer's edition, calls him Dean, the parish clerk Sexton and the *foged* Mayor.

[4] It is reported that in a conflagration he saved his archives at personal risk.

[5] II, p. 145; Archer, III, p. 51.

[6] II, p. 203; Archer, III, p. 143.

> The universal moral measure.
> You see, the State is scant of treasure,
> And wants full value for its pence.
> "Good Christians" means "good citizens".....
> The corporal, staff in hand, must knock
> The sense of Time into his flock:
> For, to our mind, the best of all
> Commanders is the corporal.
> Just as the corporal leads his men
> Into the church, battalion-wise,
> So must the priest lead his, again,
> By parishes to Paradise.
> It's all so easy![1]

If such be the spirit[2] in the 'commissioned ranks' (as in spite of the allusion to corporals we may fittingly call them), it is not offset by any virtue among the 'non-commissioned' officers in the administration. With its wit and brilliant hard versification (and *caricatura*) the dialogue between Schoolmaster and Parish Clerk at the opening of Act V is not unworthy the pen of W. S. Gilbert and shows each of the speakers as merely a self-righteous jack-in-office. We may pause to note the particularly stinging passage in which the nature of a public pledge is canvassed; it reproduces more directly than is done elsewhere Ibsen's sentiments about the promises to Denmark:

Sexton. One thing I've ponder'd many a day;
You've studied,—what do folks intend
By that same "People's Promise", pray?

Schoolmaster. A People's Promise, my good friend?
That were a long investigation;
But 'tis a thing that is pursued
By force of sheer anticipation;
A grand Idea they must make good
In *future*, be it understood.

Sexton. Thanks; I see that at any rate;
But there's another point I'd fain
Beg of you briefly to explain.

Schoolmaster. Speak freely.

Sexton. Tell me, at what date
Comes, what is call'd the future?

---

[1] II, pp. 240 and 245; Archer, III, pp. 200 and 208.
[2] The *foged* at all events, it may be remarked, has not been without admirers among those who esteem Brand as more than a crack-brained enthusiast with something of the charlatan about him (cf. Prozor, M., in *Revue des Deux Mondes*, 4th ser. CXXVI, 1894, p. 161).

Schoolmaster.	Why,
	It never does come!
Sexton.	Never?
Schoolmaster.	No,
	And only follows Nature so.
	For when it comes, you see, 'tis grown
	The Present, and the Future's flown.
Sexton.	Why, yes, to that there's no reply;
	That logic one must needs accept.
	But—when then is the promise kept?
Schoolmaster.	A Promise is a future-dated
	Pact, as I have already stated;
	'Tis kept in Future.
Sexton.	That is clear.
	When will the Future, though, be here?
Schoolmaster	You blessed Sexton! (*aloud*) Worthy friend,
(*aside*).	Must I the argument recall?
	The Future cannot come at all,
	Because its coming is its end.[1]

To summarise, then: the 'multitude', the antagonists to the 'individual' Brand, are rated as rather poor stuff, mainly deteriorated through lack of sympathetic and enlightened leadership from those who should be in a position to furnish it.

It might, however, fittingly be asked, whether Ibsen had the circumstances of his native country especially in mind. Apart from all others, geographical considerations enforce an affirmative answer: the sunless glen, giving on to the open main, the crags and glaciers above its slopes, the indigent populace of crofters and fisherfolk, the dilapidated church dating, expressly, from "King Bele's days" are designed to be typically Norwegian, to stand for Norway itself, though the observer is in candour constrained to allow that the officials and ratepayers of *Brand* behave like men and women under every flag.

*   *   *   *

On the other hand, when we turn to a consideration of *Peer Gynt*, we find it generally accepted that, as it forms the complement and counterpart to *Brand*, so it is in its hero that we must discern the personification of Norway, or, at any rate, that he must first and foremost be looked upon as representing Ibsen's conception of the typical Norwegian. Yet neither

---

[1] II, p. 227; Archer, III, p. 182.

Ibsen nor anyone else of sound wits has averred that his fellow-countrymen constitute a race completely apart or that they are informed by a morality and constitution of mind utterly unlike those possessed by the rest of mankind. So, the more intensely the character of Peer Gynt is studied, the more will universal traits in him be discovered too, and, in perusing the drama, readers, whatever their nationality, will constantly feel the impulse to exclaim: "Tout comme chez nous!"

None the less, it is with *Peer Gynt* as an essay in national portraiture and as a contribution to national criticism that we are mainly concerned here. Many other features of the poem must be passed over as irrelevant: we must leave aside the question for which *Brand* furnishes so exact a parallel, of the hero's presumed 'redemption' at the end; the shrewd observation made by the historian of nineteenth-century Norway[1] may not be out of place, however, to the effect that when it came to the point Ibsen, in his temporary capacity of Supreme Judge, shrank from damning Peer and, with him, the community of his compatriots.

Though, thanks to Ibsen's play, Peer Gynt has become something of an emblematical national figure, Ibsen did not invent him. His origins are gravely disputed.[2] Some trace them back to the eighteenth century, some to the seventeenth, some to the sixteenth. However that may be, Ibsen's conception of his authenticity is on record in unambiguous terms. To his publisher he wrote, on 28 August 1867: "Peer Gynt is a real person, who lived in the Gudsbrandsdal, probably at the end of the last or beginning of this century. His name is still well known among the people up there, but nothing particular is remembered of his doings, beyond what is to be found in Asbjørnsen's Norwegian Fairy Tales in the piece 'Highland Pictures'."[3]

In Asbjørnsen's accounts Peer is patently a remarkable man

---

[1] Keilhau, W., *Det Norske Folks Liv og Historie*, IX (1931), p. 361.

[2] Cf. Kluften, P., in *Edda*, XXX (1930), pp. 120 and 680; Bakken, H. S., *ibid.* p. 680.

[3] *Breve*, I, p. 151. During the tour which he made in 1862 under the pretext of collecting folk-lore, Ibsen may have heard a few things about Peer Gynt. The relevant passages are printed (in English) in Archer, IV, pp. 272 ff. From Asbjørnsen Ibsen took over not only the name of this personage, but many of his characteristics and a variety of other ingredients for which he found a use: notably, the story of the huntsman's wild ride on the reindeer's back, which, in the piece, Peer tells his half-horrified, half-incredulous mother; the great crooked monster, the Bøjg; and the lascivious dairymaids.

in his way; and during the present investigation we should not lose from sight the fact that Ibsen's hero is no common yokel either. He should not be taken for the *average* Norwegian, any more than Dr Faust is the average German or Don Quixote the average Spaniard. The recollection of his comparative eminence will preserve us from the error into which so acute a critic as Georg Brandes lapsed in complaining[1] that rather too much seems expected of "the wretched Peer". Indeed, there is no inherent absurdity in Koht's suggestion[2] that one of the greatest Norwegians, Ole Bull, with his unreliability and his fantastic schemes, contributed some traits. In Peer Gynt we are to see the better kind of Norwegian; in his most cynical moods Ibsen perhaps thought him a very good Norwegian, at any rate he is the raw material from which the country's philosophers, politicians, poets and statesmen might be expected. The metaphysical Button-Moulder says to him

> Now, *you* were designed for a shining button
> On the vest of the world.[3]

So the criticism implied in *Peer Gynt* will necessarily be of a different order to the censure of *Brand*; the shafts directed in the latter against defective leadership only strike obliquely, since Peer never seriously prepares to assume such a function—an implied condemnation, perhaps; constituted authorities and professional persons,[4] with their functions and their short-comings, scarcely come into the picture at all.

Having thus, as it were, disposed of what *Peer Gynt* neither is nor is supposed to be, let us proceed to a more positive appraisement. That may prove a hopeless undertaking, for this reason: even if it be argued that Solvejg, at the end, pronounces the favourable verdict of a Court of Appeal, or brings Peer a free pardon from a Higher Authority, he has before been put on trial by the Button-Moulder and the Lean One (who is the Devil, in the guise of a parson). Their verdicts agree. The essential offence of which they adjudge Peer guilty is what the Norwegians call *halvhet* (literally 'half-ness', which is near to, but not exactly the same as, 'half-heartedness'), a failure to be anything *whole* or *wholly*. He is not a saint, he is not a sinner,

---

[1] Brandes, *op. cit.* p. 96.   [2] Koht, II, p. 35.
[3] II, p. 405; Archer, IV, p. 238; he goes on: "but your loop gave way."
[4] The parson with his panegyric (II, p. 390; Archer, IV, p. 214) on the deceased deserter provides a trivial exception.

as these great words should be applied; in a sense, it was a
waste of human material to have him made at all—just as the
best of buttons serves no purpose whatever if the loop is lacking.
He ought to go back into the melting-pot, into the Button-
Moulder's casting-ladle.

Now, as we have seen, this inability to be anything positive
is not due to lack of endowment in Peer, but a failure to develop
and apply it; and the root cause of his failure must be set
down as inertia, laziness. He obeys the voice of the Bøjg[1] and
"goes round about"—he follows consistently the line of least
resistance. A refinement of this quality in Peer's character
expresses itself, after the English phrase, in the wish 'to have
it both ways at once'. Hating the word '*overtvert*' (once for
all),[2] Peer cannot bring himself to contemplate an advance to
any position from which he can see no safe retreat,[3] just as the
Norwegian parliament refused to rally to Denmark until the
adhesion of France or England made it probable that no
material disaster could overtake them. A concrete instance of
his congenital distaste for positive, irrevocable action is the
quite naïve, incredulous fright which overcomes Peer on seeing[4]
a young peasant deliberately hack off one of his own fingers
in order to escape military service. An incident of this kind
(far from uncommon in all countries relying on conscription),
of which Ibsen read in a news-sheet,[5] left a deep impression
on him. He intended in the first instance to incorporate it in
Brand,[6] and it appears that he viewed the act with detestation
of a kind quite remote from Peer's; but the youth's self-
mutilation, an act criminal maybe, if physically and morally
courageous, is admirable by contrast with Peer's disapproval
of it (and possibly also with Ibsen's departure for the Prussian
capital the day that Dybbøl fell).

The desire to 'have it both ways' combines with laziness in
Peer's fondness for quoting and arguing from[7] trite proverbial

---

[1] The Bøjg or Crooked One is not an invention of Ibsen, but a multifarious
monster well known to Northern folk-lore, glossed in Brynildsen's *Dictionary* as
a "goblin snake coiled up round a man; a mythical representation of a man's
sinful past".   [2] II, p. 340; Archer, IV, p. 126.
[3] II, p. 342; Archer, IV, p. 129.   [4] II, p. 322; Archer, IV, p. 93.
[5] *Aftenbladet* of 14 June 1864.   [6] It figured in the epical version.
[7] Boer, R. C. (*Gids*, 4th series, XI, 1893, IV, p. 98) thinks the "neiging tot
raisoneeren" (i.e. proneness to argumentation) to be a trait common to Peer and
the general Norwegian character. He names "nuchterheid" (i.e. sobriety, dryness)
in the same context, which is unfortunate, even if he means no more than a philistine
adherence to common sense.

sayings, which relieve him of the necessity of thinking for himself while, at the same time, they seem to support him with the wisdom and approbation of the ages; and Ibsen held[1] that laziness constituted the chief national vice of his countrymen, who, according to him, congratulate themselves on leading the good life if they just paddle along on the verge of bankruptcy.[2]

The catalogue of Peer's specific defects may be concluded with references to his fickleness and lust. The account of his amours is left incomplete, but his dealings with Ingrid in Act I, with the wanton dairymaids and the Old Man of Dovre's green-clad daughter in Act II, and with Anitra[3] in Act IV prove the charge. Another variety of fickleness—that variant of *halvhet*—was observable in *Brand*, but excess of eroticism and inconstancy are characteristics which Ibsen's frigid temperament never cared to dwell on again; certainly, no appraisers of the Norwegian national character who consulted his works would single out these as inordinately prevalent!

A consideration of Kierkegaard's maxim, 'Be thyself', in connection with Brand[4] involved that which the Old Man of Dovre prescribed to trolls or monsters:

Trold, vær dig selv—nok.[5]

Peer knew the former of these rules of life, since he discussed it with the Button-Moulder,[6] but he adhered rather to that which enjoyed the dubious patronage of goblins and fetches: "Troll, to thyself be—enough." It is not over-precise, but the elaboration of Wicksteed's gloss[7] scarcely falsifies it: "Peer finally learns...the art of gaining and keeping self-respect by

---

[1] Johnsen, P. R., *Om og omkring Henrik Ibsen og Susanna Ibsen* (1928), p. 15.

[2] Norwegian literature as a whole shows how common the threat of bankruptcy is (or was) in that country; but it is scarcely suggested by the writings of a Garborg, a Bjørnson or a Bojer that bodily indolence is the cause. Note the financial difficulties in the Bratsberg, Helmer, Stockmann, Ekdal, Tesman and Borkman families.

[3] Grieg's exquisite music has done something to falsify this incident (as well as others); the name given to the mercenary and sensual Moorish trull suggests that she was not even graceful, but had acquired the waddle of Oriental corpulence.

[4] See p. 89, above.

[5] Prozor paraphrases it (*Le Peer Gynt d'Ibsen*, 1897, p. 40), "chacun pour soi" (i.e. "each man for himself").

[6] How far he stands from the stern doctrine of Kierkegaard, however, appears from his comment on the funeral oration to which reference has been made: "Now *that* I call Christianity—absolutely nothing that affected one as uncomfortable" (II, p. 393; Archer, IV, p. 217).

[7] Wicksteed, P. H., *Four Lectures on Henrik Ibsen* (1892), p. 64.

means of a self-sufficiency that enables him to use all that is
foul in himself as though it were fair."

*　　　*　　　*　　　*

The imprecision of the motto "Vær dig selv nok" may in part
be a consequence of Ibsen's wish to put personal attributes and
national attributes under one hat, as it were. The self-sufficiency
of a self-sufficient man is not quite the same thing as that of a
self-sufficient community. The world knows only too well what
ensues when states take self-sufficiency for a political principle.
Economic at first and ethical by a rapid transition thereafter,
it manifests itself politically in the negative manner of refusal
to co-operate—exactly as Norway had refused to co-operate in
the war of 1864. Now, national self-sufficiency had been consistently preached for many years by one of the foremost
publicists of the country, a man of genuine gifts at the
height of his influence then, Ibsen's old acquaintance Vinje,[1]
and it is significant in this connection that 'Det Lærde Holland'
(which knew Vinje well) believed him to be the chief personal
model after whom Peer Gynt was drawn.

Vinje, one of the champions and perfecters of the new
landsmaal, addressed himself mainly to the rural population,
from whom he believed, in the old Romantic fashion, that his
nation's salvation must come, and on the peasants *Peer Gynt*
seems to be most especially severe when we remember what a
bright contrast in the first two acts Peer, unstable, contemptible, self-satisfied lecher as he is, affords to the brutish and
vindictive wedding guests whom he defies and who outlaw him.
And Peer, too, is a peasant, like his legendary prototypes.

The rural vote preponderated in the parliament that had
virtually denied help to a 'brother in need' in 1864, and it was
well known that their old leader Ueland and the rising politician who was to carry their 'opposition' into power, Johan
Sverdrup, had framed the reservation expressly directed
against Scandinavianism. A 'gamle Bonder'[2] (who was
perhaps Ueland himself) had written a notorious letter to
the editor of *Morgenbladet*, in which he declared that Norway's

---

[1] Aasmund Olavsson Vinje (1818–70) was often known as 'Dølen' (i.e. The
Dalesman), from the influential periodical of that title which he edited and almost
wholly wrote for from 1858 onwards.
[2] I.e. 'old peasant'.

concern for Denmark was no more and no less than it was for Poland and that farmers should not incur the risks which war would bring of higher taxation and the loss of productivity in their farms.[1] At no time had Ibsen evinced much sympathy for the rustic population; henceforward his enmity was positive and unappeasable. Rosencrantz Johnsen reports that, quite late in life, Ibsen, having listened to a panegyric of the peasants delivered by Bjørnson and being asked for his opinion, responded with a mocking smile: "I think they should be extirpated".[2]

If the country population were on political grounds the object of his peculiar detestation, as a literary man he came to view with corresponding distaste the new literary language that it was designed to concoct from their speech. Gone were the days when, in the libretto he set about fashioning from *Olaf Liljekrans*, he had coquetted with *landsmaal*. Kristofer Janson had a chair thrown at him in Rome by the infuriated poet during an argument on that philological topic.[3] This sturdy advocate of *landsmaal* freely acknowledges that he saw himself portrayed in Huhu of *Peer Gynt*:[4]—Huhu being one of the inmates of the Cairo madhouse to which Peer is likewise consigned, and his special lunacy consisting in the manufacture of a language from the chatter of the orang-outangs of Malabar.

Over against Peer Gynt's qualities hitherto passed under review, most of which it would not be improper to qualify as vulgar or low, stand, as we must once more observe, a certain *braggadocio* and exuberance of imagination. For, to counterbalance his base qualities, to revive the self-esteem destroyed by his compromises, retreats and humiliations, Peer draws upon his fancy. His mother, who is alive to the consequences, declares that she and Peer in their misfortunes took to fairy-tales as others take to liquor.[5] Grandiose deeds of which he has heard he proceeds to narrate as if he had been the hero of them, and he constantly dreams of, and looks forward to, a sudden turn of events which will make him an 'Emperor' (and no

[1] Bing, J., *Henrik Ibsens Brand* (n.d.), p. 56.
[2] Johnsen, P. R., *Om og omkring Henrik Ibsen og Susanna Ibsen* (1928), p. 25. Lest this should be thought momentary petulance, I adduce the wish he expressed in 1880 that there might be a revolution in Norway, so that he might have the pleasure of shooting at its yeomen from the barricades (Janson, K., *Hvad Jeg Har Oplevet*, 1913, p. 78).
[3] Janson, *op. cit.* p. 77.
[4] Janson, *op. cit.* pp. 76 f.
[5] II, p. 304; Archer, IV, p. 55.

common Emperor either,[1] but a man of taste, lofty emotions, profound thought and practical usefulness to boot).[2]

The hint for this trait Ibsen derived from Asbjørnsen.

"That Peer Gynt was a strange one", said Anders. "He was such an out-and-out tale-maker and yarn-spinner, you couldn't have helped laughing at him. He always made out that he himself had been mixed up in all the stories that people said had happened in the olden times."[3]

This is pretty well what Ibsen believed the Norwegians to be doing when they recounted the somewhat dubious exploits achieved by the Vikings of the Dark Ages. For, in his view,[4] they had no more actually in common with these than a modern Greek pirate has with the men who sailed to Troy and were helped by the gods.

The alleviating quality, as it may appear to some, of Peer Gynt's *panache* by no means serves, then, to redeem him in the eyes of his creator. If imagination justifies Peer at all, it is not his own, but that of Solvejg, the simple daughter of the pietists, who believed in him and his love and could have only the slenderest knowledge of both. Ibsen's merciless eye for the falseness in the alloy of Romantic prepossessions made him see all incarnations of the 'Gyntian self' as more preposterous even than the ensign-bearers who held aloft the flag of the ideal. In terms of human value, there did not seem, to him, much to choose between the children of Peer and the children of Brand; if the latter might provoke more grief by the thought of misdirected moral energy, the former afforded the richer objects of sardonic humour. It has been observed that Ibsen put Peer Gynt on the stage again almost immediately, in the Stensgaard of *The League of Youth*, which will be our concern in the next chapter; and in the photographer of unrecognised (and nonexistent) genius, the poetic phrase-maker who is to restore an equally chimerical family honour, Hjalmar Ekdal (of *The Wild Duck*), pampered by his simple, but devoted wife, he reappears still more degraded and diminished, just as his counterpart Gregers Werle is a Brand seen through the wrong end of a

[1] 'Emperor of England' is one of the possibilities he contemplates.
[2] Act IV (the African scenes), which many find redundant, exists largely in order to illustrate these points, by means of the 'Baedeker scenes', the *liaison* with Anitra, the talk with Begriffenfelt and the scheme for irrigating the Sahara desert.   [3] Archer, IV, p. 278.
[4] *Breve*, I, p. 91.

telescope. Rather oddly, with the scale still farther reduced Ibsen attempted a fusion of the two in Ulric Brendel, the philosopher-vagabond of *Rosmersholm*, who dreams of being Aristotle, where Peer Gynt had dreamed of being Alexander, who engages in one short, humiliating combat with reality and then vanishes for ever into the darkness out of which he came.

The grudge which Ibsen bore his fellow-countrymen manifested itself not only in the creation of the 'national type', so unfavourably viewed by him, and in the appropriate fleers of *Brand*. Profiting by a public generosity that in effect constituted an ironical and subtle counter-criticism, Ibsen shook from his feet the dust of Norway as soon as he could after the *Storthing*'s fatal decision of 1864. Not improbably a lifelong exile was under contemplation at that time, and, in effect, he did not revisit his native country for ten years nor settle in it again until 1891;[1] it was his deliberate intention that his only son Sigurd should not grow up a Norwegian, and the future *statsminister* all but became a servant of the crown of Italy. Much as he longed for home, Ibsen could not, for a very long period of time, think of it without pain. But he recognised that it was a fruitful pain.[2] In a poem called 'The Power of Memory' (*Mindets Magt*),[3] he likens himself to the bear, who, taught to dance by standing in a cauldron heated to an intolerable degree, cannot help breaking into uncouth capers every time he hears the tune which accompanied his torment. As long as he expressed himself on such a topic at all, Ibsen usually spoke of the country that pensioned him in derogatory terms. It was not his mission to propose patriotic toasts of a suitable and encouraging character. Instead, he dwelt on the unavoidable provincialism and rawness of a community both small and remote, snarling[4] that its one good piece of legislation was the law permitting quacks to practise, so that thousands of idiots had lawful licence to exterminate one another.

It must not, however, be supposed that Ibsen's published writings persecuted his fellow-countrymen with the rancour he frequently felt for them. Not to everyone does it become immediately clear that Brand incarnates a striving which had

---

[1] All the works of his maturity, therefore, were written abroad, except *The Master Builder, Little Eyolf, John Gabriel Borkman* and *When We Dead Awaken*.

[2] He publicly acknowledged this in the poem he wrote for the millenary celebrations of 1872 ('Ved tusendaarsfesten', VI, p. 407).

[3] VI, p. 327.   [4] Janson, *op. cit.* p. 78.

been peculiarly defined in the North at the time of the poem's composition or that in Peer Gynt a national type is held up to scorn. *The League of Youth* certainly is more narrowly local in its appeal than any other of Ibsen's plays;[1] but thereafter, though (as has been remarked) the scene of the modern dramas never moves outside Norway, whatever is criticised or attacked in them is nowise specifically Norwegian and rarely intended to apply first and foremost to conditions in Norway. This is true even in *An Enemy of the People*, virulent though its tone may be by reason of the treatment meted out to the author at home and rich as is its 'local colour'. This same 'local colour', unmistakable also in *Pillars of Society*, in *Rosmersholm* and *The Lady from the Sea*,[2] fitfully declines in prominence.

Before leaving the consideration of *Peer Gynt*, round which the present discussion has revolved, two topics of lesser interest should receive notice, the one regarding its purely literary inspiration, the other the author's political attitude towards a foreign country.

In the conception of the whole, Œhlenschläger's *Aladdin* must have gone for a great deal: Ibsen reproduces, in his own compass, the verbal *brio* of his Danish exemplar, and for his hero he takes over the ingratiating scamp (to whom a half sceptical old mother is wholly devoted), with abundance of imagination for his only capital; the undramatic 'episodical' construction of *Peer Gynt* is that of *Aladdin* also, and for this peculiarity, as well as for the serious tone of the end, which throws up the question of the hero's redemption, Ibsen had a farther model in Goethe's *Faust*. For certain details, and notably for hints how to bestow satirical treatment on the kind of theme which Œhlenschläger and Goethe had approached romantically and approvingly, Ibsen drew on two poems of the first post-Romantic generation, by authors whom he knew well and valued highly, Paludan-Müller and Heiberg.

About Paludan-Müller's masterpiece *Adam Homo*, especially in its relation to the final judgement upon Peer, enough has already been said in an earlier chapter. But what befalls Adam

---

[1] Hence the rather surprising fact that it proved by a long way the most popular of the author's plays at the Christiania Theatre and has kept its favour in the house that replaced it in 1899.

[2] In this connection it may be unkind to remember that the ceaseless rain in *Ghosts*, which has struck some observers as so characteristically Norwegian, was suggested by an unusually wet summer at Berchtesgaden.

Homo after his demise occupies only a fraction of Paludan-Müller's *Don Juan*-like composition. Heiberg's 'Apocalyptic Comedy' in verse[1] (which, by no means inappropriately, brings in Aristophanes), *A Soul After Death* (*En Sjæl efter Døden*, 1841), concentrates, on the other hand, entirely on this stage of the 'hero's' career. The soul of a law-abiding and respectable, but humdrum citizen is, to his vast surprise, refused admittance both to the Christian heaven and to the classical Elysium next door to it on account of the same sort of *halvhet* and nullity which Ibsen's Button-Moulder[2] reprobates; somewhat reluctantly he takes up his abode in hell on discovering that, for all practical purposes, the place with the frightening name is scarcely distinguishable from, if a trifle more boring than, the Denmark in which he has lived quite tolerably. The closest approximation between the last Act of *Peer Gynt* and Heiberg's apocalyptic comedy is to be found in an episode of the latter, where Death comes to fetch a recalcitrant actor and advises him to come quietly to hell without farther fuss, not for any outstanding vice or disability that can be laid to his charge, but simply because he has always been a poor creature in the theatre as well as in life and so can expect nothing better.[3]

Peer Gynt has two strokes which are insidiously directed at the Swedes. The mad Fellah whom, just after the scene with Huhu, Peer meets[4] in the Cairo madhouse, carrying everywhere on his back the mummy of 'King Apis', to whom he ascribes every possible and impossible glory, stands as much for the Swedes with their cult for King Charles XII as for the Norwegians and their *sværmeri* for the Vikings of 'King Bele's' day; and in the minister Hussein, who haunts the same dire precincts, Ibsen himself confessed to having delineated one of his main aversions, the Swedish[5] foreign minister Manderström, whose official

[1] It was not intended for acting.

[2] The figure of the Button-Moulder seems to have been Ibsen's original invention; research, however, has not failed to recollect biblical allusions to a metaphorical 'melting-down' (cf. Logeman, H., 'The "Caprices" in Henrik Ibsen's *Peer Gynt*' in *Edda*, VII, 1917, p. 280).

[3] There is the suggestion here as in *Peer Gynt* (and in Brand's first admonition of Ejnar) that the individual's proving satisfactory in the Kierkegaardian 'aesthetic stadium' is equivalent to proving satisfactory according to the values of the 'ethical' or the 'religious' stadium—a theory to which Kierkegaard certainly did not subscribe.

[4] II, p. 377; Archer, IV, p. 186.

[5] And, by that token, under the terms of the Union, the foreign minister for Norway as well.

notes he held responsible for the diplomatic isolation of the North in 1863 and 1864. Hussein suffers from the delusion that he is a quill (i.e. merely a writing machine, with no thought or purpose behind it) and, to the author's grim satisfaction, cuts his throat in the attempt to sharpen himself.[1]

Ibsen's attitude towards Sweden, which has no very great importance for his works, remained ambiguous. As long as the recollection of the manner in which the 'brothers' had left Denmark to its fate in 1864 was strong, he felt a special resentment towards the stronger of them. He recognised, with mixed feelings, that Sweden could constitute a potential danger of the first order to Norway. On the other hand, he clung to his 'Scandinavianism' to the end and would do nothing overt to sow seeds of discord between the Northern peoples;[2] he recognised the good will of Charles XV during the difficult years and addressed a poem of condolence[3] to him upon his isolation. In return, the house of Bernadotte was lavish in its recognition of Ibsen's genius, and he enjoyed the personal friendship both of Charles XV and of Oscar II.[4] The university of Upsala was the only one to confer (1877) on him a doctorate *honoris causa*. Altogether, Sweden treated the great *skald* of the neighbouring nation *en grand seigneur*, from the time of his first visit in 1869 onwards and contributed its part in widening his whole outlook at this critical time.[5] Ibsen appreciated all this, and the Swedish sense of style made him feel the *res angustae* of Norway the more acutely. Beyond that there is not much to say in this context. Ibsen knew a little about Swedish literature, about Tegnér and Strindberg in particular; but its effect on his own writing was quite superficial and essentially negligible.[6]

[1] II, p. 379; Archer, IV, p. 191.
[2] He contributed a poem of greeting (VI, p. 398) for Norwegian students to sing at Upsala in 1875.
[3] 'Uden Navn', VI, p. 372.
[4] Who personally contributed to the *Ibsen Festskrift* of 1898.
[5] As a community the Swedes alone showed courage over *Ghosts*. When no theatrical organisation, even in Norway, dared touch it, August Lindberg produced it, and the state theatre put it into its repertory less than two years after publication.
[6] Svensson, E., 'Brand och den Svenska Göticismen', in *Edda*, XXX (1930), pp. 316 ff., argues to the contrary, but not with much effect.

CHAPTER NINE

BJØRNSON AND IBSEN

The League of Youth (1869)

From all the richness of Norwegian literature during the last eighty-five years or so, perhaps Ibsen's writings alone have contributed to what the civilised world at large places among its classics. In Norway, however, it remains a matter for vital debate whether the primacy in that country's literary hierarchy should not rather be accorded to another name, to Bjørnson. The argument has something in common with that so persistently canvassed in Germany a hundred years after their birth touching the respective merits of Schiller and Goethe.

Bjørnstjerne Martinius Bjørnson was born four years later than Ibsen, in 1832; but his faculties ripened more quickly. He was similarly affected by the Revolution in 1848 and, though he entered into the undergraduate, journalistic, theatrical and literary worlds after his great senior, he came to his artistic maturity and reputation well in advance of Ibsen. His first story was published in 1856; already in 1857 he made two enduring contributions to the national literature, with *Between the Battles* (*Mellem Slagene*) and *Synnøve Solbakken*. Up to the time of his death (in 1910) he continued a most prolific writer of historical dramas, plays of modern society, poems, essays, short stories and novels, and his eminence was attested by the award in 1903 of the Nobel Prize for literature (a distinction never won by Ibsen). Bjørnson farthermore rendered great services to the theatre besides supplying it with pieces that were always presentable and usually popular;[1] to him were successively entrusted the artistic direction of the Norske Theater in Bergen, the Christiania Theater and the playhouse in the Møllergate, Christiania, and until late in life he served occasionally, with great effectiveness, as 'producer' of his own plays.

[1] When the new National Theatre was opened at Christiania in 1899, four pieces each by Ibsen and Bjørnson were put into the first year's programme; Bjørnson's totalled 93 performances, Ibsen's 40.

Bjørnson's peculiar eminence, however, rested only partially on the arts. What he valued in them was their 'propagandist' intention and effect: "Shakespeare, Molière, Holberg", he declared,[1] "all wrote propagandist pieces; all the great have a 'purpose'." His speech at the Nobel banquet in 1903 proclaimed[2] Victor Hugo as his idol among modern writers. He is the great composer of patriotic songs and owned that, in his historical plays, he aimed at supplying a kind of National Portrait Gallery.

In the moral history of Norway, as Ibsen's critical and pessimistic approach followed on that of Welhaven, so Bjørnson was the divinely designated speaker at the inauguration of Wergeland's statue in Christiania—and that not merely by reason of their affinity, but also because Bjørnson was the foremost public speaker of his country, indeed one of the greatest orators that the world has known. The abundance of his energy could not rest content with the indirect means of influencing public opinion which *belles-lettres* allowed in the hands of even the most consummate craftsman. His masterful mind, he confessed,[3] always had to be 'managing' something—if it could not always be Norway, then at least the microcosm of a repertory theatre. Everything that occurred in Norway, everything that occurred in the artistic world and that might have some effect on the happiness of Norwegians was his concern. To many it may seem strange that he never entered Parliament; he was probably right in adjudging his power more effectual outside.

It is tempting to give a more detailed account of Bjørnson's career as a publicist and would not be wholly irrelevant, since he occupied so conspicuous a place in the shifting background of national life which Ibsen rarely lost from his imaginative sight. Some particular aspects of it will have to engage our concern sporadically in the ensuing pages. In general terms, however, it may be said here, first and foremost, that Bjørnson must not be dismissed out of hand as a mere publicist dressing up his proposals in an aesthetically appealing guise; his artistic endowment may not have been the equal of Victor Hugo's or

---

[1] In *Verdens Gang* for 22 July 1896, quoted in his *Artikler og Taler*, II (1913), p. 335.
[2] Bull, F., 'Bjørnson' (being reprint of the article in *Norsk Biografisk Leksikon*, 1923), p. 65.
[3] Cf. a letter of his in *Gro-Tid*, II (1912), p. 278.

Mr Bernard Shaw's, but it can fittingly be judged by the same standards as theirs. In some of his poetry, such as that of *Arnljot Gelline* and *Bergliot,* he attained perfection; and something lyrical, in the widest extension of the term, informs almost all his best work, of whatever kind.

The lyrical element was incompatible with the doctrinaire. Moving from interest to interest, from public question to question, Bjørnson came, in the efflux of time, to occupy positions inconsistent with those of an earlier epoch; for a space he was almost what would to-day be called a 'fundamentalist' and then turned a convinced and persuasive agnostic; he toyed with *landsmaal* and with his peasant tales did something to promote it, only, afterwards, to denounce it with his customary vehemence. But he never sought to conceal his apostacies and new enthusiasms—indeed his zeal to bring others at once to the same new way of thinking as himself had something of the comic about it.

Most of the positions which he successively took up exposed him to bitter and persistent attacks. In 1872 he advocated a *rapprochement* between the northern nations and Germany,[1] he adopted and assailed in turn most of the religious orthodoxies of any account, he proclaimed himself a republican, he demanded the separation of the Norwegian and Swedish crowns. At certain epochs of his life he was probably the most hated man in Norway, and, when he was to deliver his oration at the unveiling of Wergeland's statue in 1882, all the 'best people' of the capital literally pulled down the blinds in the houses which he had to pass *en route.* Yet, in general, though ever open-minded towards novel ideas and frequently generous in their support, he was a man of the 'left-centre' (as continental jargon has it), defending with incomparable skill conclusions to which a substantial body of enlightened opinion had already advanced and which were soon to form planks in the liberal platforms of the day. This fluid radicalism of Bjørnson's mind proved of inestimable service to the cause of progress in his native land. Almost at every stage of his protracted public life he held together and ensured the advance of the parties of the 'left', always by their nature prone to disintegrate and become

---

[1] In metaphorical language, Bjørnson described it as an alteration in sailing-orders (*signaler*); hence the term '*signal-fejde*' (literally = signal-feud) for the ensuing controversy.

ineffectual, and Norway, thanks largely to him, was spared that extraordinary picture of political impotence which Denmark exhibited during the last quarter of the nineteenth century and to which an enquiring mind will find pendants in larger polities during the same period. The liberalism of Norwegian public life which (subject to numerous qualifications, of course) became so marked in the last quarter of the nineteenth century was not without its effect on Ibsen. Not only did it ensure a respectful hearing for his questionings of many fundamental assumptions, but it may well be argued that it also encouraged him indirectly to multiply and deepen them.

A few words may be devoted specifically to one phase of Bjørnson's religious development. The son of an orthodox Lutheran clergyman, he grew up uncritical of what was accepted for religious truth at home. In the middle of the 1850's he was brought into contact with Kierkegaard's doctrines, and Georg Brandes, who had a keen nose for Kierkegaardian vestiges, believed[1] that such psychological penetration as Bjørnson commanded (this was, as a matter of fact, his weakest point) derived from the author of *Either-Or* and *The Concept Fear*. But he seems soon to have reached the conviction that the moral demands formulated in these books were what he summed up in the title of two of his plays, *Over Ævne* (i.e. *Beyond our Powers*), and a sentiment of this order made *Brand* distasteful to him.[2] In the first half of the nineteenth century Denmark had seen the advance of another great religious force, besides that emanating from Kierkegaard, namely that launched by Grundtvig, which swept the Danish countryside in a manner recalling Wesley's ministrations in England and Wales.[3] Grundtvig's religion was almost the antithesis of Kierkegaard's: it centred not in the individual conscience, but in the church, as the centre of a spiritualised communal life, and aimed at making, in Christ, both individual and society contented, prosperous, cultivated, co-operative. An interesting and curious feature of the Grundtvigian mission was the deliberate linking of the Christian communal culture with veneration for the

---

[1] Brandes, G., *Henrik Ibsen, Bjørnstjerne Bjørnson* (trsl. Morison, M., 1899), p. 147.
[2] He evidently discerned no implied criticism of Kierkegaard in the fate of Ibsen's hero.
[3] The two men's missions were radically different in nature, of course.

pagan past,[1] in a manner not unlike that which has been described in connection with Œhlenschläger and with Ibsen's *Warrior's Barrow* and *Vikings in Helgeland*. This religious movement, the cheerful mildness of which proved almost as uncongenial to the crag-bound Norwegians as it had been acceptable to the peasants of the Danish plain, and its practical emanation, the Popular High-Schools,[2] appealed so strongly to Bjørnson when he came to give them his attention and he owned his belief in them in such glowing language that the succession all but fell upon him on the aged apostle's demise in 1872. It may be remarked in passing that as the ideals of contentment, prosperity, culture and co-operation had been unmeaning or contemptible to Kierkegaard, so Grundtvigianism and Popular High Schools struck no sympathetic chord in Ibsen either. In a poem more thoroughly permeated with contempt than any other, Ibsen dismissed "old Grundtvig" and God in a line.[3]

*   *   *   *

In the year 1850 that crammer of genius, Henrik Anton Schjøtt Heltberg,[4] had on the books of his 'student-factory'[5] the four youths Ibsen, Bjørnson, Jonas Lie and Vinje, who between them were firmly to put the staggering young Norwegian literature on its feet. Academic year and civil year do not, however, coincide; all four were not subject to Heltberg's inculcations simultaneously; and Ibsen had departed for the goal of his endeavours, even if he had not passed it, before young Bjørnson inscribed himself on Heltberg's register.[6] Though, as it seems, they met in 1850, Ibsen left the capital before the next year was out, and, indeed, he and Bjørnson rarely abode at the same place together for any considerable length of time. When, after five years and a half, Ibsen quitted Bergen, it was Bjørnson who succeeded him at the Norske Theater; and when,

---

[1] Grundtvig was a most distinguished Old English scholar and one of the early editors of *Beowulf*.

[2] Adult continuation schools, mainly concerned with the 'Modern Humanities', to which Norway took more readily than to other aspects of Grundtvigianism.

[3] Centenary Edition, XIV, p. 435.

[4] 1806–73.

[5] The point of the expression lies in the continental identification of 'student' and matriculated 'undergraduate'; a 'student-factory' implies the conversion of school-children into junior members of the university by the methods of mass production.

[6] Bjørnson came to Christiania about the same time as Ibsen, but postponed his entry into Heltberg's institution till the autumn.

after a farther two years, in the autumn of 1859, Bjørnson likewise relinquished the post and took ship for Christiania again, his stay proved only of short duration, and from the spring of 1860 to the spring of 1863 he was travelling overseas. A year after Bjørnson's return to Norway, Ibsen in his turn went abroad and thus the alternation continued. Bjørnson, who all this time stood much higher in the general esteem than Ibsen and already in his Bergen days had made himself a power in the land, publicly championed *The Feast at Solhaug*, on the beauties of which he repeatedly descanted, and thereby secured the confidence of his shy rival. But he did not belong to the inner circle of 'Learned Holland', and even in the two periods of a few months each (September 1859 to June 1860 and October 1863 to April 1864) when both, mature, were in Christiania together, there is no evidence that they saw much of one another. On the other hand, as has been remarked, Bjørnson's presence and encouragement contributed notably to shed a peculiar glory over the days which he and Ibsen spent in Bergen at the time of the choral festival in June 1863.

Not only did Ibsen admire and, in a defensible way, envy (as *The Pretenders* discloses), but Bjørnson, large-hearted as always, sympathised. Ibsen found himself in desperate financial difficulties and stood in peril of falling a helpless victim to alcoholic excess.[1] Bjørnson bestirred himself on his friend's behalf, to solicit private benefactions for the diminution of his debts, to extract a grant from the Scientific Society at Trondheim and, in conjunction with the friends of 'Learned Holland', to secure for him one of those authors' allowances (*digtergager* = poet's wages) to which the Norwegian Parliament from time to time sees fit to allocate public money and of which Bjørnson himself was a beneficiary[2]. Perhaps the best service

[1] Ibsen seems always to have relished his drink; Bergsøe and Gunnar Heiberg both give accounts, as entertaining as they are surprising, of him in his cups (*Henrik Ibsen paa Ischia*, p. 177 and *Aftenposten* for 1911, *cit.* Koht, II, p. 170, respectively).

[2] Andreas Munch had been the first in 1860. Bjørnson (like Vinje) received a travelling allowance from the Norwegian government in 1860, and a 'poet's wage' in 1863, which became an annuity in 1866. Ibsen, refused a grant in 1860, obtained a small one in 1862; the next year, a motion to treat him *pari passu* with Bjørnson and Munch was defeated in parliament, but in the spring of 1863 a small travelling allowance was granted, and a larger one in the autumn of that year and on several subsequent occasions; the annuity (of spd. 400, equivalent to about £50) followed by resolution of 12 May 1866. When he was already quite well off in 1877, Ibsen made strenuous efforts to have his annual allowance increased.

which, in the material realm, he rendered his friend was to introduce him to Frederik Hegel, the head of the great house of Gyldendal in Copenhagen; Messrs Gyldendal published all Ibsen's writings, beginning with *Brand*, and, from the outset of the association, amassed very substantial profits from them for themselves and for the author.

At the time of these important pecuniary transactions, between 1864 and 1867, Bjørnson and Ibsen were in constant and fruitful correspondence with one another, and though the answer will involve some anticipation of matter subsequent to 1867, the question may be attempted at this point: What did Ibsen the author owe to his benevolent and deeply interested junior?

*　　　*　　　*　　　*

Since Bjørnson was the impetuous man of energy, the pioneer, and Ibsen the critic who needs must have an antecedent subject on which to exercise his talents, it is natural that the investigator will occasionally, for all its originality, find anticipations of Ibsen's development as thinker and writer in Bjørnson's works. At times, however, the interesting, if not very momentous, question of priority falls hard to determine, and similar motives occurred to both men independently and simultaneously. Brandes reports[1] as a striking instance of such a phenomenon that Bjørnson struck out a sentence from his short story *Dust* (1882) because he found it, almost word for word, in *Ghosts*. Again, Professor Koht argues[2] with great plausibility, that questions canvassed by *Love's Comedy* and *Brand* could not but set up processes of fruitful thought in one who studied them so closely as we know that Bjørnson did. It is, for instance, almost inconceivable that the drama about the domination of the flesh by the spirit, about the relations between organised and unorganised faith and about the pastor as married man which Bjørnson called *Over Ævne*[3] and which some hold his dramatic masterpiece, could have been written if it had not been for *Brand* and the stimulus it imparted.

However, the other side of the account is the present business, and the first entry in it to be scrutinised is *Between the Battles* (*Mellem Slagene*), written in 1856, acted and printed in 1857.

[1] Brandes, G., *ut supra*, p. 81　　　　　　[2] Koht, II, p. 145.
[3] Bjørnson wrote two plays with this title; the earlier, known as *Over Ævne I* (1883), is here alluded to.

With it Bjørnson began that series of national plays about the Norwegian civil wars of the thirteenth and fourteenth centuries with which he persevered for a matter of fifteen years and to which Ibsen may almost be said to have contributed an item with *The Pretenders*. As important as the subject-matter of *Between the Battles* was its style; Bjørnson, somewhat uncertainly, elaborated a prose which should be quite comprehensible to the audience of his own day, but at the same time also suggest the language of the Sagas—an experiment repeated with better success in his next play, *Limping Hulda* (*Halte-Hulda*).[1] Now Ibsen (as we saw) abandoned the ballad-style of *The Feast at Solhaug* and *Olaf Liljekrans*[2] at this time precisely in favour of a saga-style of his own in *The Vikings in Helgeland* (1858). When he wrote the latter he must have known *Between the Battles* and may even have read *Limping Hulda*, though, paradoxically, the virtual identity of theme makes the supposition rather less, than more, probable.

In the case of Ibsen and *The Vikings in Helgeland* we should seemingly speak of encouragement received through Bjørnson's example coupled with essential independence—I am not aware that anyone proclaimed Ibsen to be his colleague's debtor. The same twofold phenomenon is to be seen, nearly twenty years afterwards, in the more complex case of *The Pillars of Society* (1877), but here Ibsen's dependence (if we may so call it) could be maintained with a degree of greater probability. The problem is complicated, however, by *The League of Youth* of 1869. For here Ibsen had glanced at both the subjects of commercial speculation and the improper manipulation of public opinion, which Bjørnson was to handle at length in *A Bankruptcy* (*En Fallit*, 1875) and *The Editor* (*Redaktøren*, 1875) respectively. But the subject of *A Bankruptcy* at least was revolving in Bjørnson's mind several months before he can have known anything about *The League of Youth*, and it is undeniable that each of his two plays was not only to be primarily the exemplification of the evil in question, but also to preoccupy the public conscience with it. Such a definition, though inapplicable to *The League of Youth*, fits *The Pillars of Society*, finished two years after the appearance of *A Bankruptcy* and *The Editor*. Moreover, it is noteworthy that in the later play we find a feature not repeated

---

[1] *Halte-Hulda*, finished in 1857, published in April 1858.
[2] Produced 2 January 1857.

in any other of Ibsen's plays of modern life, namely the change of heart, repentance and recantation of the main character in a speech which cannot justly be called anything but didactic; and this feature even more crudely marks the *dénouement* of *A Bankruptcy*.

So far, the slight presumption of Bjørnson's priority[1] should be allowed; in another point, certainty takes the place of presumption. Without any doubt, Bjørnson was a pioneer (as far as the literature of Norway is concerned) in plays of modern life which were written in prose and which deliberately and straightforwardly—without satire—raised questions of conduct applicable to many members of the public. The cardinal document here is not *The Editor* or *A Bankruptcy*, but the much slighter production, *The Newly-Wed*,[2] which preceded them by ten years, *The League of Youth* by four and *Pillars of Society* by twelve. In this two-act piece, a young wife persists in disregarding the precept of the gospel by putting her duty to her parents before that which she owes to her husband; she looks upon herself always as a daughter and never as a spouse, until her husband's forbearance and the deterrent effect of a piece of literature induce a change of heart. Bjørnson thus insists that a wife should be adult (as Ibsen later did in *A Doll's House*), he lavishes no sentimentality on the 'child-wife' as Dickens had recently done in *David Copperfield*, and, farther, he suggests that lack of adequate response in the wife provides an effective cause for infidelity in the husband (as Fru Alving was to do in *Ghosts*).[3]

[1] Should these arguments too strongly suggest the pupilage of Ibsen to Bjørnson, two mitigating considerations may be remembered: (i) that, though the evidence is vague (*Breve*, I, pp. 194 and 211), Ibsen immediately on completion of *The League of Youth* was revolving in his mind the 'serious modern play' which probably became, after seven years, *The Pillars of Society*; and (ii) that developments in the direction which both Bjørnson and Ibsen were taking were not peculiar to Norwegian literature, as these two writers must have known: the comedies of Danish authors, with a faithful presentation of certain middle-class peculiarities, have been mentioned, Balzac's play about financial credit, *Mercadet*, was presented at Christiania during the season 1867–8 and the newer French drama of Augier (like *M. Poirier's Son-in-Law*, 1854) and the younger Dumas (like *The Half-World*, 1855) had begun its triumphal progress over the European stages. A somewhat slender play by Fru Ibsen's step-mother, Magdalene Thoresen, *A Wealthy Match* (*Et Rigt Parti*, 1870), shows how minor playwrights were moving in the direction of their betters; it may have conveyed a hint or two for *Pillars of Society*, *A Doll's House* and even *The Lady from the Sea*. [2] *De Nygifte* (1865).

[3] Brandes (*Samlede Skrifter*, XVIII, 1910, p. 123) takes the view that Bjørnson exerted a considerable effect on Ibsen's *personality* in impelling him to be 'otherwise' and to develop the eremetic, aristocratic and European elements in it at the expense of the social, democratic and national in which Bjørnson was so strong.

The Pretenders betrays Ibsen's normal attitude towards Bjørnson: an admiration genuinely felt and based on the intellectual conviction that his friend possessed outstanding endowments; but in many of these Ibsen, if dimly, knew himself to be lacking; and the admiration that warmed him was not unaccompanied by the stings of envy, which perhaps does not justly merit the qualification of petty and which left a sense of resentment partially ineradicable. Half in jest and half in earnest, it has been said that Ibsen nurtured for his glorious junior emotions which a wife often feels for a brilliant and successful husband—love blended with a grudge at having, unfairly, been created second-best. By contrast with Bjørnson, Ibsen saw himself as Earl Skule, and the last words of *The Pretenders* say of him: "Skule Baardsson was God's step-child on earth; that was the secret."[1]

So the admiration with which Bjørnson inspired Ibsen could not but be critical. Ibsen recognised, for instance, as clearly as justly, that the artist in Bjørnson was inferior to the publicist. He compared[2] him with Schiller, as one standing ever behind the figures of his imagination and declaiming his opinions through their mouths; *The Newly-Wed* he described[3] as "no drama, only a dramatised short story"; it drove him to contempt and exasperation[4] to observe with how bearish a touch (which enraptured the general public) Bjørnson's *Gauntlet* (*En Hanske*, 1883) handled the delicate subject of pre-nuptial chastity. But he was deeply grateful for Bjørnson's championship of him, especially perhaps in the storm which *Ghosts* raised at a time when political passions ran high and the two poets stood in opposed camps; and at this epoch he acknowledged a fascination at the aspect of Bjørnson fighting like another Achilles, even if his was a cause he did not wish to see defended.[5] "That interests me", he said, "because it is an act of rebellion [*er oprørende*]." It should, he justly and nobly declared in public, be Bjørnson's epitaph that his Life was his best Poem.[6]

*   *   *   *

[1] II, p. 116; Archer, II, p. 343.
[2] Janson, K., *Hvad jeg har Oblevet* (1913), p. 80.
[3] *Cit.* Paulsen, J., *Samliv med Ibsen*, I (1906), p. 168.
[4] Koht, H., II, p. 228.
[5] Viz. the right of Norwegians to fly an ensign showing no connection with Sweden.
[6] Unfortunately, the English reproduces the original most imperfectly since *digtning* means (here) "work of imagination".

BJØRNSON AND IBSEN

Ibsen's opinion of Bjørnson was probably well enough known. Interspersed with traits perhaps suggested by the indefatigable rebel and believer in minorities, Georg Brandes, and certainly by that true-hearted, but grotesque old argufier, Jonas Lie, he presented a perfectly recognisable portrait of him in Dr Thomas Stockmann, the detector of public scandals, the Enemy of the People: the impulse at once to communicate his latest discovery to all and sundry in the hope (persistent, though perpetually disappointed) that they will at once adopt it too, the whole-heartedness, unselfishness and frequent imprudence of his championships, his readiness to trust and inability to bear a grudge, his love of a fight for its own sake, the ridiculousness of a hoary head popping up all the time "bloody but unbowed". His inability to give his admiration for Bjørnson completely without stint is illustrated also by the amusing little anecdote[1] of their later years, according to which he was, in Bjørnson's company, talking of Gossensass, his favourite little Alpine village, and its blacksmith who was the jack of all trades, even on occasion acting as district midwife: "He always made me think of you, Bjørnson." Bjørnson laughed. Indeed his behaviour to Ibsen, whom he admired and loved, was always everything that it should have been, great though he must have felt the provocation to react otherwise.[2]

This reached its maximum during the phase of their relationship which set in, under somewhat mysterious circumstances, in 1867.

Bjørnson had not liked *Brand*. But *Peer Gynt* filled him with joy. As he read it, he declared, he kept breaking into *yodels*.[3] More than that, he put together a most enthusiastic review and sent it from Copenhagen, where he was then staying, to the *Norsk Folkeblad*. One of his great friends in the Danish capital was Clemens Petersen, the foremost literary critic in Scandinavia at this time (the very eve of Georg Brandes's emergence). This arbiter, believing in a close and manifest association of art and sound ethics, had found much that was dubious and turbid

[1] Reported by Johnsen, K., *Om og omkring Henrik Ibsen og Susanna Ibsen* (1928), p. 26.
[2] It is all the more creditable to him since he disapproved of that substantial fraction of Ibsen's work which he held to be *l'art pour l'art*. Of *John Gabriel Borkman* he said to W. Schofield, "...not the kind of thing we want at all. It won't do anybody any good" (*Atlantic Monthly*, LXXXI, 1898, p. 570).
[3] This is what I take *storhauke* to mean (Koht, II, p. 52 *ex Norsk Folkeblad*).

128

in *Love's Comedy*; the stern ethical demands implied in *Brand* gained his approbation. But now, when the multifariousness and ambiguities of *Peer Gynt* were displayed before his judgement-seat, he wrote, at the great length which his prestige permitted, a critique upon the piece in which he not only voiced the uneasiness he felt on the score of morality, but in addition censured it also for its form, indeed declaring that it was "no poetry".

Ibsen, still in the state of extravagant irritability provoked by the events of 1863 and 1864, was beside himself with anger at Petersen's judgement, at the aesthetic depreciation in especial, and burst into the abundantly justified riposte: "If this is not poetry, it soon will be."[1] But, more than that, he believed the criticism to be part of a plot hatched by Bjørnson during his colloquies with his Danish friend: Bjørnson was to save his own name and preserve the valuable friendship of Ibsen by praise in private letters and the columns of a provincial news-sheet, while under the cloak of Petersen he was (more or less) to deal him a stab in the back in the literary metropolis of the North.

No evidence for this supposed conspiracy has come down, and, on every count, it is fantastically improbable. But at the time that he conceived its existence, Ibsen was harbouring some resentment towards Bjørnson on grounds which were real enough, but of a kind he did not greatly like admitting. Bjørnson had picked up a rumour to the effect that Ibsen and he were to be offered knighthoods in the Norwegian Order of St Olave; as a strict upholder of the tribunate of literature, he disdained to assume the appearance of a royal lackey and, accordingly, approached his senior with the suggestion that they should act in concert in declining the nomination. As his later career was to show, the acquisition of knighthoods, grand crosses of orders and the like constituted Ibsen's secret passion;[2] and now he perceived Bjørnson to be coming along with the proposal, on perfectly unexceptionable grounds, to seal the fount of honour before it had even begun to play! He returned a measured and, on the whole, well reasoned reply to his "carissimo", but this letter (of 28 December 1867)[3] proved to be the end of their

[1] *Breve*, I, p. 159.
[2] When he received the Grand Cross of the Swedish Order of the Northern Star in 1898, Ibsen declared that no greater honour could possibly be accorded him. (Koht, II, p. 375.)
[3] *Breve*, I, p. 163.

correspondence for ten years;[1] and the two men, who had last seen one another in the early spring of 1864, did not meet again till the summer of 1884. According to John Paulsen,[2] Ibsen heard a report about a speech in which, it was alleged, Bjørnson had divided his fellow-countrymen into the breed of nobles and the breed of slaves, among the latter of whom he ranked Ibsen; the story is not substantiated, but does not sound improbable and would well account for Ibsen's resentment.

The breach was no inert lapse of communications. For a long time Ibsen bore Bjørnson a grudge which knew of no reserve and scarcely of *ménagement*. When, soon after 1867, the Danish publicist, Rudolf Schmidt, set up a periodical, *For the Ideal and Reality*, and invited Ibsen to contribute to it, the latter declined on the grounds (*inter alia*) of the company he would be believed to be keeping: "I see," he wrote to Schmidt, "I see Hr. B. Bjørnson named as a probable co-editor of 'For Idé og Virkelighed';[3] and this circumstance would in itself be decisive...." Somewhat later he expressed his contempt of the conservative administration of Norway for permitting "fellows" like Bjørnson and the religious leader of the peasantry, Jaabæk, to remain at large.[4]

* * * *

The loudest literary repercussion of this long-echoing explosion of 1867 reverberates in *The League of Youth*[5] (*De Unges Forbund*, 1869), which was first conceived during the weeks immediately following the breach with Bjørnson. The earliest of Ibsen's plays to be written in the 'modern', conversational prose for which his new-found foeman had supplied a pattern in *The Newly-Wed*, *The League of Youth* rehearses an attorney's strenuous attempts to gain local influence in a provincial constituency and have himself returned to parliament for it. The grounds for calling

[1] When *The Pillars of Society* was published at the end of 1877, Ibsen sent Bjørnson a copy with some lines of appreciation and personal regard.

[2] *Samliv med Ibsen*, II (1913), p. 13.

[3] *Breve*, I, p. 176. Schmidt's other associate was the philosopher Rasmus Nielsen who laboured for one of the earliest 'concordats' between religion and natural science. In view of his hatred of compromise, Ibsen detested him almost as much as Bjørnson, but was presumably frightened by his academic prestige from saying so to Schmidt.

[4] Letter to J. H. Thoresen of 27 September 1872. *Breve*, I, p. 264.

[5] One would censure the usual translation of the title (which literally means The Alliance of the Young) if it were not for the reflection that the charlatan founding such an organisation in this country would be equally capable of inventing so disgusting a title for it.

him "Peer Gynt in politics"[1] are doubtless his complete lack
of moral ballast and a slippery facility for extricating himself
from the predicaments into which his over-spurred ambition
lands him—also, perhaps, because he is thought to incarnate
certain specifically Norwegian characteristics. No scruples
fetter Stensgaard, and he employs flattery, intrigue, oratorical
sophistry, amorous advances and blackmail in the (frustrated)[2]
design to gain the great end; notable in his tactics is the formation of a 'League of Youth', which, both for the founder's
political and the author's theatrical purposes, possesses the
advantage of a programme remaining altogether nebulous
except for the determination to supersede existing interests.

Vinje, one of the putative butts of *Peer Gynt*, leapt[3] forward
to identify Stensgaard with Bjørnson; at the first public reading
in Copenhagen,[4] the actor Kristian Mantzius, who undertook
the part of Stensgaard, impersonated Bjørnson;[5] and, a more
remarkable circumstance, Bjørnson believed himself to be
attacked; he wrote bitterly in a poem, significantly announcing
his solidarity with Johan Sverdrup,[6] that Ibsen had chosen the
Muses' sacred grove for a murderous ambush (*snigmord*).

One may well be excused for asking what possible grounds
there could be for identifying so virtuous a personage as
Bjørnson with the principal character in *The League of Youth*.
At the time that the comedy was written and published, Bjørnson was at the height of his 'Grundtvigian phase', a very busy
apostle among the Norwegians of this variety of Christianity,
especially concerned about the propagation of the Adult Continuation Schools which it fostered and whose prime purpose
was to educate young citizens. Now, Stensgaard is so strongly
insistent that his activities consort with the will of the Almighty,

---

[1] This is the expression of Professor Koht (Introduction to Centenary Edition,
VI, p. 341) who, as a cabinet minister of his country, should know what he is talking
about; he likewise (II, p. 78) declares Stensgaard to possess qualities common to
all political adventurers, but at the same time to be as Norwegian as Tartarin
de Tarascon is *méridional*.

[2] The frustration must be supposed to have been but temporary. In *An Enemy
of the People*, Stensgaard is referred to as *stiftsamtmand* or sheriff.

[3] Ording, F., *Det lærde Holland* (1927), p. 232, quoting Vinje's *Skrifter i Samling*,
II, p. 373.

[4] Bjørnson, B., *Gro-Tid*, II (ed. Koht, H.), p. 404; the date of the reading was
5 November 1869.

[5] Cf. letter by Bjørnson to R. Schmidt of 30 November 1869 in *Gro-Tid*, II
(1912), p. 335. On Sverdrup see p. 132 below.

[6] 'Til Johan Sverdrup' in Bjørnson's *Samlede Digter-Verker*, VIII (1927), p. 325.

9-2

whose name he frequently takes in vain,[1] that Ibsen had given his play the sub-title 'Our Lord and Co.' ('Vorherre og Cie.') until the prudent publisher counselled its omission. And then, this inchoate, vague League of Youth, with its stress on the second half of its name, suggests connection with the adult education which the Popular High Schools were to promote. Farther, the arrogance which Stensgaard betrays when, for instance, he refers to his supporters as "fellows (*karle*) like that"[2] could be imputed to Bjørnson, who was so conscious of his great abilities that he seems actually to have asked the rhetorical question put into the carpet-bagger's mouth: "Have you ever been fit to appreciate me?";[3] and more phrases than posterity can identify were recognised by *The League of Youth's* first audiences as being in Bjørnson's idiom.

It must be said at once, however, that Bjørnson was not the only real person to be reflected in this distorting mirror,[4] to the joy of some and the vexation of the rest.[5] The type of political adventurer in Ibsen's mind was probably a certain Bagger, member of the *Storthing* until 1869, whom he remembered from his boyhood in Skien. The cheapness of Stensgaard's glib oratory and private conversation is, it would seem, less Bjørnson's than that of Johan Sverdrup, the leader of the 'Left' and a future prime minister of Norway; and several more characteristics were copied from Ole Richter,[6] lawyer, politician and, at that time, friend of Bjørnson,[7] notorious for his con-

[1] An admirable instance of Ibsen's caustic treatment of such piety is afforded at the end of Stensgaard's great speech in Act I. He cries out: "And now, God be with us! For we are going about His work, with youth and faith to help us. Come, then, into the refreshment-tent—our League shall be baptized this very hour." (III, p. 15; Archer, VI, p. 28.)

[2] III, p. 37; Archer, VI, p. 69.

[3] III, p. 40; Archer, VI, p. 75. That Bjørnson made some such observation about himself is averred by Christian Collin in *Neue deutsche Rundschau*, 1907, p. 1286.

[4] Moreover, Stensgaard is not the sole reflector; the name Lundestad, it is held, derives from Lundevatnet in the native district of the veteran leader of the peasantry in parliament, Ueland, who had been delivering a valedictory speech in the *Storthing* at the time Ibsen was completing his comedy, just as Lundestad is contemplating retirement from public life.

[5] Nissen, I., *Sjelelige Kriser i Menneskets Liv* (1931), p. 62, takes the view that Stensgaard is a portrait of Ibsen himself in a state of 'power-crisis' (*maktkrisen*), whatever that may be.

[6] Richter seems also (Koht's Introduction in Centenary Edition, VI, p. 348) to have popularised the catch-phrase "the local situation" so often used by Aslaksen; it apparently means something like "our own conventions and traditions".

[7] This is not the place to speak of Richter's suicide, for which Bjørnson was largely responsible and out of which, with some *sang-froid*, he distilled one of his

descension to the rabble, for his acquisition of land as property-qualification for parliamentary candidature[1] and also for his well-known designs upon heiresses, whose fortunes might relieve his political career of financial dependence, just as Stansgaard plans to settle down in Lundestad's old constituency and, for estate and money, to marry in a descending scale of opulence Thora Bratsberg or, failing her, Ragna Monsen or, failing both, the hotel-licensee, Madam Rundholmen.[2]

The burden of the satirical attack delivered in *The League of Youth* clearly falls on the liberal leaders and their party,[3] which was just beginning to form itself as well-organised fighting opposition, associated with the peasant interest and with the least obscurantist of the religious movements in the country. The play was recognised for a major political manifesto from the conservative[4] side and as such met with a mixed and highly excited reception on its first presentation in Christiania (18 October 1869, nineteen days after publication). Ibsen may pessimistically have felt that, however much he might be applauded, he had engaged in a losing battle. For all that Stensgaard is discomfited at the end of Act V, in ten or fifteen years fellows like him (Lundestad opines)[5] will sit in the councils of the people or the king or even both—a somewhat remarkable prophecy of Sverdrup's rise to supreme power in 1884, exactly fifteen years later.

*　　*　　*　　*

Until the appearance of *The Pillars of Society* in 1877 and perhaps until later, Ibsen was generally looked upon as the 'poet of the Right', the conservative author, the rival and counter-

best plays, the tragedy *Paul Lange og Thora Parsberg* (the resemblance between the heroine's name and Ibsen's Thora Bratsberg is very striking).

[1] The Norwegian constitution provided that every member of the *Storthing* must be a *bona-fide* resident in the constituency for which he was returned.

[2] A certain lawyer called Lange believed himself aimed at in Stensgaard (cf. Loken, H., *Fra Fjordnes til Sjovinn*, 2nd ed., 1912, p. 18).

[3] "*The League of Youth* sought to turn our young liberal party (*Frihedsparti*) into a crowd of ambitious adventurers whose patriotism could be carried off by their phraseology; and, in particular, eminent men were first rendered recognisable and then were supplied with false hearts and sordid characters and had imaginary Leagues stuck to them" (Bjørnson in the letter to R. Schmidt, *ut cit.* p. 334).

[4] Jæger who gives a vivid account (*Life of Henrik Ibsen*, English translation, 1890, p. 177), takes the view (*ibid.* p. 172) that the conservatives are as sharply satirised as the liberals; I cannot share his opinion, which was dictated by 'a policy of appeasement' congenial to Ibsen's wishes at the time of publication (1888).

[5] III, p. 117; Archer, VI, p. 225.

weight to the dangerous radical, Bjørnson. The position seemed confirmed by *Emperor and Galilean*, a work highly praised as a piece of scholarship and equally unexceptionable on public grounds. Even if, as we shall shortly discover, Ibsen came thereafter to occupy a new position in the public opinion of Norway, he was always liable to what his ally and mentor Georg Brandes felt to be 'lapses'. His passion for official distinctions and perhaps the debt which he felt that he owed to stylish Sweden, ensured this; and as a private individual he subscribed to the melancholy truth that radicals are the great drawback to radicalism. But the gravamen of his impatience, even dislike, of the liberals was always, as it had already been in the days of *Andhrimner*, that they were not liberal *enough*—an imputation all the more plausible when, in Norway, the one-time opposition took over the responsibilities of government in 1884 and found themselves (as so often happens in such cases) under the necessity of tempering the fervour of the programme that had carried them to power with the exigencies of administration.[1] Ibsen preferred to them the still insignificant Socialists (probably identifying their doctrines with revolutionary communism), and he always cherished a predilection for anarchism and nihilism in all their forms, even the most anodyne. He followed with sympathy,[2] for instance, the career of Charles Bradlaugh, as an example of the solitary rebel. Could, on the other hand, nihilism go farther than the poem in which he declared that if it were in his power to save the whole of the human race he would contribute rather to its annihilation?

> They say I'm becoming conservative;
> No; still in my life-long creed I live.
> Your changing pawns is a futile plan;
> Make a sweep of the chess-board, and I'm your man.
> Was never but one revolution unfaltering
> That was not marred by half-hearted paltering.
> To that, all since were but idle menaces.
> I allude, of course, to the Deluge in Genesis.
> Yet Lucifer tripped, even then; by a later ship
> Came Noah, you remember, and seized the dictatorship.

[1] There were cross-currents here too; on the one hand, Ibsen came to admire Sverdrup who, against expectation, stuck to his guns right through the long political crisis; on the other hand, as a capitalist, he was relieved that no tumults ensued.

[2] Archer, C., *William Archer* (1934), p. 113.

Let us go, next time, to the root of the matter.
It needs men to act as well as to chatter.
You deluge the world to its topmost mark;
With pleasure I will torpedo the Ark.[1]

A strong outbreak of his radical sympathies followed upon his visit to Norway in 1885, and we shall have to study it in connection with *Rosmersholm*. It may be looked on as the culmination of a line of development which will next engage our attention, that which, on the plane of art, led to the great series of plays after *Emperor and Galilean*.

Before proceeding to this aspect of our subject, we may dismiss the history of Ibsen's relations with Bjørnson. The acutest phase of his displeasure passed fairly quickly, though, when Bjørnson spoke in favour of a pro-German outlook in 1872, Ibsen contemptuously referred to him in a poem as the "weathercock on the vane".[2] But *Pillars of Society* provided an excellent pretext for the first overtures of reconciliation; and, when Bjørnson threw over Grundtvigian Christianity in favour of a loudly avowed agnosticism a few months afterwards, the chances of *rapprochement* increased. Bjørnson had behaved with characteristic charity throughout the crisis, refusing for instance, to flay *The League of Youth* in *For Idé og Virkelighed*.[3] The men met again (in 1884) and fraternised as much as Ibsen ever could fraternise, a seal being placed on their friendship by the marriage, in 1892, of Ibsen's only legitimate child, Sigurd, with Bjørnson's daughter Bergljot.

[1] 'Til min Ven Revolutions-Taleren!' (VI, p. 371), translated by Garrett, F. E. (*Lyrics and Poems from Ibsen*, 1912, p. 34).
[2] "Vejrhanen paa Fløjen har ændret Signalerne" ('Nordens Signaler' *cit.* Brandes, G., *Samlede Skrifter*, XVIII, 1910, p. 123).
[3] Cf. his *Gro-Tid*, p. 327; the most he did was in a private letter to warn Hegel against Ibsen (*ibid.* p. 356) with the observation: "He is ungrateful, and he who is that is capable of anything."

CHAPTER TEN

GEORG BRANDES AND IBSEN[1]

Emperor and Galilean (1873), *Pillars of Society* (1877)

IBSEN'S journey to Italy in 1864 obviously implied, in the literal sense, a vast widening of his horizon. True, he had been in Copenhagen and Dresden for a few weeks in 1852, but the poverty-stricken, self-conscious youth rarely looked round the blinkers of duty which he felt that the managers of the Bergen theatre had clapped to his eyes. Now he had grown into a mature man, perhaps too mature to be radically affected by the new sights that opened up to his view and the new kind of people with whom he came into contact. But the evidence for this may, in its paucity, be misleading. We know little about the impression which the pictures of the Renascence masters at Venice, Rome and Florence, the classical statuary in the palace of the Vatican made upon him. Yet his old interest in painting did receive a stimulus (as no doubt it had also done at Dresden long ago), and the principal extravagance in which he indulged himself was to be the acquisition of paintings, a circumstance sufficiently well known to ensure his nomination to a jury of awarders at the International Exhibition in Vienna in 1873. He confessed[2] that he preferred the reliques of medieval and *barocco* art to those left by classical antiquity. Still, he took some pains to acquaint himself with the latter, and in preparation for his drama on the Roman Emperor Julian was fired sufficiently to plan an excursion to Greece (which was never realised).[3]

Nevertheless, congenial as he found Italy for working, he does not appear to have established any but superficial relations with the natives or to have acquired enough of their language to use its products for mental sustenance. His acquaintance in Rome, where he was moderately sociable, was confined, pretty nearly, to the membership of the Scandinavian Club.

[1] The interesting essay by Bull, F., 'Henrik Ibsen og Georg Brandes' in his *Studier og Streiftog* (1931) is perhaps more valuable as an indication of what Brandes owed to Ibsen than vice-versa.

[2] *Breve*, I, p. 89.   [3] Koht, II, p. 21.

In 1868, with *Brand* and *Peer Gynt* completed and *Emperor and Galilean* temporarily shelved, Ibsen moved to Dresden, where he had his headquarters till the spring of 1875. These were then transferred from the Saxon to the Bavarian capital. He was domiciled in Munich from 1875 to 1880 (with a year's break at Rome and Amalfi, 1878–9) and again from 1885 to 1892.[1] Here the difference of tongues raised no barrier round him. German had been the sole subject in which he had gained first-class marks in his matriculation examination, and he acquired, it seems, perfect mastery of it.[2] He even made a few German acquaintances, for instance with the literary dictator of Munich, Paul Heyse, with his own enthusiastic young champion Otto Brahm, and with Julius Elias, the co-editor of the collected edition of his works in German translation.[3] Through the German periodical press[4] (as well as the Scandinavian, of course) he was enabled to follow the intellectual and artistic controversies which reflected those of Europe at large. Life in Germany, he declared[5] "in many points carried with it a transforming power for me". He was well placed for observing the general ferment of promises and hopes in the moral sphere which in modern times great wars are apt to engender and which the German campaign of 1870–1, with its constitutional consequences, set up in abundance. His imagination, preoccupied with the problem of Julian the Apostate could not but be engaged by the protracted struggle (1872–80) between the German chancellor and the Roman Catholic hierarchy, which went by the name of the *Kulturkampf* (i.e. Civilisation-Fight).

On his visit to Stockholm in the summer of 1869, Ibsen was *fêté* for the first time in his life and found the doors of opulence and birth opened to him. The sense of a freer existence and his own right to a share in it was farther enhanced when the King

[1] It has been observed (by Meerkerk, J. B., *Om het derde Rijk*, 1906, p. 27) that Ibsen preferred to live among papists, though there is no evidence or likelihood of sympathy with their practices.

[2] One of his most famous epigrams was originally composed in it:

> "Leben, das heisst bekriegen,
> In Herz und Hirn die Gewalten;
> Und dichten; über sich selber
> Den Gerichtstag halten."

[3] Elias is said to be portrayed as Jørgen Tesman in *Hedda Gabler*.

[4] How much Ibsen picked up through books is doubtful; he declared that he left book-reading to his wife and son (with the former of whom, at least, he was quite conversational); Sigurd Ibsen was a German schoolboy, Fru Ibsen very well read in many languages.

[5] *Cit.* Koht, II, p. 100.

of Sweden and Norway procured him an invitation as one of
the Khedive of Egypt's guests for the protracted and sumptuous
ceremonies which inaugurated the Suez Canal in the autumn
of the same year.[1] The pyramids, the desert, the black beauty
whom, pasha-like, he had at his pleasure,[2] the vast new piece
of engineering and financial enterprise had the effect of putting
into contrast the smallness, the pettiness of conditions in Norway, all the more forcibly as the experience of them coincided
with the storm in the teacup blown up by the first performance
of *The League of Youth* in Christiania. Contemplation of the
antique civilisation of Egypt also raised in Ibsen's mind valuable
reflections about the relation of material achievements to personality, of mass to beauty. He extended them to the world
of his own day and was impelled to draw a parallel between the
civilisation of the Pharaohs and that of the Hohenzollerns.[3]
The nullity of a Bismarck and a Moltke, by contrast with the
magnitude and energy of the machinery they constructed and
set in motion, striking and appalling him, confirmed his fanatical
insistence on the primacy of personality.

*   *   *   *

The widening of Ibsen's visual horizon thus involved an increase
also in his moral experience, which, at the same time, was
worked on in other ways. By contrast with the almost mechanical
regularity of his literary activity between 1877 and 1899, with
the richness and *élan* of his work between 1850 and 1867, the
ten years bounded by these periods show him as a writer
relatively hesitant and unfruitful. He persevered, but almost
all the novelties involved immense labour, endless re-casting:
he devoted himself extensively to the process of mental stock-
taking, re-writing and re-issuing his poems,[4] publishing revised
versions of older plays.[5] Evidently what may be called the
'intake' into his mind considerably exceeded its 'output', his
best energies went to the process of assimilation.

The strongest single influence brought to bear upon him at

[1] Enfantin, the disciple of Saint-Simon who coined the expression 'Emancipation
of the Flesh', was an engineer by profession and one of the promoters of the Canal,
on almost mystical grounds.
[2] The only purpose she seems to have served was to vex Fru Ibsen. It must
be borne in mind that *Peer Gynt*, with its African scenes, preceded the poet's visit
to them.   [3] vi, p. 387.   [4] *Digte (Poems)*, 1871.
[5] *Catiline* (second edition, with an introduction, 1875) and *Lady Inger* (second
edition, 1874) were extensively altered, though the alterations may all be called
verbal.

this crucial period probably emanated, neither from Italy nor from Germany, but, once more, from Denmark, from Georg Brandes. The qualification 'probably' is in place, because in many ways Brandes presumably acted as a conduit only and conveyed to his friend by letter, conversation[1] and reference the notions of others without leaving much or anything of his own impress on them; and the caution is necessary for the farther reason that obviously about many of the ideas which occupied Brandes's mind and Ibsen's the latter may well have reached his conclusions quite independently. Nevertheless, the stimulating effect of discussing them, whether they were completely or only partially formed, with someone so versatile, well-informed and brilliant may almost rank as an influence in itself. The two men did not meet often, even in the years (1877–8 and 1879–82) when they were both in voluntary exile in Germany; but for several years they corresponded busily and they had at their earliest meeting memorable days together in Dresden in 1872, at the end of which Ibsen said, as he saw his friend into the train: "Now you go home to provoke the Danes, while I stay behind to annoy the Norwegians."[2]

Although Carlyle would most likely have seen in him another "blackguard Heine", Brandes might exemplify the Hero as Man of Letters as well as Dr Johnson. Georg Morris Cohen Brandes (1842–1927) was above everything a critic, but at the same time, indubitably the director of his country's intelligence in the agitated generation coming to maturity after the national disaster of 1864. The critic with whom he can most fitly be compared is Lessing. He took all modern European literature for his province, and in its turn the interest roused by his critiques and the ideas they implied extended far beyond the frontiers of Denmark and of that phase in its moral life which, in an ill-advised hour,[3] he called the *Gjennembrud* (or 'Break-Through') of 1872. In Scandinavia it was that he, naturally, left the deepest mark, both as a principal and as an intermediary, bringing to the notice of the northern kingdoms recent literary developments elsewhere at the same time that their own men

[1] The three occasions on which Ibsen and Brandes had most opportunities for prolonged and private conversation were in July 1872 at Dresden (their first actual meeting), in September 1885 and in the summer of 1891 at Christiania.

[2] *Cit.* Andersen, V., *Det nittende Aarhundredes anden Halvdel* (1925), p. 173.

[3] It was at once rather pertinently asked *what* there was in 1872 to break through; and the word 'Gjennembrud' became a most irritating parrot-cry, often used, as the German uses the word 'Kampf', for the most trivial exercise of energy.

of genius were contributing substantially to the common stock; for advertising such contributions his good offices were often employed.

Bearing in mind the *caveats* already made, we may consider Brandes's influence on Ibsen under two heads, as it affected, respectively, his artistic methods and his thought.

(I) The first discussion of his work by the Danish critic which Ibsen read was the essay devoted to him in *Aesthetic Studies* (*Æsthetiske Studier*, 1868), completed just after the appearance of *Peer Gynt*. It is there conceded that he is a genius and has written one of the finest scenes in dramatic literature, but he is also blamed for "lack of motivation",[1] with concomitant laxity of construction, for over-indulgence in symbolism that is more powerful than lucid[2] and for proffering "incarnate ideas", with correspondingly sententious speech, in place of personages.[3] It can hardly be a coincidence that much of the great difference discernible between *The League of Youth* and the two precedent 'dramatic poems' can fairly be summed up as a correction of these faults. Indeed, in his review of *The League of Youth*, Brandes made it a matter for complaint that too much attention had been paid to form, a phenomenon which he alleged to occur commonly in artists at the junction between their apprentice work and their mature manner; and, as a matter of fact, Ibsen's construction hereafter,[4] though impeccable, never relied again on the intrigues and misunderstandings which lend the impress of farce to the last act of *The League of Youth*.

This review was re-issued in *Criticisms and Portraits* (*Kritiker og Portraiter*, 1870), which contained also two other papers that must have been of great interest for Ibsen.[5] In 'The Infinitely Small and the Infinitely Great in Poetry'[6] Brandes adduced Shakespeare's Hotspur for a demonstration of the supreme method of character-drawing through which a personality as great and truly heroic as Homer's Achilles is rendered vivid and actual by innumerable touches like his stammering speech

[1] *Æsthetiske Studier* (1868), p. 270.   [2] *Ibid.* p. 271.
[3] *Ibid.* p. 274.
[4] I exclude *Emperor and Galilean* from this argument; it had already been conceived for some time back.
[5] "I have received your book", he writes to Brandes on 24 September 1871 (*Breve*, I, p. 235); "I can tell you it is reading to which I return over and over again."
[6] *Illustreret Tidende*, XI (1869–70), no. xxiv, reprinted in *Kritiker og Portraiter* (1870).

or his bantering affection for his wife; he is as far removed as
may be from being an "incarnate idea". Nora's macaroon-
eating, Hjalmar Ekdal's preoccupation with the butter-dish
while his life lies in ruins about him, the reminiscence of Hedda
Gabler's pulling Thea's hair at school—things for which there
is no parallel in *The League of Youth* or earlier—presumably
owe their remote origin to Brandes's analysis of Hotspur.
The critique of *The Newly-Wed* in the same volume praises
Bjørnson for the kind of subject which he chose and for his
method of 'observation' (rather than intrigue), but comes down
severely upon the crudeness both of the manners presented and
of the inartistic way in which realistic speech and action are
blended with a 'madrigal-style'.[1] While *The League of Youth*
could not be subjected to such harsh strictures, yet *Pillars of
Society* and its successors, agreeing in range of subject-matter
and in the 'method of observation' with *The Newly-Wed*, advance in refinement on *The League of Youth* and nowhere err,
as Dr Fjeldbo of *The League of Youth* does, towards sentimentality
of thought and expression except in a definitely satirical purpose.

In sum, as far as aesthetics are concerned, Brandes, on the
one hand, warned Ibsen against the excess of 'technique' such
as that in which, at the expense of probability, *The League of
Youth* indulged; on the other hand, his critiques, in *Criticisms
and Portraits*, of Brun's *Marie Antoinette* and of Munch's *Lord
William Russell* buoyed the Scylla and Charybdis between which
the serious modern playwright must steer a course: he must
command a philosophy of life, otherwise he cannot count in the
world of to-day; but, equally plainly, this must transpire in an
imperceptible fashion: if it is inadmissible to let a personage
directly inform the audience of all the latter needs to know
concerning that personage's character and opinions, how much
the more so to convey the author's philosophy in the same way?

(II) Knowing next to nothing about Ibsen's personal
history Brandes had, in his first study of his writings,
remarked upon the uncertainty of aim betrayed in them. The
prime question, he averred, which should be posed about an
author: "Where lies his discovery, what is his America?"[2]
could not in his case receive a satisfactory answer. Beyond this
Brandes did not say very much about the content of the early

[1] *Kritiker og Portraiter* (1870), p. 279.
[2] *Æsthetiske Studier* (1868), p. 239.

plays of a nature to point Ibsen to his America: but he did let fall two observations which produced, in all probability, some effect. Brandes described[1] Ibsen's mind (*aand*) as profound rather than comprehensive, and, in conjunction with one or two other observations, that remark could be construed as an animadversion on a certain narrowness of range both in the realm of ideas and in the variety of dramatic situations; and, farther, he protested[2] that the tendency of *Brand* was too narrowly religious, inimical to the imagination. It is certain that henceforth Ibsen, already (as 'To the Fellow-Culprits' shows) intent on breaking away from his older preoccupations and stimulated by his new life, was at great pains to extend his mental horizon and that he came to display extraordinary dexterity in varying his dramatic themes and personages, even where underlying ideas and traits might be very similar.[3] And as for the other point, the conflict between religious prepossessions and artistic imagination, he may be said, up to a point, to have dramatised it in *Emperor and Galilean*.

The third major impulse, after *Aesthetic Studies* and *Criticisms and Portraits*, which Ibsen underwent from Brandes's printed words was imparted by the famous inaugural lecture[4] at Copenhagen, published (1872) as introduction to the first volume of his great *Main Currents of Nineteenth Century Literature*.[5] In many a passage there, Brandes virtually addresses Ibsen himself, and we have good reason for believing that he forged arrows bearing legends like 'Brutus, thou sleep'st: awake' in the confident expectation that they would strike deep.

The programme which Brandes promulgated in this lecture was both negative and constructive. His aim was to shake out of their lethargy his fellow-Scandinavians, whom he saw before him represented by a cultured *élite*. However fine a masterpiece *Adam Homo* may be, he declares, the age of Romanticism is over, especially when little but its trappings and its idlest dreams remains. In the recent literature of the North "men outbid one another in piling up ideals, from which reality can

---

[1] *Æsthetiske Studier*, p. 244.   [2] *Ibid.* p. 265.

[3] Cf. the antagonism of the individual reformer and the vulgar herd in *An Enemy of the People* and in *Rosmersholm*, or the loquacious good-for-nothings with 'a great future behind them', Hjalmar Ekdal and Ulric Brendel.

[4] Most oddly, this is omitted from the English edition; the translations from it are therefore my own.

[5] *Hovedstrømninger i det 19de Aarhundredes Litteratur.*

only be discerned as a distant black spot". "Wherein has the current issued?" he asks; and replies: "In shapes like Paludan-Müller's *Kalanus*...and like Ibsen's *Brand,* whose moral, if realised, would lead half of mankind to starve to death from love of the ideal." How strong must the current be if it has carried a powerful revolutionary nature like Ibsen's along so undesirable a channel, where the reader, "first with a kind of horror, later with a kind of voluptuousness, may properly feel what a worm he is, how wretched and disheartened".

Over against this literature, remote from reality or inimical to life, he sets up his own ideal in the memorable sentence: "That in our days a literature is alive is shown by its submitting problems to debate";[1] the 'problems', he at once proceeds to make clear, are not transcendental matters which (Ibsen might have pleaded) *Brand* and *Love's Comedy* had quite effectively submitted to debate, but questions affecting the lives of ordinary men and women. "In this way, for instance, George Sand submits marriage to debate, Voltaire, Byron and Feuerbach religion, Proud'hon property, the younger Alexandre Dumas the relations between the two sexes and Emile Augier the social relations." Brandes ended his lecture with a call to raise the red flag on that northern outpost of art and thought: "Our principal labour will be to direct hither, through a multiplicity of channels, the currents originating in the Revolution and in the ideas of Progress and to halt the Reaction at every point where, historically, its mission is at an end."[2]

Though its clauses probably contained nothing that was completely novel to him, this manifesto shook Ibsen profoundly. It kept him awake at nights;[3] the first volume of *Main Currents,* he described as "one of the books that sets a yawning deep between yesterday and to-day."[4] The main programme, it is evident, he accepted at once; it was the programme of the future, which did not stand in need of any defence. He renounced verse,[5] the medium of an effete romanticism and, after completing *Emperor and Galilean,* whose long gestation was

---

[1] "Det, at en Litteratur i vore Dage lever viser sig i, at den sætter Problemer under Debat" (*Hovedstrømninger i det 19de Aarhundredes Litteratur,* I, 1872, p. 15).

[2] *Hovedstrømninger, ut cit.,* p. 28.

[3] This phenomenon does not seem to have been common, as a recurrence is reported as significant, on Ibsen's first witnessing of *Brand* at Copenhagen in 1898.

[4] Letter to Brandes of 4 April 1872, *Breve,* I, p. 249.

[5] All Ibsen's poetry after 1875 could be written on a single sheet of notepaper.

nearing its term, he resolutely turned to the present, one much more concrete and familiar than that foreshadowed in 'To the Fellow-Culprits' and that to be supposed in *Brand* and *Peer Gynt*; for in the latter there might be talk of steamships and other manifestations of Anglo-Saxon industry, but rural deans still spoke the language of the Age of Reason and the wars which recruits sought to avoid might as well be those of Buonaparte or even Charles XII as Bismarck's. Ibsen now broached problem after problem of the present-day world.[1] Not only George Sand, it was to appear, submitted marriage to debate, but *A Doll's House* and *Ghosts* as well, *Ghosts* and *The Lady from the Sea* were to canvass the relations between the sexes no less than the younger Dumas, *An Enemy of the People* and *Little Eyolf* the social relations, as Augier had done.

Brandes had even, should it be necessary, indicated stepping stones for his friend by including the two living dramatists among those who realised his ideal, adding the observation that pieces like *The Natural Son*, *Giboyer's Son* and *The Brazen*[2] revealed conditions and posed problems which had never been treated in Northern literature, but which, all the same, existed in and for Scandinavian society. ("For to our moral fury we add a corresponding moral prudery.") The hint, however, was probably superfluous. *The League of Youth* shows that Ibsen had sufficient knowledge of Dumas and Augier for his purpose.

By encouraging Ibsen's deliberate 'modernity', Brandes rendered his friend the sovereign service of strengthening a bridge (as it were) which he believed to be no less than his life-line, the bridge over the Gyntian chasm separating 'dream' from 'deed', imaginative literature (which was his *forte*) from action (which he was intellectually convinced should be a man's work). For submitting problems to debate, widening their terms of reference,[3] meant supplying active life with ideas to propel it. Ibsen had long realised what his mission was, but Kierkegaard had taught him to despise the æsthetic. Now that Brandes had laid the worst ghost which haunted his mind, the self-assurance which his outward deportment had assumed permeated his whole being; and after the terrific wrestling with

---

[1] Brandes had impressed on him the ominous urgency of the need, and he had vividly responded: "I think we are sailing with a corpse in the cargo" ("Jeg tror vi sejler med et lig i lasten!" VI, p. 406).

[2] The younger Dumas's *Fils Naturel*, Augier's *Fils de Giboyer* and *Les Effrontés*.

[3] "Flytte grænspælerne" (i.e. "move the frontier-posts"), he called the process.

the matter of *Pillars of Society* he 'never looked back', as the popular saying is.[1]

*   *   *   *

It may be asked whether Brandes's own personality and ideas exerted a more specific influence than this. They almost certainly did,[2] though it is difficult to lay a finger on any definite conception, let alone a single passage, in Ibsen's writing and positively say of it: 'But for Brandes, this would not have been.' Brandes flattered himself[3] that his applause of Selma's outburst (in *The League of Youth*) at her neglect and humiliation ensured the full development of this explosive theme in *A Doll's House*. It is pardonable vanity, but the fact remains that Ibsen had thought of Selma's position before Brandes saw fit to expatiate upon it.

Nevertheless, in all he wrote, Ibsen had the bracing assurance of meeting the sympathetic and searching, though not always approbatory, interest of an expert for whose judgement he cherished the highest respect, and he owned to having ever present to his mind: "What will Brandes think of this?"[4] He not only studied Brandes's three critiques of his own work,[5] but he perused many of his other writings as well. A small proof of this is afforded by *John Gabriel Borkman* (1896), where the interest in things English raised by the recently published monograph of Brandes, *William Shakespeare* (1895–6), suggested an English Christian name for the hero and also the surname of the adventuress Fanny Wilton, taken from the family seat of the house of Pembroke. It is moreover not unlikely that his individualistic, radical reformers, his Stockmann and love-tangled Rosmer, derived touches from Brandes's monograph on Lassalle.[6]

[1] In another sense, Ibsen did look back in *When We Dead Awaken*, though the style and ideas of the piece betray no radical break with what had gone before. It is full of regrets, though not necessarily regrets at the way Ibsen thought he had used his talents. He cherished at that time the notion of writing works in quite a different vein again, but nothing came of it.

[2] The preceptor was pleased: in 1882 he wrote (Brandes, G., *Henrik Ibsen, Bjørnstjerne Bjørnson*, English trans. 1898, p. 79) that Ibsen by degrees had made himself "the most modern of the Moderns. This, I am convinced, is his imperishable glory and will give lasting life to his works."

[3] *Op. cit.* p. 76.

[4] So at any rate Brandes himself declared; see his autobiographical *Levned*, II (1907), p. 103.

[5] Published in 1867 (in *Dansk Maanedsskrift*, and then reprinted in *Æsthetiske Studier ut supra*), in 1882 (*Det moderne Gjennembruds Mænd*) and in 1898 respectively, and printed together in a volume, *Henrik Ibsen*, of the latter year.

[6] *Ferdinand Lassalle* (1881).

CHAPTER ELEVEN

MODERN PROBLEMS

Emperor and Galilean (1873), *Pillars of Society* (1877),
A Doll's House (1879), *Ghosts* (1881)

AT a time when Brandes and his ideas began to affect Ibsen he was at a pause, a Hercules at the cross-roads. Despite all the great issues raised by *Love's Comedy*, *The Pretenders*, *Peer Gynt* and, especially, by *Brand*, these were works not merely centred in Norway topographically, but written with specifically Norwegian conditions in view. The holiday from deep problems which the author now permitted himself in writing *The League of Youth* might divert itself with abundant satire at "the local situation", but was still completely bound up with it. Henceforth a profound change was to be observed. Ibsen, it may be said, after some tarrying and much self-debate turned from being a Norwegian to being a European. Modern he had made himself beyond qualification or peradventure in the last comedy, and to the Norwegian scene he remained unswervingly faithful in the dramas conceived after this date. But the themes, the situations and the personalities which came under his pen were no longer suggested to him, living in exile as he was, by purely local preoccupations and literary traditions, but by the interests of the civilised world at large and his observation of it, however much life and individuality might still accrue from the Norwegian guise in which he finally saw and presented the generalities.

That Brandes exerted no specious or unnatural influence upon him is attested by the nature of the great work on which Ibsen was intermittently engaged throughout most of the critical years and which had begun to engage his thoughts as far back as July 1864. *Emperor and Galilean* (*Kejser og Galilæer*, 1873), in its choice of subject and theme, shows that Ibsen's spirit, unaided, was prepared to transcend all the limits of space (as well as of time) in which so far it had kept itself confined. The problems to which it owes a great part of its formation and which in turn it was to transform for later debate had an urgency no greater

146

for Norwegians than for anyone else, and their country is not so much as mentioned.

To begin with, it would seem, Ibsen was attracted to the Eastern Roman emperor Julian, the hero of this vast drama, by apprehending him to be, first and foremost, a rebel of almost Miltonic grandeur, since his repudiation and persecution of the religion of Christ could be little less awful than Lucifer's defiance of the first person of the Trinity. Plans for treating this subject alternated in Ibsen's mind with those for a drama on the pirate-king Magnus (or Mogens) Heinesen. But, as he absorbed himself in it and in some of the secondary sources which he consulted, its complexity and farther implications were borne in on him,—precisely those implications in fact to which a somewhat widespread interest in Julian was due at that epoch.[1]

In the middle third of the nineteenth century the Christian religion, firmly established in the statute-books and conventions of all civilised nations outside Asia, was sustaining attacks not always realised by its adherents, but of a seriousness in comparison with which the criticisms of a Bayle or a Voltaire had been mere skirmishes. Geology, biology, mathematics and philology—all the advancing sciences of the day—combined to undermine the foundations on which the Christian edifice was reared. Ibsen took little interest in the labours of Lyell, of Colenso, of Huxley or of those who represented their point of view in the North; he had very likely never heard of Bishop Wilberforce's animadversions upon evolutionary biology;[2] it is probable that the culmination of Renan's scholarship in *The Life of Jesus*[3] (like the similar efforts of Strauss and Feuerbach) left him indifferent, since he neglected the easiest possible opportunity for making the author's acquaintance.[4] We need therefore not consider the avenues of approach to the religious problem which they opened farther than to remark on the extensive interest and heated controversies which they were arousing,

---

[1] Recent studies had been D. F. Strauss's *Der Romantiker auf dem Thron der Cäsaren* (1847), A. de Broglie's *L'Eglise et l'Empire au IVe siècle* (1859), E. Lamé's *Julien l'Apostat* (1861); there were plays by Hauch (1866) and Molitor (1867).

[2] Which were echoed by a Northern bishop, D. G. Monrad.

[3] 1863.

[4] It must really be a unique circumstance that, not at mutual enmity, two of the foremost spirits of the age should on two occasions be beneath the same roof (at Bergen in 1856 and apparently for some time in 1881 at Sorrento) without making one another's acquaintance.

but proceed rather to the viewpoint which revealed that problem most clearly to Ibsen.

It is not improbable that Brandes impelled or helped him to occupy this standpoint. Brandes's campaign against stagnation, prejudice, tradition and convention axiomatically assumed their impermanence; he was far from enunciating or insisting on any eternal verities; already at the end of the 1860's he was declaiming that the world of thought had entered the constellation of relativity. There was nothing that might not be susceptible to its laws.[1] Mutability, the supersession of the old by the new were, of course, no new conceptions. Before the theory of evolution and progress had become fashionable, Hegel's philosophy of history had made great play with them on an elaborate system of successive 'thesis', 'antithesis' and 'synthesis'. The all but religious awe with which Hegel was regarded at Christiania[2] had impressed even so unconventional and unphilosophical a mind as Ibsen's; and, in so far as he ever thought philosophically,[3] he was prone to do so in Hegelian terms. The religious problem of the time accordingly presented itself to him somewhat in this guise: What if the Christian religion were not the final 'synthesis' which for so long it has seemed to be (to those who systematize the course of history like this), but an 'antithesis', waiting, as it were, for a later 'synthesis' as it had confronted an earlier 'thesis'?[4] To one formulating the problem in terms such as these questions like the age of the patriarchs, Noah's flood, the special creation of man, the irreconcilability of the gospels, the prevalence of thaumaturges in Palestine would be ancillary, if not otiose.

Not only does Ibsen seem to have contemplated the religious problem in terms of this order, but he conceived of his hero Julian as doing so similarly. The rebel becomes something of a Hegelian—in a way the course of the action drives him into

[1] Cf. Dr Stockmann's belief that "a normally-constituted truth lives—let us say—as a rule, seventeen or eighteen years; at the outside twenty" (IV, p. 338; Archer, VIII, p. 135).

[2] It was the same at Copenhagen, when Georg Brandes's adherence to the French and British thinkers caused a correspondingly disturbing scandal; that it was the same at Upsala Strindberg's reminiscences attest.

[3] At any rate until after the completion of *Emperor and Galilean*. To Hoffory he wrote (*Breve*, II, p. 169) that this was the first work he wrote under the influence of German intellectual life; "and the only", Gosse adds (*Ibsen*, 1907, p. 141).

[4] A 'scheme' like this and the actual subject-matter would have been very congenial to Hebbel; there is, however, no indication that Ibsen had recourse to him for any of the inspiration of *Emperor and Galilean*.

that position. Threatened, repressed and terrified by the religion which Constantine had officially established, Prince Julian turns against it with a violence equally great. He endeavours, as his less virulent antagonists have always maintained, to put back the hands of the clock. Soon, however, he discovers that this cannot be done, or cannot fruitfully be done. If the old truth (Christianity) is, as he believes, true no more, so the old beauty of paganism, represented by the intoxication of de-bauchees and the caperings of harlots, is no longer beautiful. Something new, a *tertium quid*, a synthesis, must supersede both.[1]

An impetus to meditate on the nature of such a synthesis was imparted to Ibsen by certain important political or semi-political events of the day. His old 'Scandinavianism', dis-credited but not dead in his bosom, had betrayed a predilection for large polities;[2] he could not therefore remain indifferent to the creation round about him first of united Italy and then of re-united Germany. He saw the fashioning of two enormous political bastions where hitherto there had been little more than a heap of stones; at the same time the papacy, at the Vatican council (1870–1), was embarking, through the decree pro-mulgating its infallibility, on a policy of strengthening the doctrinal and administrative structure of organised religion. The results, to Ibsen's sight, were not completely satisfactory, far from it. The new Rome was never so good as the asylum which had received him in 1864, and Bismarck's *Reich* as such repelled him, however many fine institutions and laborious citizens it might contain.[3] He saw at close quarters the most

[1] Julian's master Maximus formulates the matter thus: "First that empire which was founded on the tree of knowledge; then that which was founded on the tree of the cross.... The third is the empire of the great mystery; that empire which shall be founded on the tree of knowledge and the tree of the cross together, because it hates and loves them both..." (III, p. 184; Archer, v, p. 114). This passage gives the clue for the underlying confusion of Ibsen's argument: the 'second empire' is always, clearly, the Kingdom of Christ; but that against which it was set up, the 'first empire', is things as divergent as the dispensation of the Old Testament, a rationalistic universe, Bismarck's *Reich* and the cult of Aphrodite and Dionysos.

[2] As the individual might the more easily lose himself in one, he believed it perhaps to afford a better guarantee for his independence than a small com-munity.

[3] I paraphrase some lines (VI, p. 385) from his verse 'Balloon-Letter to a Swedish Lady' of December 1870, when the trend of events had become clear to him in his observation-post at Dresden: calling to mind his recent experiences in Egypt, he says: "Once again a King is God on his throne, once again the individual melts away in a swarm which bustles, yearns, worries, builds, broods, ponders all around and underneath us. Once again the pyramid is raised as the product of

far-reaching experiment hitherto made to give to the state the functions of universal provider, in the realms not merely of order and security, but also of communications, health, even of art, education and religion. One of the first acts of the new centralised government at Berlin was to embark (1872) on what was called the *Kulturkampf* (or Civilisation-Fight) against the Roman Catholic Church. Was, Ibsen pondered, this *Reich*, this *rige*,[1] as the Danish-Norwegian equivalent is, the desired synthesis between the old military rule of the Caesars and the Christian rule of life? And, if not, what was the *tredie rige*, the third empire, to be?

The intellectual kernel of *Emperor and Galilean* lies perhaps in this dialogue:[2]

Julian. . . .Emperor and Galilean! How reconcile that contradiction?

Yes, this Jesus Christ is the greatest rebel that ever lived. What was Brutus—what was Cassius compared with him? *They* murdered only the man Julius Caesar; but *he* murders all that is called Caesar and Augustus. Is peace conceivable between the Galilean and the Emperor? Is there room for the two of them together upon the earth? For he lives on the earth, Maximus,—the Galilean lives, I say, however thoroughly both Jews and Romans imagined that they had killed him; he lives in the rebellious minds of men; he lives in their scorn and defiance of all visible authority.

"Render unto Caesar the things that are Caesar's,—and to God the things that are God's!" Never has mouth of man uttered a craftier saying than that. What lies behind it? . . .

Maximus. Both the Emperor and the Galilean shall succumb.

Julian. Succumb—? Both—?

Maximus. Both. Whether in our times or in hundreds of years, I know not; but so it shall be when the right man comes.

Julian. And who is the right man?

Maximus. He who shall swallow up both Emperor and Galilean.

Julian. You solve the riddle by a still darker riddle.

the whole age. Once again every vein swells, once again blood and tears flow in order that the world may see the King-God's mausoleum great. This is the caravan of the present day, with its Hathor, with its Horus and, for parliament, its chorus swearing blind oaths of fealty. What monuments rise along the level path of victory! What power in the onrush of the people! How Egyptian, the way all and each fit their little stone in its place in the fabric of the whole! How faultless is the plan and how accurate the calculation! Yes, in truth, it is great, great, so that the world stands and gapes: yet there trembles a 'but' in the gape's open void."

[1] No quite satisfactory English equivalent of this key-word exists since *rige* means *kingdom* or *empire* without any monarchical implications.

[2] III, pp. 334 f.; Archer, v, pp. 369 ff.

To *Emperor and Galilean* Ibsen was always disposed to look reverentially as his most important work; his regard for it may be pardoned, since perhaps more protracted and fatiguing labour went to its composition than to any other and it embodied the result of more abstract and philosophical ratiocination. "Alone I did it", he could also reflect.[1] It has not, however, so favourably impressed its readers, who have been content to repeat the last words of Maximus just quoted and hold it a reproach to Ibsen that, having embarked on so stupendous a quest, he carried it no farther. The fact is, that he tired of his theme before the end, and the progressive loss of control over character, situation and plot betrays it. In the letter to Georg Brandes of 4 April 1872,[2] which has already been quoted from, Ibsen says of the volume containing his critical friend's introductory lecture: "A more dangerous book could never fall into the hands of a breeding author." Ibsen was pregnant of *Emperor and Galilean*, and it is highly probable that *The Main Currents of Nineteenth Century Literature* produced nothing less than a miscarriage. True, the subject of *Emperor and Galilean* was important, and Ibsen had his own independent attitude towards it. It was big, perhaps too big, but, even if read in the light of the *Kulturkampf* (which it might not occur to everyone to direct upon it), it was scarcely modern; it certainly did not exhibit the modern world. Then it was, in origin, Hegelian, and, great as Hegel might be, the world lay not now with Hegel any more than with the fathers of the Christian Church; it lay with Darwin and Spencer,[3] or at least with Hartmann. In waking hours of the night Ibsen may have seen *Emperor and Galilean* respectable, remote and grandiose, but, if applicable to actual conditions, only quite indirectly. It just did live, it just did submit problems to debate. But of such half-and-half things there were to be no more.

✳   ✳   ✳   ✳

When, with Ibsen, we now turn away from the past, we may commence the next stage of the present enquiry by revolving the question: What lessons had Brandes's own teachers to

[1] He deliberately left Hauch's drama, *Julian the Apostate* (1866), unread, so that his conception should not be affected.
[2] *Breve*, I, p. 249.
[3] The Norwegian scholar J. E. W. Sars was just making a major application of Spencer's theory of development with differentiation in his *Udsigt over den Norske Historie*, of which the first volume appeared in 1873.

impart to him? In the realm of pure aesthetics their influence on
Ibsen must have been nil: it would be vain to seek for any
echoes from Sainte-Beuve or Philarète Chasles in the technique
and ideas of his plays. The aesthetic philosophy of Taine, however, by which at one time Brandes was profoundly impressed,
which he carefully expounded[1] and to which he gave currency
in northern Europe, raised issues that far exceeded the bounds
of art. Ibsen would scarcely be touched by the famous doctrine
of literature as the product of *milieu, race* and *moment,* but the
wider question with which it was bound up, of determinism
and the freedom of man's will, remained one of serious concern
to him. That question not only tinges the whole catastrophe of
Emperor and Galilean,[2] but is placed into the focus of the memorable
spirit-raising scene (in Act III of the first Part), which ends with
Julian's outcry:

I defy necessity! I will not serve it! I am free, free, free![3]

Shortly before that, the shade of Judas Iscariot[4] had appeared
and the following dialogue taken place:

The Voice. But for me, whither had the chariot rolled?
Julian. Whither did it roll by means of thee?
The Voice. Into the glory of glories.
Julian. Why didst thou help?
The Voice. Because I *willed.*
Julian. What didst thou will?
The Voice. What I must.
Julian. Who chose thee?
The Voice. The master.
Julian. Did the master foreknow when he chose thee?
The Voice. Ah, *that* is the riddle![5]

This was not the first riddle with which the occult world had
answered Julian's frantic interrogations. Earlier, when he had
asked, "What is my mission?" the 'Voice in the Light' had
made reply:[6]

---

[1] In *Present Day French Aesthetics* (*Den Franske Æstetik i vore Dage,* 1870).
[2] Which no doubt accounts for Ibsen's writing to Brandes (*Breve,* I, p. 234)
that over the work he had become a "fatalist".
[3] III, p. 188; Archer, v, p. 123.
[4] The significance of Judas is also treated in a short poem by Ibsen (*Efterladte
Skrifter,* I, p. 211), of which the second half runs: "We know that, lulled in a torpor
of conscience, he went straight and gave the Redeemer the kiss. Then both heaven
and hell were advantaged. But what if Judas now hadn't *wanted*?"
[5] III, p. 186; Archer, v, p. 119.   [6] III, p. 183; Archer, v, p. 112.

To establish the empire.[1]
Julian. What empire?
The Voice. The empire.
Julian. And by what way?
The Voice. By the way of freedom.
Julian. Speak clearly! What is the way of freedom?
The Voice. The way of necessity.
Julian. And by what power?
The Voice. By *willing*.
Julian. *What* shall I will?
The Voice. What thou *must*.

Beyond this Ibsen himself does not go. The whole trend of his romantic upbringing—in so far as he enjoyed a literary upbringing at all—and the deep striving of his nature to liberate himself and his fellows from trammels of every kind made him unwilling to abandon the conception of free will. On the other hand he could not disown the strength of the deterministic argument or claim that the human mind was exempted from it. In a letter[2] in which he takes up Georg Brandes's discussion of the treatment of necessity in his own *Emperor and Galilean* and in Paul Heyse's novel, *Children of the World*,[3] he observes that it amounts to very much the same thing to say "he is free—under necessity"—and to say "it lies in his blood". The observation suggests that, after a fashion which Taine would have approved, Ibsen admitted physiological causes of heredity and the like as mediate between ultimate necessity and individual volition. That he brooded on these causes and their bearings on tragedy is especially evident in *Ghosts*, on which an eminent classical scholar of the day[4] fastened at once as a translation into modern terms of the hereditary curse handled with such effect by the Greek dramatists when they too were confronted with the incompatibility of *Ananke*, necessity, and human responsibility.

Not only as a tragedian, but as a moralist also Ibsen continued to concern himself profoundly with questions of individual responsibility, for which the absolute necessitarian has so facile an answer. It is not without significance that the life's work of the most serious professed philosopher in any of his dramas, that of Alfred Allmers (in *Little Eyolf*), should be 'On

[1] *Riget.*   [2] Letter to Brandes of 30 January 1875 (*Breve*, II, p. 25).
[3] *Kinder der Welt.*
[4] Schjøtt, P. O., in the first number of *Nyt Tidsskrift*.

Human Responsibility'.[1] Responsibility presented itself to Ibsen in two different guises. The first is the degree of obligation for the well-being of his neighbour and, to a less extent, of himself too which each individual should take upon himself, the problem which Alfred and Rita Allmers propose practically to solve by their school for the riff-raff of the water-front and which Hedda Gabler consistently shelves with consequences more catastrophic than Dr Stockmann's ill-requited exertions on behalf of his fellow-townsmen; it is this conception of responsibility which flashes upon Ellida Wangel's mind when she realises that she has been sick through neglecting "freedom ...under full responsibility"[2] and that she can regain her health by repairing the neglect. The second aspect of Responsibility may be defined as the degree to which everyone is the deliberate director of (and on that ground should be accountable for) his own actions, when these are the manifestation of a personality moulded by a chain of causes as old as the world. Ibsen cast this into the dramatic form in *A Doll's House*, where Nora's frivolity and even her crime are explained and palliated by her temperamental inheritance from her father and by her upbringing at his hands. (How close the two aspects stood to one another in Ibsen's mind is shown by the fact that her breeding produced in Nora a lack of responsibility in the other sense of the word, and the whole of *Ghosts* may be interpreted as a protracted examination of Responsibility in both of its guises.)

Taine imparted a shock to the settled notions of his time not only by his philosophy of necessity and his rigorous application of it to aesthetics, but also by his theory of the nature of man with which his disciples, *les naturalistes*, associated it. Man was a mammal, and a particularly powerful, ferocious and libidinous mammal at that, and, if the proper study of mankind should still be man, it should take the form of a natural history as free from moral preoccupations in its approach as in its findings.

[1] "Det Menneskelgie Ansvar" (VI, p. 102; Archer, XI, p. 33). I take it that *Ansvar* and *ansvarlig* in Dano-Norwegian correspond exactly to 'responsibility' and 'responsible'.

[2] v, p. 289; Archer, IX, p. 349 (*The Lady from the Sea*). Compare Ellida's outburst just before: "Responsibility! This transforms everything." The interfusion of free will and determinism in Ibsen's philosophy is well illustrated by Ellida's sudden exercise of volition and her remark on it: "do you not understand that the transformation came, that it *had* to come—when I could choose in freedom" (v, p. 287; Archer, IX, p. 345).

To Brandes, the admirer of Sainte-Beuve and Philarète Chasles and the predestined adorer of genius, the rigorism of Taine's aesthetics had only made a very partial and evanescent appeal; and he took up a highly ambiguous attitude towards Naturalism by so wide and, in a sense, old-fashioned an interpretation of the term as, for instance, to include Wordsworth and Shelley among its foremost professors. Neither in his plays nor elsewhere did Ibsen intrude speculations on the nature of man in zoological terms. His preoccupation with the problem of responsibility is an index of his remoteness from any wish to write 'Natural History'. As much as he knew of the great propagandist of this narrower Naturalism he thoroughly detested: "Zola descends to the sewer to take a bath, I do in order to scour it."[1] The timidity and chastity of his temperament kept him away from scenes of violence and passion, even though (as puritanical opponents were not slow to point out) his plays might involve concubinage, incest, homicide, fraud, self-slaughter and arson. But for such the devoted reader of the Bible, whose art followed in the line begun by Aeschylus and made illustrious by Shakespeare, had no need to incur any debt to a Zola or a Taine.

*　　　*　　　*　　　*

The ferment which engendered the *Gjennembrud* or "Break-Through" in Georg Brandes's mind during the years on either side of 1870 was supplied to him from Great Britain as well as from France. For a short while, indeed, he adopted the private slogan "Read Mill and turn Anglo-Saxon". He made the acquaintance of the English thinker, visited him at Blackheath and by translating them into Danish (with prefaces by himself) gave to two capital works of his, *The Subjection of Women* and *Utilitarianism*,[2] a very notable circulation in the North.

When, in his educational design, Brandes attempted to infect Ibsen with his own admiration for *Utilitarianism*, he encountered a recalcitrance, however, which seems rather strange. For though, in later life, Ibsen is never reported to have mentioned Mill again in praise or disparagement, he came to assume towards many capital concerns very much the same attitude,

[1] *Cit.* Koht, II, p. 199.
[2] *Kvindernes Underkuelse* (1869) and *Moral Grundet paa Lykke- eller Nytteprincipet* (1872); the literal re-translation of the latter title might be noted, 'Ethics based on the Principle of Happiness or Utility'.

and the imperceptible process by which this came about suggests that he was congenitally pre-disposed. In Ibsen there was, often overlaid or qualified, a deep strain, probably derived from Rousseauistic romanticism, which made the happiness of the individual the ultimate criterion in morals—precisely the tenet of the 'hedonistic calculus' propounded by Jeremy Bentham, Mill's great predecessor. Just at the time that Brandes was translating *Utilitarianism* (1872) Ibsen was wrestling in *Emperor and Galilean* with the problem of adjusting pagan hedonism to the demands of spiritual religion and the future commonwealth (*rige*), a problem that had not been very far below the surface in *Brand* and *Love's Comedy*. Though some of its manifestations were so shocking, as none could appreciate better than herself, Mrs Alving meditated profoundly whether sufficient importance were attached to *livsglæde*, the 'joy of life', a problem which she at once submitted to the most animated debate in all Northern countries. The desperate striving of later heroines and heroes, of Rosmer, of Ellida Wangel, of Solness, for instance, to shake off their *trolde*, the monsters that constrict and hold them down, issuing in the radiant song of Maja—the last words of Ibsen which an audience was to hear:

> I am free! I am free! I am free!
> No more life in the prison for me!
> I am free as a bird! I am free![1]—

and the main theme of the play in which she figures (*When We Dead Awaken*) raise more directly than its author ever did before the question whether, in the teeth of the demands put upon him by ethics, by art and his mission in life, a man should not first and foremost clutch at sensual delights, emancipate the flesh, as Enfantin put it.

In view of what has been said about his preoccupation with human responsibility, it is unnecessary to remark how deeply Ibsen reflected on the bearings of one person's welfare and happiness on the welfare and happiness of those with whom he has immediate contact—an aspect of hedonism to which Mill devoted particular attention, insisting that, if the happiness of a community were measurable by the aggregate happiness of the individuals comprising it (as the older utilitarians had

---

[1] VI, p. 295; Archer, XI, p. 456.

urged), then reciprocally the happiness of the community promoted and increased also that of each constituent member.

*   *   *   *

Several reasons may be alleged for Ibsen's dislike of Mill.
The very coincidence of their views may be one of them; Ibsen,
intent on independence and, therefore, on 'originality' of
thought, disliked the notion that Mill had already been enunciating his doctrines for a lifetime and might be adjudged his
preceptor; his reverential awe for the name of Hegel may have
been perturbed by one who could easily dismiss some of his
Metaphysics as "nonsense"; for all his interest in his bank-
balance and investments, he remembered perhaps the contempt
for 'utility' as a criterion of moral values which came natural
to the great exponent of the Christian paradox; philosophy
should have about it the sublime and the cryptic of a Delphic
oracle, and it jarred on Ibsen to hear it exposed in intelligible
sentences appealing to the highest common factor of human
understanding: Mill, to him, was another philistine Cicero,[1] for
whom his vexation and contempt had not yet been slaked.

But the most singular of Ibsen's objections to the hierarch
of utilitarianism was Mill's chivalrous acknowledgement[2] that
he owed many of his ideas to the gifted woman who ultimately
became his wife. The ideas in question are those informing
that other work on which Brandes had exercised his talents as
a translator and expositor, *The Subjection of Women* (1869).

Nowhere else perhaps had dissatisfaction with the position
of women in a rapidly changed and changing society been felt
more acutely than in the Scandinavian countries. On the one
hand, as the old literature abundantly shows, they had enjoyed
the respect and comparative freedom which the Teutonic-
speaking peoples were prone to accord to their women-folk, so
that the energetic Lady Inger and ruthless Hjørdis of Ibsen's
youthful fancy struck his audiences as nothing abhorrent in
nature; their education had not been utterly neglected; and
the ideas of the Romantic Age[3] had presumably tended to raise
their *self*-esteem. On the other hand, the material backwardness
of Norway in particular at the beginning of the nineteenth

---

[1] *Breve*, I, p. 276.
[2] Which, with bitter irony, Ibsen declares himself quite prepared to accept
(*Breve*, I, p. 277).
[3] Tinged with misconceptions of the Middle Ages and their 'chivalry'.

century and the corresponding rapidity with which it made up leeway during the next two generations often produced an adverse effect. Jonas Lie's faithful delineations in *The Family at Gilje*[1] show how a squire's lady (as we might call her) in a remote, but not uncharacteristic country neighbourhood during the 1840's presided in almost medieval fashion over highly varied and complicated domestic functions, so that her confinements procured her her only holidays: under her supervision the products of dairy, sheep-farm, vegetable-garden, orchard, lake, brewhouse, poultry-yard were converted into almost everything required for the consumption from January to December of her own family and the considerable retinue maintained by her husband and herself. The industrial revolution, the steamship, the new roads and railways changed all that; and someone like Fru Jæger might, economically, become quite superfluous in the realm in which she had reigned supreme, or at any rate might have many of her functions reduced largely to their ornamental aspect.[2] Not only her environment would come to realise that, but she herself would do so too, in the enhanced leisure for reflection and reading which simultaneously accrued; and nowhere was this more apparent than in the rising middle class of the towns. What was true of the married woman was even more self-evident in the case of her unmarried daughters. Hence sprang dissatisfaction and unhappiness, as well as the mischief with which, according to the saying, Satan compensates for idleness, and concomitantly therewith a desire, evinced by the more resolute women, for entrance into other activities, the professions and the arts.

Camilla Collett had been a victim to this nascent dissatisfaction and a pioneer in diagnosing and liberating it. From biographical reasons (her unrequited passion for Welhaven), it was natural that in *The Sheriff's Daughters*, the novel that left its mark on *Love's Comedy*, she should devote her attention to the sentimental restrictions put on girls by being allowed no more than the negative choice of a spouse. But the publication of her grievance established also the valuable right of women to plead their own cause, and throughout a long life she con-

[1] *Familien paa Gilje* (1883).

[2] Even her inalienable functions as a mother were threatened and restricted by practical malthusianism (after the birth of her only child, Fru Ibsen declared that there would be no more) and by the extensive employment of wet nurses and children's governesses, against which many moralists declaimed.

tinued to exercise it on a variety of subjects. Round about 1870 and again towards the end of the decade she came into fairly frequent personal contact with Ibsen, and the diatribes to which she gave voice undoubtedly made an impression upon him, though in talk he usually assumed an extremely conservative attitude, partly to tease her, but principally perhaps to stimulate her into stating her case in its extremest form.

In the meantime Camilla Collett received reinforcement from Mathilde Schjøtt[1] and the painter Aasta Hanstein. The former published a critique of Mill from the female point of view, *The Women-Friends' Discussion of The Subjection of Women* (1871), the latter carried on in 1874[2] an overt campaign against male arrogance, championing a Swedish noblewoman who had been unable to gain redress for the 'insult'[3] inflicted by a Norwegian undergraduate, delivering feminist lectures all over the country and striding about with a riding-whip for the prevention of any such insult as had befallen her *protégée*. The campaign for extending women's rights and opportunities took shape and produced results. In 1882 they were admitted as matriculated members to Christiania university, and in 1884 a petition was presented to the *Storthing* for a bill giving married women a legal right to property and earnings.

Among the signatories of this petition was not only Bjørnson (as anyone might expect), but also Ibsen. In the main, however, this aspect of the feminist movement does not appear greatly to have concerned him, and he took no notice of it in his imaginative work.[4] Perhaps his dislike of the great utilitarian's labours may in part be due to his apparent preoccupation with status, rights, political and economical considerations. Yet fundamentally Mill and Ibsen were at one here also; Mill believed that women's disabilities elsewhere were only clung to in order to maintain their subjection in domestic life,[5] and he concentrated on the causes so that the effect would follow of itself; that ultimate effect, in his view, would before long make marriage an alliance of equals or at any rate of

[1] Daughter of Bernhard Duncker, lawyer, benefactor to Ibsen and model for Berent, the representative of society in Bjørnson's *Bankruptcy*.
[2] Just about the time that Ibsen was in Norway on a short visit.
[3] No doubt the same vulgar euphemism in Norwegian as in English.
[4] It is true that Asta Allmers and Petra Stockmann are professional teachers; Martha Bernick works in a school as a form of 'charity'.
[5] *Subjection of Women* (1869), p. 91.

potential equals [1]—morally much the same thing; such a change would vastly benefit society at large, settling it on a firmer basis of justice and equal opportunity, tapping a reservoir of immense social energies, and in the benefit to society, husbands and men in general, would of course share.

An attitude analogous to this Ibsen unfeignedly discloses in the short speech which he made on 26 May 1898 at a banquet of the Norwegian Society for the Woman's Cause.[2] On the one hand, he defends himself against the ascription of feminism, but, on the other, he wishes it to be known that any aim he has had outside his art has been for mankind in general and the mankind inhabiting Norway in particular:

I thank you for drinking my health, but I must reject the honour of having consciously worked for the woman's cause. I am not even clear what the woman's cause really is. For me it has been an affair of humanity.[3]

Later on his words are equally significant, and, though they may not have proved palatable to all his listeners, they take a positive form:

I have always looked on it as a mission[4] to elevate the nation and give the people a higher status. Two factors come into play in this process; and it rests with the *mothers* by means of strenuous and protracted exertions to rouse a conscious sense of *culture* and *discipline*. These must be created in human beings before the people can be raised higher. It is the women who shall solve the problem of humanity. As mothers they are to do it. And only *so* can they do it.

These deliberately chosen words show that the last speech of Bernick in *Pillars of Society* is not the sentimental clap-trap that it is sometimes thought to be—"it is you women who are the pillars of society".[5] On one plane Bernick's words represent the author's conviction, though he would equally have acquiesced all his lifetime in the sentiment with which a woman then proceeds, as it were, to trump Bernick's card: "the spirits of Truth and Freedom—*these* are the Pillars of Society". The

[1] *Subjection of Women* (1869), p. 89.
[2] 'Ved Norsk Kvindesagsforenings Fest', printed in Centenary Edition, xv (1930), pp. 717 f.
[3] "For mig har det staaet som en Menneskesag."
[4] The phrase ("for mig har det altid staaet som en Opgave at løfte Landet...") has a slightly ambiguous meaning, for Ibsen carefully refrains from saying that he looked on it as *his mission*.
[5] IV, p. 104; Archer, VI, p. 409.

specifically feminine is very important in his view, but in the last resort it is no more than ancillary.

In the indictment against modern society of which Ibsen delivered himself in play after play, beginning with *Pillars of Society*, one of the counts was that it disregarded in its communal assumptions and institutions one half of itself and depressed the ancillary to the servile. Lona Hessel, who speaks the lines about Truth and Freedom and in whose ungainly deportment and provocative speech contemporaries were not slow to recognise Aasta Hanstein, puts the former point quite precisely: "your society is a society of bachelor-souls; you have no eyes for womanhood";[1] but, at one time intended to have equal prominence in *Pillars of Society* with the criticism of commercial morality, the feminist argument was only slightly developed there and relegated to fuller treatment in its successor, *A Doll's House*.

Among Ibsen's preliminary notes to the last-named occurs the following:

There are two kinds of spiritual law, two kinds of conscience, one in man and another, altogether different, in woman. They do not understand each other; but in practical life the woman is judged by man's law, as though she were not a woman but a man.... A woman cannot be herself in the society of the present day, which is an exclusively masculine society....[2]

The disagreement on which the drama of *A Doll's House* is built accordingly is not so much that between a wife and a husband as one between a woman and the society in which she lives, the society which imposes its laws upon her; Nora leaves her home and family in the last act not as a declaration of war, but in order that she may meditate in peace upon her position as a woman and member of the human community. The prominence which Ibsen gave to women in his plays is due not to any preponderating interest he may have taken in them as a sex[3]—there is no hint of this in the annals of his life—nor because, like his northern colleague Strindberg, he thought the private relations of women and men and the antagonisms to

---

[1] IV, p. 103; Archer, VI, p. 408.
[2] *Efterladte Skrifter*, II, p. 327; Archer, XII, p. 91.
[3] One may infer from the contrast between Rebecca West and Rosmer, between Alfred Allmers and his two women, perhaps also between Hilda Wangel and Solness, that he thought women more strongly endowed with the dramatic virtue of energy.

which they give rise to be of special dramatic interest, but because women afforded him specimens of humanity peculiarly trammelled by their conventional disabilities in the struggle for personal emancipation which formed his passionate preoccupation. Nora Helmer becomes the typical representative of the individual whose free development has been checked and who has been driven into courses which both society considers criminal and the individual eventually finds uncongenial. The claims of freedom and personality in general could best be vindicated in women, because in women they were most persistently denied. The word 'slaves' which Mill had applied to the female half of humanity must have evoked the loudest echo in Ibsen.[1]

* * * *

With the doctrines of John Stuart Mill, lay opinion on the continent commonly associated those of Herbert Spencer and with the latter the biological theses first formulated by Charles Darwin in *The Origin of Species* (1859).[2] In view of the currency which some of their conclusions enjoyed, Ibsen must have known about them, but there is no evidence that he studied[3] their works themselves, and philosophy and biology were naturally less congenial to him than morals.[4] It has been noted how he disdained the construction which the French

[1] When at the end of his career Ibsen considered the cases where the individual was at issue with himself rather than with society, his examples are chiefly men, and John Gabriel Borkman, Rubek, Alfred Allmers, even Halvard Solness, are brought into conjunction with comparatively uncomplicated women, for whom the living of a happy life depends on simpler conditions. It may be observed that in his analysis of one woman, possibly two women who are their own worst enemies, Hedda Gabler (and Ellida Wangel), Ibsen played with an idea to which he did not commit himself, namely that the psycho-pathological concomitants of pregnancy were responsible for their extravagant acts and outlook.

[2] It is probable that Ibsen read in *The Origin of Species* and *The Descent of Man*; since 1872 and 1875 respectively those two books were accessible to readers of Danish in the translation of Jens Peter Jacobsen, who enjoyed (in Ibsen's eyes) the combined advantages of being a scientist by education, a friend of Brandes and an original author. Jacobsen and Ibsen were in Rome in the winter of 1878–9 and discussed science together (Centenary Edition, VIII, p. 261). Darwin had the good fortune to be introduced into Norway by the thorough and understanding study of his theories which P. C. Asbjørnsen contributed to the magazine *Budstikken* for February and March 1861.

[3] The remark which Darwin makes on wild ducks in captivity in *The Variation of Animals and Plants under Domestication* (II, 1868, p. 278) may have come to his direct notice and contributed something to *The Wild Duck*.

[4] It is significant that Fru Alving, in *Ghosts*, ranks the inheritance of ideas *pari passu* with physical inheritance (IV, p. 228; Archer, VII, p. 225).

naturalistes placed on the new evolutionism. Nevertheless, the order of speculations to which the latter gave rise had points of interest for him. His depreciation of the Norwegian national character made him (who had implied no criticism of the Vikings in *The Vikings in Helgeland* or of the Vikings' next descendants in *The Pretenders*) scrutinize the belief in an almost automatic progress which some thought that the doctrine of evolution justified. In meditating upon the hindrances to freedom and happiness, as well as on other occasions, he had to take into account hereditary disease and degeneracy. If certain strains improved and proliferated, others deteriorated and languished; a congenital disability could by itself stultify every striving after happiness and freedom.

Considerations of this kind were very prominently in the public eye of Norway during the 1870's, because of the controversy which was taking place about the proper treatment of lepers. Of all the civilised countries of Europe Norway suffered perhaps proportionately most at that date from the incidence of leprosy, which indeed seemed to be on the increase. In 1875 there were more than 2000 sufferers from the dread and incurable disease, and opinion, both among men of science and others, was sharply divided about its nature and transmission. Was it contagious and eradicable therefore by isolation, or was it a hereditary disability communicable only by parent to child? In 1873 Gerhard Armauer Hansen of Bergen discovered the leprosy-bacillus, eventually discredited the theory of hereditary transmission and inaugurated an agitation which culminated in the forcible segregation (when necessary) of sufferers, whose numbers subsequently decreased to about one-eighth.

The disease of syphilis offered some analogies to leprosy and, though it was sufficiently well appreciated that it was communicated in sexual intercourse, many of its effects could also be construed as the visitation of the sins of the fathers upon their children. It is possible that Ibsen's interest in venereal disease had been roused by Strodtmann's biography of Heine (1867–9),[1] who had been one of the idols of *Andhrimner*'s staff

---

[1] Cf. in particular II, p. 529. Perhaps a guiding influence was exerted also by Ibsen's exact contemporary, Mrs Josephine Butler, whose campaign against the supervision of prostitutes was begun in 1869, and attracted much notice outside Great Britain.

in his early youth, and the poignant paradox of the great hedonist's complete paralysis from *tabes dorsalis* presented precisely that aspect of disease, hereditary or otherwise, which would most profoundly affect him. The first case which Ibsen presented was that of Dr Rank, the family friend of the Helmers, in *A Doll's House*, and with him, as with Heine, it is the central nervous system which is attacked. Rank himself attributes his illness entirely to paternal excesses.[1]

In *Ghosts* the illness no longer remains on the second plane, but is advanced into the forefront and is handled more comprehensively. The late Captain Alving, we are to suppose, contracted it by contagion during the cheerful promiscuity of his youth; the heir to his body bears about with him the uncontagious sequelae, which are manifested in his brain and which will reduce him to idiocy. Oswald thereby provides a clear instance of physical degeneration, and the enigmatic conclusion poses the question whether the degenerate members of the stock should not at a certain stage undergo extermination,[2] an extension of the measures which society, in its own real or supposed hygienic interests, was prepared to take against lepers.[3] In throwing up this question Ibsen also canvassed the original responsibility of society, its crime against the individual, in constraining a man like Captain Alving to a course of life so dreadfully visited.[4] After many years of anguished meditation on the subject, Mrs Alving has evidently reached the conclusion that the puritanical morality and cramped environment in which she herself had been bred, and which Pastor Manders represents as an ideal, had turned the sparkling, gay, energetic young man whom she had married into a furtive sot and profligate, capable of playing disgusting practical jokes on his own infant son; it was these things which brought the curse on the house both in that manner and by refusing to let her herself escape from it when the mischief to her husband had been done.

Ibsen used contagious disease thus as an illustration of an

[1] "My poor innocent spine must do penance for my father's wild oats" (IV, p. 151; Archer, VII, p. 81).

[2] It is not clear whether Ibsen believed that Oswald was capable of communicating his disease; Regina evidently holds this error.

[3] Oddly enough, the playwright Dumas (the younger) had advocated the elimination of moral degenerates by private initiative in *Claud's Wife* (1873), which caused a great stir.

[4] The analogy to his indictment of society in the case of Consul Bernick (IV, p. 67; Archer, VI, p. 354) will be apparent.

argument about private and public morality. He was not concerned to suggest pure physical loathsomeness or to construct any argument, as one of the *naturalistes* might have done, to exonerate a malefactor on account of impairment of his faculties through inherited or acquired disease.[1]

On the other hand, though he did not regard *belles-lettres* as a branch of natural history, he accepted what so many of his contemporaries could not bring themselves to accept from the newer biology, man's unprivileged position in the evolutionary process. He nowhere hints at any belief in a special creation, with special prerogatives and special obligations of a supernatural order. Not even a clergyman or pedagogue ever in his plays calls to mind that God created man in his own image.[2] The calm manner in which Mrs Alving and the horrified fury with which great sections of the public contemplated the possibility, even the desirability, of an incestuous union between Oswald and Regina—which no one would have condemned in the case of domestic animals—betrays the distance by which Ibsen had outstripped most of his co-evals in the acceptance of the new science. He not only drew his own conclusions from it, but interested himself in some of its details. In *The Wild Duck* Hjalmar Ekdal is convinced of Hedvig's bastardy on the evidence of the defective eyesight which she shares with Werle senior. Ellida Wangel's sick love of the sea (in *The Lady from the Sea*) receives a curious illumination from some observations[3] by Ibsen to the effect that the evolutionary process went astray in removing the higher animals on to dry land, so that they carry about with them an unsatisfied yearning for the element to which they belonged—a notion apparently suggested[4] by Ernst Haeckel's demonstration that the fishes stand in the direct evolutionary line leading down to man.

*   *   *   *

[1] It is possible to argue, as Strindberg does, that Ibsen meant to acquit Nora Helmer of forgery, on the grounds that she had inherited her father's irresponsibility.

[2] Brand comes nearest to doing so (II, p. 232; Archer, III, p. 26). A sad figure is cut by all parsons and accredited teachers in Ibsen's plays after *Emperor and Galilean*: Adjunkt Rørlund, Manders, Molvik, Kroll, Tesman.

[3] E.g. the sentiment which Ibsen wrote in Count I. Milewski's album: "The development of the human race took the wrong turn from the start. Our dear fellow-men ought to have evolved themselves into maritime creatures" (Centenary Edition, XV, p. 381).

[4] Cf. Centenary Edition, XV, p. 36.

Many of the ideas and tenets of Ibsen which have received consideration in this and earlier chapters, profoundly shocking the orthodox among his contemporaries, were not infrequently lumped together as 'pessimism': such were his notions of torpedoing the Ark; the implied denial of a special creation and the acceptance of man's position in the long and incompleted evolutionary process, with no suggestion of any supernatural privileges such as are promised by the Christian faith; the prominence which he gave in his speculations on heredity to degeneration and the inheritance of undesirable characteristics; the delineations of the weakness of the individual and of the actions of a society which is created to promote and protect, but in effect thwarts and crushes the individual; the defeat of human effort and aspiration, which in a high degree all tragedy-writing involves. The question naturally presents itself whether Ibsen's speculation was directly affected by the consciously pessimistic thinkers in which the nineteenth century abounded.

Here Georg Brandes may be acquitted of immediate responsibility and, as far as the evidence reaches, of indirect responsibility too. His strenuous, reforming nature might, for professional purposes, acquaint itself with doctrines that, in the main, are inimical to effort, and his study of Shakespeare shows how sympathetic a knowledge he possessed of the springs of tragedy. But round about 1870 it is most unlikely that he preached pessimism or would have acted as Ibsen's director of studies in that department of philosophy. Indeed, it will be remembered that the gravamen of his charge against *Brand*, and a capital reason for diverting his friend to another order of artistic creation, was precisely the enmity to life which that play might inculcate and the stimulus it might give to Christian pessimism already so powerfully furthered by Kierkegaard.

Romantic pessimism, as it is called, was of course familiar to Ibsen, since he grew up with it, and there is reason to believe that, speaking relatively, he cherished a high regard for its chief exponent, Byron,[1] in whom Brandes's brilliant study (in the fourth volume of *Main Currents of Nineteenth Century Literature*) roused a renewed interest; and on *Adam Homo*, an outstanding successor to *Don Juan*, he drew, as has been seen, heavily. But there is probably no more specific influence here.

[1] Cf. *Breve*, I, p. 245, where he urges a Norwegian translation.

Schopenhauer, with his 'English' style and manner, his contempt of women and yearning for Nirvana, would seem less of a kindred spirit.

What Ibsen learned about Eduard von Hartmann (whose *Philosophy of the Unconscious* appeared in 1869) may well have been more congenial to him. The saturnine paradox in which Hartmann's pessimism can be summed up—that this is the best of all possible worlds, but that it is a damned bad one—was of the sort to enchant him. The greater part Hartmann allotted to the intellect and his recognition of biological evolutionism as part of the cosmic process would appeal to him; and Hartmann's belief that we all, singly and collectively, strive perpetually after happiness, which is unattainable, seems to be paraphrased in a note of Ibsen's to the effect that man in his more natural aspirations shows himself a megalomaniac. But closest of all, perhaps, Ibsen may later have felt himself drawn to the Prussian pessimist by the large allowance which the latter made for the operation of unconscious will and unconscious thought—the powers that actuated an Ellida Wangel and a Hedda Gabler, and in which, seemingly, Solness and Borkman and the Rat-Wife of *Little Eyolf* believed. None the less, it would be an abuse of the term to write Ibsen down a disciple of Hartmann.

*   *   *   *

The first of Brandes's famous problems to which Ibsen applied himself, when the long fermentation set up by his leaven was beginning to settle, was not of so vast a scope as those just sketched. Self-knowledge had kept even step with knowledge of the outside world, and after the unsatisfactory immensities of *Emperor and Galilean* (1873) Ibsen clearly felt he should attempt a less ambitious task and execute it more perfectly. In *Pillars of Society* (*Samfundets Støtter*, 1877) he submitted to debate certain problems of commercial morality. This may be thought the stranger as Ibsen betrayed very little interest in the great issues of economics and sociology which, at that time, were as prominent in the public eye as any others. What John Stuart Mill had written on these topics he very likely had not so much as heard of; he paid no heed to Carl Marx; the struggles of free traders and protectionists in the new Germany in which he lived left him completely cold. His hatred of peasants rendered him indifferent to the plight of the poor, while he could scarcely cherish much sympathy for those who were supposed to exploit

167

them. The 'social question' *par excellence*, as it came to be called, hardly obtrudes itself into any of his plays, and when it does so, as, for instance, in the scheme of social welfare which Alfred and Rita Allmers propose to inaugurate at the end of *Little Eyolf*, it is unaccompanied by zeal or conviction.

Nevertheless, Ibsen had good reasons for undertaking a theme bordering on economics. As often happens after a major war, the seventies (until near the end) were a period of great commercial activity, and Ibsen was in a particularly favourable position for observing it, in Germany, where gigantic projects and gigantic failures characterised the so-called Founders' Years.[1] But on a smaller scale, as Ibsen's visit to Norway in 1874 would show him, similar things were happening at home, and they were of a kind to be familiar with a peculiar vividness to the sections of the public from which theatre audiences were then drawn. Farthermore, these audiences had, with Balzac's *Mercadet*, some of the plays of Augier and, especially, with Bjørnson's *Bankruptcy* before them, become accustomed to the dramatic presentation of situations in which an economic element preponderated.

Ibsen chose the narrower field of *Pillars of Society* with an equal tact. The 1870's witnessed an energetic effort to extend the exiguous Norwegian railway system, and Bernick's double piece of sharp practice, first in ruining the project of a railway line which would have competed with his own coasting vessels and then in privily buying up land through which a less dangerous inland line would run, was a transaction that could probably have been nearly paralleled more than once.[2] To this matter Ibsen joined the more melodramatic theme of the *Indian Girl*, sent out in the same unseaworthy condition as the 'coffin-ships' against which Samuel Plimsoll was just then (1875) successfully declaiming in the British House of Commons. Plimsoll's labours for the inspection and codification of sea-going vessels[3] were followed with great interest in the wealthy and extensive[4] ship-

---

[1] *Gründerjahre*; the term has reference to the founders (many self-appointed) of the new German empire.

Certain details of Bernick, his activities and his sister were taken from a Grimstad magnate, Smith-Peterson, who died in 1872 (Centenary Edition, VIII, p. 25).

[3] The Merchant Shipping Act was passed in 1876.

[4] It is reported (Due, C., *Erindringer fra Henrik Ibsens Ungdomsaar*, 1909, p. 15) that in Ibsen's youth at Grimstad the very servant-girls used to put their savings into shares of ships and cargoes.

ping circles which Norway had fostered in the course of the nineteenth century,[1] while the artisan Aune's protest against the use of machinery faintly echoes perhaps a certain uneasiness felt by more opulent members of these circles at the threatened supersession of the wooden sailing-ship, which Norway could produce cheaply, by the new-fangled iron steamer, which it had neither the materials and skill to build nor the coal to work on.

Ibsen's cunning lent in this way a considerable actuality to the complicated transactions unfolded in *Pillars of Society*. But, as has been seen, they remained essentially subordinate in his interest and dramatic scheme, which, in accordance with his invariable rule, turn upon the moral problems thrown up by the chances and changes of the phenomenal world problems of freedom, guilt and responsibility.

[1] The commissioning of badly repaired ships was brought up at the annual meeting of the Norwegian Marine Assurance Company 'Veritas' in 1874 and 1875 (Centenary Edition, VIII, p. 21).

CHAPTER TWELVE

THE LAST WORKS AND THEIR WORLD

An Enemy of the People (1882), *The Wild Duck* (1884), *Rosmersholm* (1886), *The Lady from the Sea* (1888), *Hedda Gabler* (1890), *The Master Builder* (1892), *Little Eyolf* (1894), *John Gabriel Borkman* (1896), *When We Dead Awaken* (1899)

ONCE IBSEN had approved the fifth draft of *Pillars of Society*, the troubled period of uncertainty about the precise course of his 'mission' as artist and leader of thought,[1] of conflicting and impetuous claims on the reflective and formative functions of his imagination had come to an end. There was always to be plenty of wind in his sails, and the wind was to blow from diverse quarters, but the waters were less agitated, the hands of the helmsman never faltered. As time went on his work reveals fewer and fewer obviously external impulses.

* * * *

The full study of the manner in which one work of his bred another, of how a late work serves, probably consciously enough, as a corrective and criticism of works that precede it,[2] has not yet been written; nor is it to the present purpose to add to the tentatives made in that direction. A partial exception, however, should be made in connection with *An Enemy of the People* (*En Folkefiende*, 1882). For here Ibsen was, as it were, taking up a public quarrel, and it can be considered an accident that he himself had provoked it. It is not fantastic to imagine that if not he himself, but some other writer near to him, like Jonas Lie, had written *Ghosts*, the outcome would have been the same. Indeed, the satire on Peter Stockmann may be faintly coloured by suggestions from Kielland's novel *Working*

---

[1] Though Ibsen was no propagandist and vehemently resented any such imputation, he had not been unduly hypocritical in declaring to the king in 1866 that he desired to make the people of his country think loftily (cf. *Breve*, 1, p. 114); he used similar language as late as 1898.

[2] I mean, for example, the way that some of Lona Hessel's problems were left over for Nora and Nora grew into Fru Alving, or the fashion after which the man who stands alone is approved in Stockmann and disapproved in John Gabriel Borkman.

Men (1881),[1] which had also provoked an outcry among the right-thinking.

At the root, then, of *An Enemy of the People* lies the reception accorded, in Norway as in other countries, to *Ghosts*, which the censorious branded as smutty, immoral, impious and subversive. As in the older play Ibsen had shown what pestilent and lethal vapours could mount from a scrupulously observed Christian marriage, from family piety and from charitable organisations,[2] now he presented the fate of a medical officer, who, discovering a taint in the water-supply essential to his community's health and prosperity, announces the fact, and suffers nothing but the vilest obloquy and most rancorous persecution for performing what he looks upon as a public duty.

His own cause was not the only one which stirred Ibsen's mind in the unusually swift[3] composition of *An Enemy of the People*. Allusion has already been made to the spectacle of *Bjørnson contra mundum*, which thrilled Ibsen in 1879 and reflections from which play on the figure of Dr Stockmann. Besides this, some minor touches came from the long feud which a certain apothecary Thaulow waged against the Christiania Steam Kitchen Company, with uproar at the annual meetings, motions from the chair and so forth, much as in Act IV of *An Enemy of the People*.[4] An infinitely deeper mark is left on the play by the grave constitutional struggle in which, precisely at this time, Norway was engaged.

The name under which the momentous struggle is known is the Affair of the Councillors of State (*Statsraadssagen*). When the constitution of the new Norway after 1814 was sketched above,[5] it was remarked that it exhibited a complete division of powers and allowed of an all but perfect bureaucracy, the heads of the civil service, as Councillors of State, forming the executive cabinet and avoiding all contact with the legislative body. On paper, there was nothing to prevent Councillors

---

[1] The 'Working Men' of the title are the bureaucrats who are represented not merely as thinking, but also as proclaiming themselves the only true 'working men' in the land.

[2] It is only through his labours on the woodwork of the new orphanage that Engstrand collects enough money to set himself up as a brothel-keeper.

[3] Only a year, instead of the usual interval of two years, had elapsed between its publication and that of its predecessor.

[4] I cannot help feeling that more illegalities than Ibsen was aware of were committed at the meeting in Captain Horster's house, while the corresponding transactions, as the result of which Thaulow was silenced, seem completely in order.   [5] Pp. 8 f.

from attending meetings of the *Storthing* (though they might not vote), and, indeed, the crown, familiar with this arrangement in Sweden, was more prepared to sanction the custom than the timid ministers were themselves. But it wished to couple the innovation with certain others, and, when the *Storthing* rejected these and pressed by way of constitutional amendment an Enabling Bill of its own, the question of the king's absolute veto was raised. Parliament rejected the government bill *nemine contradicente* in 1877; but over its own measure and the methods requisite for securing its passage opinion was hotly divided.

Since the late sixties and those political excitements which Ibsen had turned to account in the satire *The League of Youth*, something like a party system had developed in Norway, or, to speak more accurately, one party in the country had organised itself as such—the essentially oppositional party of the Left (*Venstre*),[1] of which the peasants formed the gross, skilfully marshalled by Ueland's successor Jaabæk, and receiving invaluable help from professional men like Bjørnson, Richter and the Sverdrups. This party held that laws affecting the constitution were like all other laws, in that the crown could only exercise a temporary, a suspensive veto. Accordingly, when in 1880 the king, acting on the advice of his Norwegian ministers, again pronounced his veto on a bill admitting ministers to parliament which had been passed in three successive sessions,[2] the *Storthing* declared it to be law and proceeded against the royal advisers by the established means of impeaching[3] them before the supreme court (*rigsret*); in 1884 they were found guilty and sentenced, with costs, to various penalties.[4] King Oscar had to recognise that in his Norwegian kingdom the centre of political gravity had passed from himself in council to parliament and sent for Johan Sverdrup, the leader of the majority, who thus became the first Norwegian prime minister under the new dispensation.

In 1877, before King Oscar had inauspiciously taken a hand

[1] The conservatives, somewhat hampered by their constitutional doctrines, were for long too proud to form a proper party of their own and suffered for the omission.
[2] Beginning in 1871 there were annual parliaments with a fresh election to each.
[3] The main accusations were tendering illegal advice to the crown concerning the exercise of its veto, and refusing to implement subsequent acts of parliament.
[4] Eight were declared incapable of holding public office, the three others fined Kr. 8000 each.

in the political game, virtual unanimity had prevailed in parliament, at least outwardly. But the servants of the crown and their friends, whom we may properly call the conservatives, had not been blind to the consolidation of the Left and became gravely alarmed on witnessing an agitation for abolishing what they looked upon as the last bulwark against demagogy in a unicameral constitution. They commanded a considerable body of support[1] and could naturally exercise a power greatly in excess of their numerical strength. Everything of which they disapproved was lumped together as 'subversive', in the realm of education, religion, morals, art and literature, as well as government: hence, indeed, part of the indignant fury with which *Ghosts* was greeted. Where subversive activities were in question, they made no great secret of approving repression.[2] They put obstacle after obstacle in the way of the cabinet ministers' legal conviction.

Very naturally, an almost febrile excitement accompanied the protracted political crisis at several of its stages. That repression was no empty word even in a civilised polity was evident in neighbouring Denmark, which for twenty-seven years (1874–1901) exhibited the extraordinary spectacle of unconstitutional rule against the reiterated wish of the electorate. A *coup d'état*, perhaps even with Swedish help, was seriously apprehended, and the song which Bjørnson wrote[3] for the numerous and enthusiastic corps of volunteer riflemen made it abundantly clear that they were ready to fire for the protection of parliament and civil liberties. Fear begot fear, and fear hatred. An article in the newspaper *Morgenbladet*[4] declared: "Even into private life this political fever has penetrated, producing division and gloom: friendships are dissolved and family bonds broken through adhesion to different parties, every company becomes a debating-club, and there is as good as no neutral ground on which people can meet in peace."

It was into this combustion that Ibsen cast the inflammable matter of *An Enemy of the People*. An amusing triple cartoon

---

[1] At the critical elections of 1882 they gained 28,411 votes and 31 seats against 42,881 and 83.

[2] The assassination of Alexander II of Russia in 1881 helped to appal the timid.

[3] 'Opsang for de Norske Skytterlag' in *Samlede Digte-Verker*, VIII (1927), p. 385.

[4] Quoted by Keilhau, W., in *Det Norske Folks Liv og Historie*, X (1935), p. 113; the writer was Professor Monrad, who long ago had reviewed young Ibsen's *Catiline* with some approval.

of the comic paper *Vikingen*[1] portrays him first jabbing with his quill at the kidneys of lawyer Stensgaard, while the Conservatives stand applauding, then delivering a well-aimed kick at the posteriors of Consul Bernick, to the joy of the 'Left', and finally in 1882 brandishing a scorpion in either hand and routing the hosts on each side. That, fortunately, was the way in which contemporaries in Norway[2] looked upon *An Enemy of the People*; it was not taken as a contribution to the great debate, for all the actual appeal made by its scenes of public meeting and the intrigues of publicity, and on a more general view it became clear that the severity with which the sympathetic figure of Dr Stockmann inveighed against the compact Liberal majority was matched by the figure of his Conservative brother Peter's turpitude.

None the less, the constitutional struggle itself left a profound mark on Ibsen's mind. The first picture in *Vikingen*'s triptych, just referred to, and observations made farther back in this study showed that during a substantial space of time—the time of his acutest alienation from the radical Bjørnson—Ibsen, in so far as he was politically valued at all, stood before the public eye as 'the conservative poet'. His visit to Norway in 1874, the resumed contact with his ossifying friends of 'Learned Holland' (now *minus* Botten Hansen), after the heady draughts which Georg Brandes had poured out for him, had a doubly sobering effect. He could not fail to note that toryism, however honest, might involve in a small community what he most hated, intellectual repression. The exposure of Bernick and his associates was construed as a 'radical gesture', and it was no accident that the publication of *Pillars of Society* afforded the occasion for the first *rapprochement* to Bjørnson.

The fact, however, that many of the leaders of the Left joined the chorus of denunciation when *Ghosts* came out once more gave its author pause. They do not want liberty, he growled,[3] only liberties. The three years of manœuvres and counter-manœuvres for passing and vetoing the Enabling Bill struck him as a silly and dishonest political game, played as an

---

[1] Reproduced in *Boken om Bøker*, II (ed. Sommerfeldt, W. P., Oslo, 1927), p. 133.
[2] In Denmark, on the other hand, it was believed that he had thrown in his lot with the reactionaries, and that was resented. The rancour engendered at this time did not rapidly subside, but was rather aggravated by later political occurrences.
[3] Letter to G. Brandes of 3 January 1882 (*Breve*, II, p. 101).

excuse for shirking effective action. But when Johan Sverdrup finally issued an order to ministers in the *Storthing*'s name, on their disregarding it, instead of seeking some face-saving formula, proceeded to impeachment and then assumed the responsibilities of office (1884), like many another sceptic Ibsen realised that he meant business and that sneers against the cowardly inertia of the "compact Liberal majority" had ceased to be appropriate. Sverdrup's ministry might be a sad disappointment;[1] still, he had passed beyond mere criticism, manœuvre and opposition, and at the same time no one thought more of dubbing Ibsen 'the conservative poet'.

In *The Wild Duck* (*Vildanden*, 1884) there is, almost for the only time in twenty years, no allusion to things of topical interest. Ibsen had not done with them; while he was meditating the drama he proposed to Bjørnson the foundation of a new radical party[2] in which he intended to be left fugleman on the left wing. *The Wild Duck*'s successor *Rosmersholm* (1886) clearly mirrors recent events and the dramatist's association with them. The time of action must be presumed to be near the present, and the conservative headmaster Kroll uses language very similar to the *Morgenbladet's* when he speaks of "the civil contest—I might almost say the civil war—that is raging among us"[3] or declares that "discussion and revolt have crept into my own house—into my own quiet home. They have destroyed the peace of my family life."[4] He believes that the very palladium of civilisation is threatened since the Radicals have prevailed and that it is of the utmost consequence for its defenders to gain the active support of the great magnate of the neighbourhood, Rosmer of Rosmersholm, a man of learning, principle and religion. But Rosmer neither sees a future for their cause nor finds any moral worth in them, and the time-serving of the agitator Mortensgaard—editor of the radical 'Light-House', to which Kroll's own children and the brightest boys at his school subscribe—fills him with equal disgust, the same as Ibsen felt at the externalities and *sequelae* of the party strife which he witnessed during his Norwegian holiday in

[1] The majority of his supporters were peasants who, together with their clerical mentors, often took up an obscurantist attitude.
[2] Letter of 28 March 1884 (*Breve*, II, p. 132).
[3] v, p. 112; Archer, IX, p. 9.
[4] v, p. 117; Archer, IX, p. 18.

the summer of 1885.[1] Since the blind violence of such strife can indirectly but positively bring about the death of fine souls, capable of good deeds, like Rosmer[2] and Rebecca West, a *tertium quid* again is called for, even if a Johannes Rosmer is not the man to realise it, or an Henrik Ibsen either. What it is, the latter formulated in a speech which he delivered just at this time to the artisans of Trondheim, and the way he formulated it is especially illuminating:

> An aristocratic element must come into our political life, into our parliament and into our press. I am of course not thinking of aristocracy of birth, emphatically not of that of money, not of the aristocracy of knowledge, not even of that of ability and talent. But I have in mind an aristocracy of character and mind and will. It is that alone that can make us free.[3]

Rosmer's ideal amounts almost to an expanded paraphrase of this:

> I am not in love with the spirit that is in the ascendant, nor with either of the contending parties. I will try to bring together men from both sides—as many as I can—and to unite them as closely as possible. I will devote my life and all my energies to this one thing—the creation of a true democracy in this country . . . making all the people of this country noble-men.[4]

And

> When I heard of your violence on the platform—when I read of all the rancorous speeches you made—your bitter onslaughts on your opponents . . . then my duty stood imperatively before me. Men are growing evil in this struggle. Peace and joy and mutual forbearance must once more enter into our souls.[5]

* * * *

[1] Ibsen was profoundly vexed at the government's refusal to pension Kielland. At Molde (where he spent six or seven weeks from the middle of July and subsequently laid the scene of *The Lady from the Sea*) Ibsen observed the coldness shown him by the right-thinking (of which his wife had given him warning previously), and soon after it came to a violent rupture between himself and one of their foremost representatives, his old friend Lorentz Dietrichson, now professor at Christiania. An indirect consequence of this was a split in the university Union Society, and the establishment of a radical 'secession' society, with Ibsen as one of its honorary members. (The story is fully told by Koht, II, pp. 255 f., drawing on Wallem, F. B., *Norske Studenter-Samfundet*, 1916).

[2] Many traits for the character of Rosmer were derived from Ibsen's friend Count Snoilsky, the foremost Swedish lyricist of his day, aristocrat and ex-diplomat, who had turned an avowed radical. The Snoilskys were at Molde in the summer of 1885.

[3] *Cit.* Koht, II, p. 249.   [4] V, p. 129; Archer, IX, p. 41.

[5] V, p. 130; Archer, IX, p. 44.

Georg Brandes was inclined to twit Ibsen, whom he had brought to the arena, with an unwillingness to throw himself into its dust and turmoil, with his preference for watching from a raised seat, on the fence. At any rate, Ibsen was spared the fall which their contemporaries witnessed when, a few years later, Brandes made himself the advocate of quite a different form of aristo-cracy,[1] much less humane or compatible with the beliefs which he had fostered, and became the prophet of Nietzsche. It is clear that a Johannes Rosmer, his heart on "all the people of this country", would feel little sympathy with the single aristo-crat, the 'super-man' excogitated in Sils Maria and Turin.

In the controversy with the Danish philosopher Harald Høffding in which his new beliefs involved Brandes and which was fought out mainly in the pages of the Copenhagen review *Tilskueren* for 1889, Ibsen took, as might be expected, no direct part. It is probable, however, that he followed it and pondered its implications.[2] In Halvard Solness of *The Master Builder* (*Bygmester Solness*, 1892) and in the hero of *John Gabriel Borkman* (1896) he presented two full-length portraits of self-appointed supermen,[3] to whom ordinary men and women (or those they esteem so) are mere hewers of wood and drawers of water. These two come to grief, through their egoism, and the author not only shows how that naturally ensues, but gives clearly to understand moreover that the world will be no poorer for their departure from it.[4]

One step and an interesting step, nevertheless, Ibsen had taken on the road which was to lead Brandes so far—even if it might be argued that Rosmer's programme is a disavowal of that step. It was quickly observed and made a matter for indignation and regret that in *The Wild Duck* Ibsen had utterly relinquished the idealism, expressed or implied, of all his earlier plays; indeed, the most vital and clear-sighted figure in it, who more than any other seemed to stand at the

---

[1] It seems it was Brandes himself who coined the expression "aristocratic radicalism".

[2] I say no more than that it is probable, because the nature of tragedy has at all times involved a consideration of megalomania. The Greeks needed no Nietzsche for their *hubris*, or Shakespeare for his Coriolanus, or Corneille for his Horace.

[3] I do not think that Ibsen anywhere uses a term corresponding to 'super-man'; but of his enemy Hinkel Borkman says (VI, p. 187; Archer, XI, p. 224) that he has "overskurkens moral" (the ethics of the super-rogue).

[4] The Nietzschians may object that these two are but spurious specimens of the super-man, even if they have his morals.

author's point of view, Dr Relling,[1] rounded savagely on "the confounded duns that keep on pestering us, in our poverty, with the claim of the ideal".[2] Equally plain, however, is the descent in the social plane which Acts II to V of *The Wild Duck* make; they are the only scenes limned by Ibsen in which squalor of life and manners takes the place of opulence and culture. The inference to be made from these two novelties is as legitimate as it is startling,[3] namely that 'ideals' are a luxury, demanding a substantial competence for their upkeep, and that a decent standard of life is as little to be expected of the poor and lowly in the moral as it is in the material sphere.

*   *   *   *

When Ibsen left it after his holiday of 1885 he declared[4] that Norway was inhabited not "by two million men but by two million cats and dogs". Indeed, for a matter of ten years, beginning about 1879,[5] one major controversy followed another, row succeeded to row; though the terrain and the number of the disputants might vary, the uproar and the acrimony remained constant. Some of the quarrels have been mentioned: the great constitutional issue for instance; the split in the ranks of the university club, which was directly due to Ibsen; and the wrangle about the Norwegian flag, in which he took no part.

In a fourth quarrel he did not figure as an active disputant either, like his colleagues Bjørnson, Arne Garborg and Kielland or like Georg Brandes, but in some degree the responsibility for it may be laid at his door.[6] It raged around questions of sexual behaviour and ultimately became known as 'The Morality Dispute' (*Sedelighedsfejden*). It has been remarked that the location of the national university of Norway in the capital had the effect, as it has in other centres of learning (like Paris, for instance), of bringing undisciplined young students, many of whom of course were poverty-stricken, friendless and brutish in their tastes, into close propinquity with prostitutes and other women of light virtue. Oswald's description of them in *Ghosts*

---

[1] He may have been suggested by the young medico Borg in Strindberg's novel, *The Red Room* (1879).

[2] v, p. 106; Archer, VIII, p. 400.

[3] It is almost in the vein of Samuel Butler and the Bernard Shaw who learned so much both from him and from Ibsen.

[4] Jæger's *Life of Henrik Ibsen* (English translation, 1890), p. 238.

[5] The constitutional storm had been brewing several years before.

[6] Bjørnson's play of *Leonarda* (1879) was a similar remote cause.

showed that the ensuing unions might not always be as disgusting to the humanitarian as they were reprehensible to the orthodox moralist, and it gave an impetus to informal discussions on the linked problems of continence, pre-nuptial chastity, illegitimacy, prostitution, venereal disease, love and the like. It is not unnatural that the next step should have been taken within the academic body, when in 1882 Hans Jæger,[1] a violent young anarchist, gave a paper on sexual ethics to the still united Students' Club. The succeeding stages of the debate, which spread to the other Scandinavian countries,[2] were marked by Bjørnson's play, A Gauntlet (En Hanske, 1883), by Arne Garborg's sarcastic reference to it in the short story, 'Youth', of 1885,[3] by Brandes's entrance into the arena with an essay on Garborg and his 'Youth' (later the same year) and by the prosecution, in 1886, of Hans Jæger and Christian Krohg, whose respective novels From Christiania's Bohemia (Fra Kristiania-Bohêmen) and Albertine had been confiscated for indecency.[4]

With his hatred of scandal, Ibsen held aloof from a dispute which so often turned on matters highly indecorous. At the height of the excitement he told[5] Brandes (who had just been severely heckled on the topic during a visit to Christiania) that he had never been "more repelled, never more unpleasantly affected" by the antics of his fellow-countrymen. But a matter with so close a bearing on liberty in both male and female could not but concern him. He studied it and obliquely made some comment. Like the works of the equally reticent Henry James, those of Ibsen abound in unusual and abnormal erotic relations, and the fact that an effort is often needed to realise their enormity proves the easy lack of prejudice with which he contemplated them. Never again did he parade his interest as he had done in Ghosts. But the incest contemplated between Regina and Oswald seems to have been actually consummated between Rebecca West and the late Dr West in Rosmersholm,

[1] He is not to be confused with Ibsen's biographer Henrik Jæger.

[2] Something was contributed independently in Strindberg's short stories, Giftas (1884–6)—some of which were conceived in reaction to Ibsen's Doll's House.

[3] 'Ungdom', one of Forteljinger og Sogur. In the meantime Bjørnson had tackled the problem both from the positive and the negative point of view in the long novel Det Flager i Byen og paa Havnen (1885, known in English as The Heritage of the Kurts).

[4] The circumstance that the confiscation and prosecution were undertaken by the new liberal government complicated the political excitement.

[5] Breve, II, p. 164.

and the problem is not far below the horizon in *Little Eyolf*. In both these plays there are clear indications of female sexual erethism which, in the case of the deceased Beata Rosmer, tended to lesbianism, and, in *When We Dead Awaken*, perhaps to insanity. The opposite case of feminine frigidity (to be postulated, very likely, in *The Lady from the Sea* likewise), which seeks a sort of vicarious compensation by luxuriating at second hand in scenes of debauchery, is set out in *Hedda Gabler*. It is unlikely that Krafft-Ebing's *Psychopathia Sexualis* (1893) had much to teach Ibsen.

The calmness and reticence with which all these more or less morbid cases are presented correspond to the depth to which the abnormality, in general, lies concealed within the patient. Eduard von Hartmann, it was noted above[1], had, a Canning in philosophy, called in a new world to redress the balance of the old, to the plight of which Schopenhauer had opened his eyes. Unconscious promptings, of course, were not unknown to students of human nature before his time, the Romantic poets of Germany, for instance, showing a marked predilection for what occurs in and through sleep, dreams and visions. Ibsen admired Kleist's *Katie of Heilbronn*, invoked, as we have seen,[2] against Hertz's *Svend Dyring's House*, but in general he steered clear of the shoals of 'dream-romanticism'; he resisted all temptation, for instance, of suggesting that Peer Gynt's adventures, even the most grotesque and improbable, take place during his sleep.[3] Nevertheless, as has been remarked, Hartmann's *Philosophy of the Unconscious* (or what he knew about it) must have struck sympathetic chords in Ibsen's breast and strengthened an interest in certain aspects of mind there opened to view.

It is thus not unreasonable to suppose that, without pursuing any profound studies,[4] Ibsen, like many other laymen of his time, followed intently the researches and theories in unconscious psychology which, so commonly believed to be a discovery of the twentieth century, were in fact advanced with great boldness and success during the preceding generation. The main interest centred on the labours of the French, among whom Jean Martin

[1] P. 167.   [2] See p. 30 n., above.
[3] Even the beautiful scene, intercalated in his African adventures, where Solvejg is presented, singing her song in the Norwegian fells, is probably to be taken as a real presentation, not a vision. Act II, scenes vi and vii, may form an exception.
[4] There is absolutely no evidence for this.

Charcot (1825–93) was the great pioneer and teacher.[1] Charcot, a practising neurologist, was mainly concerned, like his followers Janet and Binet, with morbid conditions and their ameliora-tion, and thanks to him catch-phrases, in which 'hysteria' and 'hypnotism' figured, enjoyed an uncommon vogue for the explanation of all unusual mental phenomena. Thus, Dina Dorf (who is prepared to throw her cap over the mill in *Pillars of Society*), Nora Helmer (who leaves her husband and babes), Rebecca West (who falls in love with a married man) and Hedvig Ekdal (who commits suicide)[2] were commonly labelled hysterical subjects, whom judicious treatment in La Salpêtrière would soon reduce to a normal frame of mind.

Beginning with *The Lady from the Sea*, however, Ibsen clearly entered upon studies of abnormal psychology which could not be swept aside in a catch-phrase or two. Indeed Ellida Wangel provides a very remarkable and deeply ramified psycho-analyst's 'case'[3] (and cure) *avant la lettre*, so to speak[4]—and the outstanding overt factor in it is her haunting, compelling susceptibility to the lure of the sea, which appears to have no bearing on her rational consciousness and indicates a fissure in her personality. Hers is the kind of case which Janet's studies of dissociation made familiar.[5] Hedda Gabler may conceivably be regarded, similarly, as a specimen of feeble personality in whom Janet for preference found his instances of this phenomenon. For all the suggestions, however, and even perhaps small factual data which Ibsen may have derived from his first-hand or second-hand knowledge of the French psycho-logist and worked into his Hedda, his Solness (who has a half-incredulous belief in preternatural "helpers and servers" and in his power over the volition of others), his Borkman (who hears the natural resources of the country crying out to him for liberation), his self-tormenting Rubek, it would be over-bold

---

[1] Among his pupils was Sigmund Freud.

[2] Ibsen, to be sure, goes out of his way to hint through Dr Relling (v, p. 74; Archer, VIII, p. 336) that Hedvig is suffering from the onset of puberty.

[3] And as such has been fully presented again, for instance by Goitein, P. L., *The Lady from the Sea* (1927).

[4] Freud and Breuer's *Studien über Hysterie* did not appear till 1895, Freud's *Traumdeutung* till 1900.

[5] There are some curious parallels between the case of Ellida Wangel and the actual case fully described by the psychiatrist William Preyer in *Ein merkwürdiger Fall von Fascination* (1895). The early (but not the latter) part of the history related by Preyer antecedes *The Lady from the Sea* apparently and may possibly have been known to Ibsen.

to range Ibsen among the professed adherents of the new psychology.

*   *   *   *

Still less close were his relations with the poetic and artistic development towards the end of the century which derived part of its inspiration from delvings in the unconscious working of the mind and from the occult generally—the ramified movement that goes by the name of 'symbolism'. There is no evidence or likelihood that Ibsen took the slightest interest in a Verlaine, a Villiers de L'Isle Adam or a Maeterlinck, subjects of many young enthusiasts' talk and adulation everywhere from 1890[1] onwards. His own literary use of symbols (which he himself always minimised) has nothing in common with theirs and is quite independent of their sources.

At first sight it might appear that the specifically 'aesthetic' ideals, summed up in the motto *l'art pour l'art*, which simultaneously enjoyed an uncommon vogue, had equally little to do with him, the great poser of social and ethical questions; and to the aesthetic movement as such Ibsen could only be related very factitiously.[2] But it may be remembered that even at the moment when Georg Brandes enlisted him under his banner and persuaded him to submit problems to debate, one of the things that had attracted Ibsen to his programme was its bearing on the relation between the artist and his work. Brandes had convinced Ibsen that he could yet do a man's work by devoting himself entirely to imaginative writing, so long as without derogation from its own perfection that writing might be held to subserve practical purposes, might induce the public to think energetically and to act on its thoughts. With a devotion that would have impressed Flaubert, Ibsen gave himself up for five-and-twenty years to the mission that had then finally become clear to him. Art subserved life, and by devoting himself utterly to the perfection of his art, he paid life the highest tribute in his power. There was, however, one aspect of life which Brandes and he had overlooked, the life of the artist himself, and Ibsen, always intent on the whole man (and the whole woman), betrayed increasing uneasiness at the omission.

[1] A little earlier in France.
[2] Only a little less factitious would be (on the strength of *When We Dead Awaken*) an affiliation with Tolstoy in his latter phase.

The Master Builder shows it, and finally, to crown all, came
When We Dead Awaken (*Naar Vi Døde Vaagner*, 1899), in which
Ibsen puts his own question directly and seemingly condemns
himself with the answer. To live for art, even when that art
subserves life, may kill life. But this personal problem has
nothing to do with current debates about 'art for art's sake';
it comes from the profoundest depths of Ibsen's own personality
and experience.

INDEX

Abel, Niels Henrik, 34 n.
Abildgaard, Theodoor Frederik Scheel, 11, 14
Aeschylus, 155
Alexander II, emperor of Russia, 173 n.
Amalfi, 137
Andersen, V., 57 n.
Andhrimner, see *Manden*
Arbeider-Foreningernes Blad, 11
Archer, C., 134 n.
Archer, W., x, 134 n., *et passim*
Aristophanes, 50, 81
Asbjørnsen, Peter Christian, 36 f., 39 n., 41, 61 n., 107, 113, 162 n.
Augier, Émile, 55 n., 75 n., 126 n., 143 f., 168

Bagger, Herman, 132
Baggesen, Jens, 23, 30
Balzac, Honoré de, 78, 126 n., 168
Bentham, Jeremy, 156
Berchtesgaden, 63, 115 n.
Bergen, 32, 39 ff., 44, 68, 69, 98 f., 118, 122 f., 147 n.
Berggrav, E., 2 n.
Bergsøe, Jørgen Vilhelm, 123 n.
Bergwitz, J. K., 4 n., 20 n.
Bernadotte, Charles, *see* Charles XIV John
Beyer, H., 82
Beyer, Sille Henrikke Christine, 27 n.
Binet, Alfred, 181
Bing, J., 112 n.
Birkeland, Michael, 64
Bjarme, Brynjolf (*pseud.*), 2 n.
Bjerregaard, Henrik Anker, 39 n.
Bjørnson, Bergljot (*later* Ibsen), 135
Bjørnson, Bjørnstjerne Martinius, 12, 15, 38, 40 n., 43 n., 60 n., 65, 66, 67 ff., 99, 110 n., 112, 118 ff., 141, 159, 168, 171, 172, 173, 174, 178 f.
Blanc, T., 39 n.
Blytt, P., 41 n., 51
Boer, R. C., 33 n., 109 n.
Bojer, Johan, 110 n.
Borgaard, Carl, 32 n.
Borkedalen, Else Sofie Jensdatter, 5

Botten Hansen, Paul, *see* Hansen, Paul Botten
Bradlaugh, Charles, 134
Brahm (*or rather* Abrahamssohn), Otto, 137
Brand, Ibsen's, 20 n., 55, 57 n., 66, 75 n., **79** ff., 83, 94, 100, 102, 103 ff., 114 f., 124, 128, 142 f., 146, 156
Brandes, Georg Morris Cohen, 26 n., 29, 37 n., 48, 56 n., 108, 121, 126 n., 128, 134, 136 n., 139 ff., 146, 162 n., 166, 167, 174, 177, 178 f., 182
Britain and the British, 113 n., 144, 145, 155
Broglie, Jacques Victor Albert, duke de, 147 n.
Brontë, Anne, Charlotte and Emily, 70
Browning, Robert, 78
Brun, Johan Nordal, 22
Brun, Michael Wallem, 141
Bruun, Christopher Arnt, 83, 100 f.
Bugge, Elseus Sophus, 36
Bull, F., 2 n., 42 n., 130 n.
Bull, Ole, 32, 40, 108
Butler, Josephine Elizabeth, 163 n.
Butler, Samuel (author of *Erewhon*), 178 n.
Bygmester Solness, see *Master Builder*
Byron, George Gordon, lord, 56 f., 143, 166

Cæsar, Gaius Julius, 3
Catilina, Lucius Sergius, 3 ff., 24
Catiline, Ibsen's, **2** ff., 13, 40 n., 52 n., 54, 66 n., 138 n.
Charcot, Jean Martin, 181
Charles XIV John, king of Sweden and Norway (*formerly* Bernadotte), 94, 95, 98
Charles XV, king of Sweden and Norway, 96, 99, 117, 137 f., 170 n.
Chasles, Philarète, 152, 155
Chesnais, P. G. de la, 79 n., 86 n.
Christiania, 1, 4, 8, 10 ff., 18, 28 n., 32, 34, 41 n., 45, 46, 63, 69, 115 n., 118, 123, 139 n., 159, 176 n.
Cicero, Marcus Tullius, **3** f., 157

184

INDEX